THE YUGOSLAV ECONOMY UNDER SELF-MANAGEMENT

By the same author

KOMMUNISTISCHE AGRARPOLITIK UND ASIEN
(COMMUNIST AGRARIAN POLICY AND ASIA)
NESMISEL IN SMISEL (NONSENSE AND SENSE)
ECONOMIC DEVOLUTION IN EASTERN EUROPE
OUTLINE OF INTERNATIONAL TRADE
OUTLINE OF INTERNATIONAL FINANCE

THE YUGOSLAV ECONOMY UNDER SELF-MANAGEMENT

Ljubo Sirc

St. Martin's Press New York

St. Martin's Press, Inc., 175 Fifth Avenue, New York, NY 10010
Printed in Great Britain
First published in the United States of America in 1979

ISBN 0–312–89832–0

Library of Congress Cataloging in Publication Data

Sirc, Ljubo.
The Yugoslav economy under self management.

Includes index.
1. Yugoslavia – Economic policy – 1945 –
I. Title.
HC407.S5 1979 330.9′497′02 79–11374
ISBN 0–312–89832–0

TO MY MOTHER *who typed the first version of this book but died at the age of 84 while I was finishing it in May 1978*

THE THEME:

Question: 'Do you find the exercise of power more difficult than you had expected?'

Answer: 'Of course, it is more difficult than I thought. And not only I but others also thought that it would be easier. I believe it is easier to wage war than to organise the government and direct social development, because these are complicated matters.'

President Tito interviewed by Henry Fairlie on 18 September, 1962. (*The Queen*, no. 5497)

Contents

List of Tables xi
Preface xiii
Acknowledgements xviii
Abbreviations xix

1: INTRODUCTION 1

1.1 The Background to Reforms 1
1.2 Reasons for Economic Reforms 2
1.3 Shortcomings of the Centralist System 4
1.4 Understanding the Shortcomings 6

PART ONE: DISMANTLING CENTRALIST PLANNING (1952–1960) 11

2: THE ROLE OF PLANNING AND 'AUTOMATISM' 13

2.1 Gradual Change in Approach 13
2.2 The New Planning 16
2.3 The Socialist Market 20
2.4 International Trade 23

3: INVESTMENT PRIORITIES 26

3.1 Decentralisation of Investment 26
3.2 Investment Criteria 28
3.3 Investment Finance 30
3.4 Rate of Investment 31
3.5 Investment Patterns 34
3.6 Special Tendencies 37

4: ORGANISATION AND WORKING OF ENTERPRISES 39

4.1 Workers' Self-management 39

4.2 Enterprises in a Wider Context 41
4.3 Working of Enterprises 43
4.4 Establishment and Winding-Up of Enterprises 45

5: RESULTS UP TO 1960 AND INTERIM CONCLUSIONS 48

5.1 Growth of Output and Consumption 48
5.2 Low Wages 51
5.3 Efficiency of Labour and Capital 56
5.4 Conclusions on the Reform up to 1960 58

PART TWO: IN SEARCH OF AN ECONOMIC MECHANISM FOR SELF-MANAGEMENT (1961–1965) 61

6: FALSE STARTS 63

6.1 Ideological Hesitations 63
6.2 'Cold Collectivisation' 64
6.3 Investment in the Social Plan 1961–1965 66
6.4 More Power to Workers' Councils 69
6.5 Disproportions in the Economy 74

7: TAKING STOCK 83

7.1 Criticism of Monetary Stringency 83
7.2 Credits Abused for Investment 87
7.3 Effects on Enterprises 92
7.4 The Role of Public Finance 95
7.5 Planning or Market Solutions 97

8: THE DECISIVE REFORM 104

8.1 Preliminary Change in the Constitution 104
8.2 Reform 1965 105
8.3 Re-alignment of Prices 107
8.4 Taxation and Stabilisation 111
8.5 The Will to Reform 113
8.6 Reorganisation and Integration 115
8.7 Cooperation Especially with Foreign Enterprises 117
8.8 'Personal Work with Private Means' 118

PART THREE: FUNDAMENTAL PROBLEMS (FROM 1965 ON) 123

9: INFLATIONARY INCOME DISTRIBUTION 125

9.1 Rising Prices 125
9.2 Personal Incomes Explosion 127
9.3 Dissaving in Enterprises and Private Saving 133
9.4 Personal Incomes Policy 137
9.5 Conditions of Work and Social Payments 140

10: FINANCIAL INDISCIPLINE 146

10.1 Banking and Credit 146
10.2 Illiquidity 150
10.3 Debts and Losses 155
10.4 Stabilisation 160

11: FOREIGN DEFICIT 162

11.1 Problems before the 1965 Reform 162
11.2 Foreign Indebtedness 165
11.3 Persistent Incomprehension 168
11.4 Convertibility of the Dinar 170

12: PROBLEMS OF ORGANISATIONAL POWER 173

12.1 Difficulties with Self-management 173
12.2 Solutions Suggested by Sociologists 178
12.3 Attitudes to Managers and Specialists 183
12.4 'Politicians' and 'Businessmen' 186

13: STRIKES AND UNEMPLOYMENT 193

13.1 Strikes 193
13.2 Unemployment 197
13.3 Work Abroad 199
13.4 Reasons for Lack of Employment Opportunities 203
13.5 The Right to Work 204

PART FOUR: MORE INSTITUTIONAL CHANGES (1970s) 207

14: ORGANISATIONAL REFORMS 209

14.1 Reorganisation of Enterprises 209
14.2 Agreements and Planning 213
14.3 Capital Markets and 'Past Labour' 218
14.4 Alienated Capital 219

15: CONSTITUTIONAL CHANGES 224

15.1 Nationalist Revival 224
15.2 Federation Dismantled 225
15.3 'Democratic Centralism' in the League of Communists 228
15.4 The Longest Constitution in the World 223

16: CONCLUSIONS 238

16.1 Quantitative Economic Conclusions 238
16.2 Theoretical Economic Conclusions 242
16.3 Political and Moral Conclusions 243

Postscript 248

Bibliography 253

Index 261

List of Tables

1.1 Total productivity of labour and capital in 1952 4
1.2 The living standard of an average four-member manual worker family 5
2.1 Retail price indices 1952 and 1962 21
3.1 Percentage share in total investment funds 27
3.2 Allocation of gross social product in percentages 32
3.3 Share of social gross investment in the gross social product 1948–1950 33
3.4 Sector shares in total 'economic' investment 34
3.5 Regional shares of fixed capital and social product 36
5.1 Rise in output, income and consumption 1947–1960 49
5.2 Indices of nominal and real earnings 1952–1960 52
5.3 Wages and salaries 1952–1955 53
5.4 Total productivities of labour and capital till 1960 56
5.5 Comparative survey of simultaneous marginal and average capital coefficients in Yugoslavia 57
5.6 Capital–output ratios in Yugoslavia before and after the war 57
6.1 Harvest of wheat and maize 64
6.2 Rates of growth of some components of GSP 75
6.3 Comparative growth rates of inventories 76
6.4 Capacity utilisation and rates of growth 80
6.5 Capacity utilisation of industrial activities 81
8.1 Reform of prices 109
8.2 Retail price indices 1962, 1964 and 1965 109
9.1 Average net personal earnings and indices of money and real earnings 128
11.1 Yugoslav foreign balances 166
15.1 External flows, by republics, 1968 227
15.2 Inter-republic flows, 1968 227
16.1 Yugoslav growth rates 240

Preface

Preparations for this book go back a long time. Although I was studying the combination of law and economics then usual in Central Europe when the Nazis invaded Yugoslavia in 1941, I had no inkling of what could possibly be wrong with communist economics. In fact, I joined a left-wing resistance group which admired Stalin's Soviet Union even though my father owned a textile factory which he had started himself. But this factory had in any case been confiscated by the German authorities in occupation of my home town.

My resistance group soon allied itself with the Communist Party within the Slovene Liberation Front. However, this alliance turned out to be a very uneasy one. To our intense amazement, when we embarked on the preparation of plans for post-war socialisation the communists attacked this as superfluous. While working on the programme, I personally began to wonder about how the abolition of private property was going to improve the lot of ordinary people almost instantly, as both the communists and my own group were promising. It was obvious, to me at least, that it was impossible to redistribute what the capitalists invested or paid in taxes but only what they consumed, and that appeared to be very little.

Another point of conflict between ourselves and the communists was their insistence that nobody should be allowed to fight the occupying German and Italian troops unless he belonged to the Liberation Front which the communists dominated. A Liberation Front 'decree' in December 1941 provided that they would 'liquidate' any such combatants, and the communists proceeded to kill would-be resistance fighters not accepting their command. We were horrified and protested, for which we were expelled from the Front at the beginning of 1942.

Alarmed by this experience, my group was determined to warn the Yugoslav government in exile in London about what was happening. I succeeded, but not until 1943, in escaping via Italy to Switzerland; however, nobody there would listen to me. When I was able to walk again—I incurred a complicated leg fracture when crossing the border — I, therefore, returned to Yugoslavia via France and Southern Italy and enrolled with Tito's partisans.

In 1945, I was used as an interpreter by the communist authorities and became very worried by the hatred and rudeness with which they treated the British, the French and the Americans. Mass executions and arrests of political opponents, amongst whom were many friends or acquaintances, filled me with revulsion. Finally, I could not understand the rapid economic deterioration. While the shops were still full of goods when we partisans liberated Ljubljana, they were all empty by mid-1946. Nobody could give me an explanation.

In May 1947 I myself was arrested and subjected, with some other members of my wartime group, to a show trial, allegedly for spying and conspiracy against the State, in fact for being friendly with foreigners and intending to take part in elections, jointly with the democratic opposition in Serbia and Croatia, which should have been legal under an agreement concluded between Marshal Tito and the Yugoslav government in exile in London. Three of us were sentenced to death, but only Dr Nagode was executed, while the death sentences on Professor Furlan and myself were commuted to twenty years' forced labour. (See *The Times*, 13, 21, 23.8.47.)

In fact I spent seven and a half years in prison, during which I took advantage of my 're-education': we were encouraged to read communist newspapers and publications, which I did so meticulously that I discovered to my own satisfaction what was wrong with Marxism and its application in Yugoslavia. Violence was necessary because otherwise no country would stay communist for very long. In 1948 and 1949 communist secret policemen sometimes visited me in prison to discuss the political and economic situation and sound out my views. I was foolish enough to tell them frankly what I thought. I say foolish because this sincerity probably prolonged my imprisonment. They had no answer to my criticisms, which did not prevent them from contemptuously waving their hands: 'Oh well, that is what you think, Sirc!' They must have been amazed when a few years later, in 1952, their own leaders started saying exactly what I had claimed earlier about centralist planning.

Nonetheless I became accustomed to being accused of bias by precisely those people who themselves suffer from preconceptions, both in the East and West. For instance, all the *Economic Journal* (March 1970, p. 223) had to say about my book *Economic Devolution in Eastern Europe* (London: Longmans, 1969) was: 'This is a polemical discussion of the recent slow-down in the rate of growth in East European countries. Although there are useful observations and information here the author has allowed his strong political feelings to determine his selection of evidence.' I would have liked to know what evidence I had omitted.

Because of such persistent accusations of prejudice, I have developed the habit of supporting my views by continuously referring to what the communists themselves write. As a rule, their detailed criticisms are valid although they cannot do much about them since they are a consequence of the system which they are bound to praise as a great success and achievement. This continuous use of quotations is a difficult method because one is forced to allow one's train of thought to be guided by the material available, which sometimes interferes with the exposition. Nevertheless, I persisted because I feel that this way of writing is in many respects more 'original' than if I told the story of the Yugoslav economy in my own words. I have also to a large extent used daily and weekly newspapers because in my opinion they offer a more immediate and genuine expression of views than books or journals, which are less a spontaneous reaction to events and can be more easily adapted to the requirements of ideology.

The many references constitute a firm basis for what one claims. In this book practically everything I say has been said by somebody in Yugoslavia. The exceptions are some theoretical elucidations and ultimate conclusions which Yugoslavs living in Yugoslavia hardly care to draw although they are—or most certainly used to be—freer to write what they think than elsewhere in Eastern Europe.

In his review of my *Economic Devolution* in the *Slavic Review* (September 1970), Professor John M. Montias took me to task for believing 'that it is sufficient to quote repentant East European planners, many of whom were as ready to heap abuse on the old system as they had been once eager to uphold it, to clinch the case for market-type decentralisation'. He thought that 'this proposition should be tested statistically, not rejected a priori on the basis of casual observation'. In my view, economic success cannot be measured in physical terms and that is what statistics in the end amount to; economic success depends on how a system meets the needs of the population and this is best shown in the satisfaction people derive from it. So many communists, including the Yugoslavs, were 'converted' to the market precisely because they became aware, while running the system, that the needs of the population remained unsatisfied, contrary to the original communist promises. For Eastern Europe, Yugoslavia today is a paradise in spite of all its shortcomings. It may be true—as Professor

Montias claimed — that the centralist system is better when a country is preparing for war but even this is by no means certain — after all the United States and Great Britain were very successful in turning out munitions when they set their minds to it in the Second World War although they did not go all the way to Soviet-type centralist planning. And who wants his country's economy to be exclusively geared to war preparations?

For all these reasons, I am still of the opinion that those who run an economy know best whether the system functions or not. That applies to the views of East European reformers and also to the Yugoslav leaders, economists and businessmen. To the latter it also applies under the circumstances of self-management; they are best placed to know what is happening and put their finger on shortcomings which may not show in any statistics.

Another problem when writing this book was how to organise the material — historically or systematically. A systematic approach would appeal to me most, but there have been so many changes in Yugoslavia over the last 25 years that I had to divide the book into periods which, however, overlap because the subject matter would be excessively divided otherwise. The result is not entirely satisfactory, but I do not see any other better approach. This lay-out does give some idea about the prevailing uncertainty of how to solve problems and the ensuing continuous changes.

I was released from prison in 1954 and escaped from Yugoslavia in 1955. Since then I have lived in the West and become thoroughly acquainted with what is thought here about the Soviet Union and Eastern Europe, including Yugoslavia. For the public and even for experts, with some exceptions, the conditions in these countries are something abstract for which they do not seem to have much understanding. I cannot blame them because I was no better in understanding the Soviet Union before I learnt in practice what communism is. But this abstract approach is one of the reasons why I did not use to any substantial extent the literature on Yugoslavia by Western authors. They tend to miss many important points and get involved with technicalities. Some of them also still suffer from idealistic illusions.

Originally I intended to devote this work 'to all those Yugoslavs who tried and partly succeeded in pulling the economy out of the quagmire of centralist planning, and ideological dogmatism'. But since then Yugoslavia has again turned away from pragmatism and 'liberalism' and got enmeshed in a labyrinth of words manipulated by ideologists.

Nonetheless I wish to say a word of praise for those of my fellow countrymen who during all these years valiantly defended economic and political common sense.

I have used the material available to me by the end of 1977. A postscript covers the events in 1978, but on the whole there is no chance that the development in Yugoslavia would suddenly take a new turning. There is not much comparison with other countries because Yugoslavia is very different from the rest of Eastern Europe. As for the West. Yugoslavia seems to show what happens if enterprises are managed by people who are not dependant on those legally linked to their capital. In this respect, it also shows where the West is heading if many ideas tried out in Yugoslavia and found wanting nevertheless gain currency here.

My aim is to show the Yugoslav economy under self-management as it appears to Yugoslavs who have to live with it, so as to help outsiders to comprehend better what is happening there. The Yugoslav communist authorities do not like my endeavours, which they showed in 1975 when they took away my mother's passport and threatened that she would not see me again if I did not stop writing about my home country. They only desisted when there appeared signs of international concern about such treatment of an old woman to stop open discussion even outside Yugoslavia.

Glasgow, May 1979 Ljubo Sirc

Acknowledgements

I am grateful to Roger Clarke who edited the final version of this book and vastly improved on the text, and to Dr Janusz Zielinki who read the first version and amply commented on it. Both are members of the Institute of Soviet and East European Studies in the University of Glasgow. My departmental colleague Robin Milne and an anonymous reader for the publishers also contributed by their criticism. The publishers' editor, John Winckler, helped me with his encouragement.

The final version of the script was competently and patiently typed by Mrs Terry Campbell and Ms Joyce Stillie.

My wife Susan and my little daughter Nadia bore with me while I was working.

Abbreviations

B	*Borba*, daily, Belgrade
D	*Delo*, daily, Ljubljana
Dn	*Dnevnik*, daily, Ljubljana
Ep	*Ekonomska politika*, weekly, Belgrade
JP	*Jugoslovenski pregled*, monthly, Belgrade
K	*Kommunist*, party publication, irregularly at first, then weekly, Belgrade
LP	*Ljudska pravica*, daily, Ljubljana
NR	*Nasi razgledi*, fortnightly, Ljubljana
NIN	*Nedeljne informativne novine*, weekly, Belgrade
NZZ	*Neue Zurcher Zeitung*, daily, Zurich
OECD	*OECD Economic Surveys – Yugoslavia*
P	*Politika*, daily, Belgrade
RIA	*Review of International Affairs*, fortnightly, Belgrade
SP	*Slovenski porocevalec*, daily, Ljubljana
Sl	*Sluzbeni list* (*Official Gazette*), Belgrade
SG	*Statisticki godisnjak* (*Statistical Annuary*), Belgrade
V	*Vjesnik*, daily, Zagreb
Vus	*Vjesnik u srijedu*, weekly, Zagreb
YS	*Yugoslav Survey*, quarterly, Belgrade
CPY	Communist Party of Yugoslavia
YLC	League of Communists of Yugoslavia
CC	Central Committee
GSP	Gross Social Product
	One billion = 1000 million

Basic data on Yugoslavia

number of inhabitants, 1977 — 21,775,000

GSP 1976 dinars 592 billion (approx. $30 billion)
1977 dinars 736 billion

1: Introduction

1.1 THE BACKGROUND TO REFORMS

After seizing power in 1945, the leaders of the Yugoslav Communist Party took over from the Soviet Union what was later called the 'administrative system', which at the time they considered the ultimate goal in the building of a socialist society (121, p. 158). Public ownership of capital and centralist planning were to be the two main pillars of the new order, as stressed by Marshal Tito when introducing the First Five-Year Plan to the Federal Assembly on 26 April 1947.

But as early as 1948 Stalin expelled Tito's Yugoslavia from the Cominform, the organisation of the ruling East European plus Italian and French Communist Parties. The immediate reaction of the Yugoslav communist leaders was to try to prove that they were true communists and even good Stalinists. There was a second round of nationalisation, now embracing all enterprises of any importance, and a campaign for the collectivisation of agriculture (cf. 31, p. 148).

However, when these moves failed to mollify the onslaught of the other East European Parties and governments, the Yugoslav leadership began looking for a way to counter Stalin's challenge. Djilas describes (31, p. 137) how he began to re-read Marx's *Capital* and discovered many previously unnoticed ideas about a future society in which the immediate producers, through association, would themselves make decisions on production and distribution. In the spring of 1950 he suggested to Kardelj and Kidric that Yugoslavia should introduce Marx's free associations of producers. They thought it a good idea, but one that should not be put into effect for another five or six years. However, a couple of days later, Kidric telephoned to say that they were ready to go ahead at once with the first steps.

Tito was apparently informed of the idea somewhat later and his first reaction was: 'Our workers are not ready for that yet'. Then he realised that it would be seen as a radical departure from Stalinism and exclaimed: 'Factories belonging to the workers — something that has never yet been achieved'. The Workers' Self-Management Act was adopted by the National Assembly on 27 June 1950.

However, this Act did not alter the nature of the centralist system itself, so there was not much scope for either management or self-management of individual enterprises (cf. JP 69, p. 431). The situation changed only in 1952 with the introduction of the so-called 'economic automatism', when the relevant Acts gradually implemented the transition to the new economic system with more independence for enterprises, broader rights of self-management and clear market elements.

1.2 REASONS FOR ECONOMIC REFORMS

President Tito said in 1971 that self-management had been 'so to speak forced' on Yugoslavia (B 9.5.71), presumably to provide *ex post* a plausible Marxist justification for the resistance to Stalin. But the Cominform attack was also an opportunity for Yugoslav communists to reconsider their ideological position creating conditions for the emergence of a Yugoslav version of socialism (53, p. 75).

However, the early 1950s were also a time of economic crisis for Yugoslavia, which further fostered rethinking. In 1952 the national income fell to below the 1948 level, back to the level of 1939 (see Table 5.1), stocks of unsaleable goods were accumulating, existing capacities were underutilised, the efficiency of labour and investment was low and individual consumption was declining. Even unemployment reappeared.

Some claimed that the crisis was due to the economic blockade by East European countries rather than to the deficiencies of central planning, and indeed the blockade can hardly have helped. *The United Nations Survey of Europe* (UNO, Geneva 1954, p. 113) attributed Yugoslav difficulties partly to the change in political climate and partly to Yugoslavia's own failures in planning, but some Yugoslav assessments were far less cautious, as exemplified by Rudolf Bicanic: 'To those who lived through it, the expense in human and economic terms of the system of centralised, bureaucratic normative planning is as obvious as the damage that it can inflict at all levels of the economy' (14, p. 125).

Turning to the figures (58, pp. 202–5), it transpires that the value of Yugoslav imports fell from 88.4 billion dinars in 1949 to 69.2 billion in 1950, but rose again in 1951 to 115.1 billion dinars, 30 per cent more than before the blockade, and subsequently remained at that level. This recovery was due especially to the USA and Western Germany (under

Allied control) which stepped up their supplies considerably. Many of these imports were not paid for by exports and thus worsened Yugoslav indebtedness abroad, but economic aid ran at a level of $100 million (dinars 30 billion) a year starting from 1951 (JP 57, p. 38).

Obviously, some disruption must have been caused by the switch from East European suppliers, who in 1948 provided 48 per cent of Yugoslav imports (23, p. 273) to American and West European suppliers, but if one is to believe Vladimir Dedijer, this switch could not have been entirely unwelcome. Dedijer (29, p. 73 ff) recounts in great detail how, from the very beginning in 1945, the Soviet Union was out to exploit Yugoslavia in manifold ways through trade. A further disruptive effect must have been due to the psychological shock inflicted on the Yugoslav leaders by the break with the Soviet Union and Stalin whom they had considered their mentor and inspiration.

The simultaneous military threat forced Yugoslavia to raise her defence expenditure from 6.4 per cent of the national income in 1948 to 21.4 per cent in 1952 (calc. SG56, p. 239). Later it was gradually reduced to 8 per cent in 1960 (calc. SG61, p. 232). But Yugoslavia was in receipt of Western military aid which, according to an American estimate (49, pp. 349 and 354), amounted to about another $100 million a year up till 1958.

All in all, it would seem that Western aid went a long way to compensate Yugoslavia for the disruption caused by Stalin's orders. Besides, economic difficulties continued through the 1950s and 1960s although the acute pressure from Eastern Europe stopped after Khrushchev's visit to Belgrade in 1955.

By the early 1950s the Yugoslav communist leaders themselves had little doubt about the deficiencies of the centralist planning they had been practising. The Chairman of the Planning Commission himself, the late Boris Kidric, said at the Sixth Party Congress in 1952: 'Who can guarantee that our plans are correct, if they are not subject to the checks and corrections of objective economic laws? I personally cannot do so . . . .' His suggestion for the future was: 'The new economic system should be based on objective economic laws and avoid, if possible, the administrative throttling of these laws. The administrative "struggle" against objectively existing economic laws is fundamentally fruitless and irrational.' Another economic Minister, Svetozar Vukmanovic, thought that the previous Yugoslav planned economy had been built 'on an unrealistic basis' (V 5.1.1953).

As the crisis of the 1950s began receding into the past, recognition of the flaws inherent in centralist planning became more blurred. Kardelj now claims (61, p. 28) that the original 'State ownership and bureaucracy were a historical necessity' and does not admit that this was 'the Stalinist system' (61, p. 15).

1.3 SHORTCOMINGS OF THE CENTRALIST SYSTEM

The inconsistency of plans and their uneven implementation led to accumulation of abnormally large stocks of all kinds of machinery, and especially agricultural machinery, at the beginning of the 1950s. This was widely reported in the newspapers but no exact data were produced. Costs of production in the new machine-building industry were very high so that it was difficult to sell its products once a semblance of economic calculation was introduced. Tractors, for instance, needed a state subsidy amounting to 70 per cent of their costs of production to make their use profitable for agricultural cooperatives (B 22.6.52). There was a similar stocks problem in the consumer goods industries, where the main difficulty was the wrong product mix and bad quality due to hurried production to fulfil the plan. The term 'unsaleable commodities' came into use.

Plant capacities could not be fully utilised (Dn 25.8.52), which contributed to the low efficiency of investment and labour shown in Table 1.1.

Table 1.1: Total productivity of labour and capital in 1952

	1939	*1952*
Industrial output	100	170
Industrial labour force	100	201
Value of capital	100	212

Source: Calculated from 58, p. 142 and 23, p. 199.

From this table it follows that by 1952 the index of the total productivity of industrial labour had fallen to 85 and the total productivity of industrial capital to 84 in comparison with 1939. If it is assumed that in pre-war plans productivity remained the same, it must have been substantially lower in the new plants. This impression was confirmed by official sources (JP 61, p. 158) which put the incremental capital–output ratio in 1948–52 as high as 10:1 (see p. 239). The figures for 1952 would have been even worse, had non-agricultural employment not been reduced by 14 per cent between 1949 and 1952, marking the end of the previous indiscriminate employment policy (see p. 14).

Of course, the 1947 Five-Year Plan had prescribed a fall in production costs and a rise in labour productivity, but the targets could not be implemented. It was difficult to establish what was going on in individual enterprises because their accounts were so complicated that they were months and sometimes years in arrear and sometimes could not be worked out at all. Even the existing level of production was only maintained by labour intensification and deterioration of quality. 'In the struggle for quantitative fulfilment of the Plan, enterprises often forget quality. If workers are blamed for bad quality, they tend to say: "Yes, but what about the norm?"' (LP 24.11.48).

Personal consumption fell from about 76 per cent of what it was before the war in 1948, to about 70 per cent in 1952, and personal consumption per capita from about 75 per cent to about 67 per cent (see Table 5.1). President Tito thought it necessary to stress in his New Year speech in 1949 that government policy was to raise the living standard, not to let it fall.

A necessary consequence of the low production of consumer goods was low wages and particularly salaries. In the 1950s the Federal Statistical Institute did not publish any general wage indices because they were 'not reliable' and could have led to 'wrong and harmful conclusions' (LP 6.3.54, cf. 58, p. 64). But in 1952 indices of real incomes of four-member families were published to prove that there was no reason for anybody to be dissatisfied (SP 6.5.52).

Table 1.2: The living standard of an average four-member manual worker family

	Total income Dinars	*Cost of a given standard of living Dinars*	*Index of living standard*
1939	978,	1.889,	100
March 1952	13.301,	17.214,	148

Source: SP 6.5.52, cf. p. 5

In 1952 the allowance for two children was dinars 6000, so that an average worker's wage without this allowance would have been dinars 7301, which is equivalent to a living standard of 81 per cent of what it was before the war. In that year 1,399,401 child allowances were paid to 1,808,807 social insurance members (SG 56, p. 344), which means 77 per cent of one child's allowance per member. The average wage, including the average child allowance, then amounted to 106 per cent of the pre-war wage.

The corresponding figures for a four-member white-collar employee family show that in 1952 his total income allowed a living standard amounting to 77 per cent of what it was before the war. His average salary amounted to 41 per cent of the corresponding pre-war salary and to 59 per cent if the average child allowance is taken into account.

More than half of the population were still peasants. According to Bicanic, in 1952 industrial prices in Yugoslavia were 81 per cent above the world market level and agricultural prices 45 per cent below it (14, p. 127). Since before the war Yugoslav industrial prices were also 10 per cent higher and agricultural prices 20 per cent lower than in the world market (JP 61, p. 355), the 1952 industrial prices must have been 130 per cent higher in relation to the level of agricultural prices than before the war. As a consequence the money income of peasants before tax was down to some 42 per cent of their pre-war average money income. Then the land tax amounted to 3–4 per cent of an average peasant's total income, while it rose, under the communist government, to between 10 and 20 per cent 'and more' (71, p. 357) and even to 50–70 per cent in some cases (SP 9.7.52). But often there was nothing the peasant could buy for his money (SP 3.6.52 and V 25.6.52). Compulsory purchases also cut into the peasant's consumption of the produce of his own farm (see p. 13). The rest of the population fared similarly.

The most spectacular sign of the dire state of the Yugoslav economy under centralist planning was the fall in the national income. In real terms, it fell from 116 in 1951 to 100 in 1952, i.e. back to the level of 1939 and below the level of 1948 (58, p. 77). Industrial output fell by 5 per cent from the peak in 1949, while the index of agricultural production fluctuated: 1947 — 120, 1948 — 138, 1949 — 135, 1950 — 101, 1951 — 142, 1952 — 100, which means that it fell to almost half of the 1939 level (58, p. 97) and 75 per cent of the average for 1930–39 (58, p. 98) (see p. 13).

1.4 UNDERSTANDING THE SHORTCOMINGS

It is of some interest to find out what understanding the Yugoslav leaders themselves had of the reasons for these shortcomings since their comprehension of the causes obviously guided them in their efforts to improve the functioning of the economy.The reasons fall into three groups: those inherent in the centralist planning system itself; reasons connected with Stalinist development strategy; and thirdly, Yugoslav exaggerations of this strategy. Only the faults pertaining to the first group appear to have been understood by the Yugoslav leaders at the beginning of the 1950s. The consequences of the Stalinist concentration on 'heavy industry' were not initially comprehended and neither were the distortions caused by very high growth rates under Yugoslav conditions. Their elimination will therefore be discussed later rather than in this section (see pp. 35 and 91).

In order to draft a plan it is essential for the planning commission to have a clear idea of the existing state of the economy and also of each of its basic units — the enterprises. In 1948 Marshal Tito complained that there were no statistics to speak of and Kardelj criticised the lack of precision in enterprises' reports to higher authorities (LP 26.4.48).

But even had the reports been correct, their sheer bulk was such that they could not be scrutinised. Kardelj complained that, in the general directorate of the iron and steel industry for instance, nobody used the comprehensive monthly reports. Apparently there were too few employees in spite of the huge administrative apparatus, to deal with the flood of paper.

On the other hand, the orders issued by central planners could not be made sufficiently precise so that, while the letter of the plan was formally executed, the spirit was flouted. 'Industry tended to produce those articles by the production of which it was easiest to fulfil and overfulfil the plans, or to carry on year in year out the same sort of production because this was cheapest.' (LP 27.3.48). There were usually discrepancies between financial and physical plans, so that it was even possible to make cost increases look like plan fulfilment and overfulfilment. 'Unfortunately, so far some enterprises have been taking little notice of the financial plan. Some directors believe that they should produce regardless of financial elements. Many a director thinks that he has implemented his plan as long as he delivers the planned quantity of product to his own warehouse.' (LP 28.3.48).

General legal provisions were a good illustration of how difficult it is for those in authority to communicate their wishes down to grass roots, especially if speed is required. The flood of legal provisions caused so much confusion that, in 1952, only 150 Acts out of 3,500 could be left in force (SP 18.7.52, see p. 20). Laws were usually drafted in a hurry (Tito, B 15.7.62) so that they had to be amended within a very short time. Even later it was claimed that 'the unstable market was due to unstable legal provisions' (Ep 29.6.61).

If a new Act only caused trouble, it used to be said that the idea was correct but that it was wrongly implemented by the lower authorities. An example of this was the hasty introduction of agricultural cooperatives (Dn 18.5.1952). The constant changes were explained as a consequence of 'the dynamism of Yugoslav economic development' (Ep 29.6.61), but serious people apparently wondered what to make of a State where nothing is stable (B 10.6.53) and where legal provisions were often retroactive (SP 4.4.1954). On the whole, they were written 'in a heavy and confused style', so that enterprises had difficulties in interpreting them (SP 4.4.54).

Up till 1952, the system was run by command from above without any incentives, which led to a complete lack of initiative. People avoided taking independent decisions if they could. Supervisory organs had to push the system forward—public prosecutors and political police interfered with everything. For a considerable time there was a representative of the political police in every major enterprise. Kardelj himself eventually scorned this omnipresent supervision: 'To make one person work, three persons were needed to supervise him' (B 6.5.59). And Vukmanovic wrote about supervisors who had 'to supervise the work of other supervisors' (121, p. 132).

However, the Planning Commission not only lacked correct and up to date information and a method to pass unequivocal orders down to production units, it also had no economic criteria to apply to the data which were available. Of course, the Commission was bound by the targets determined by the Party and State leadership on the basis of the laws of social development and of political economy (20, see also p. 28), which meant on the basis of their understanding of Marxist philosophy of history. But with the possible exception of the establishment of a desired growth rate these targets were vague ideological statements.

These statements were used by the Planning Commission to establish the desired relationship between agricultural and industrial production and between consumption and investment. Then the Commission alloted investment to the various sectors of the economy and tried to 'balance' it. The communist economist Krasovec later wrote (68, pp. 26–7) that the planners used to establish endless lists of requirements for industry, transport, mining, etc. in physical terms without taking any notice of prices. All they had to match them with were figures for the so-called 'capacities', possible output of industrial plants, frequently not connected with each other. The best that such balancing could possibly achieve was consistency of plans, but certainly not optimality.

For that scarcity prices would have been required, but Tito rejected them (87, p. 13) in 1947 and insisted that he wanted production for people's needs instead of for profits, without explaining how such needs can be calculated in the absence of a market and profitability. The result was that no economic criteria were applied at all. In the words of the economist Aleksander Bajt 'the law of value was replaced by planned fixing of production structure and by planned distribution at fixed wages and prices' (5, p. 173). Another professional economist, Rudolf Bicanic, was more explicit (15, p. 42) when he said that under centralised planning, the country was at the mercy of the political arbitrariness and bureaucratic whims of the central planning authorities which concealed the fact that the top political decision-makers had no economic criteria while their economic back-room men bore no responsibility and blocked the initiative of those below.

After the expulsion from the Cominform, the political leaders realised that it is impossible to run an economy without economic criteria (see p. 3). More than that, in his memoirs Vukmanovic quotes Kidric as saying that the best weapon Yugoslavia could use against the United States would be to send them two Yugoslav planners who would ruin their economy (121, p. 150).

Part One

Dismantling Centralist Planning (1952–1960)

2: The Role of Planning and 'Automatism'

2.1 GRADUAL CHANGE IN APPROACH

As late as January 1950, the Conclusions of the CC of the CPY on the Current Tasks in the Struggle for the Five-Year Plan (K 50, p. 8) seemed to claim that the main targets were being successfully implemented despite the blockade and other pressure from the East. There was a hint that all was not well in agriculture since inadequate organisational and political preparations for State purchases and the establishment of further production cooperatives were mentioned, but these were blamed, as always, on the lowest echelons.

The accompanying speech by Kidric (K 50) pointed out that 'a number of "sectarian" mistakes' might seriously endanger agricultural production in the coming year. In reality, 'some peasants had been deprived of all their wheat to the last grain' (11, p. 47) so that they were left without even seed for sowing. Compulsory purchases together with one-sided investment policy, droughts, the land reform, confused legal relationships, and the establishment of production cooperatives (80) completely disorganised agriculture. Production fell (see p. 6) also because the cultivated area was reduced by about 7 per cent as compared with 1939 (58, p. 97). Veselinov, the leader from the most fertile region of Vojvodina, apparently said to Kidric:

> The simple truth is that there is no wheat and we want the peasants to produce it out of nothing. Therefore, we are waging a regular war on them. Thousands of peasants have been arrested and sentenced to imprisonment. Some were killed. People are defending with axes the small amounts of wheat they have harvested . . . In the liberation war they were on our side, now they are our enemies. (121, p. 128)

Compulsory purchases had to be abolished in 1952 and the peasants were allowed to withdraw from production cooperatives. Almost all landowning peasants left although they had to leave their cattle behind (79, p. 126). The 6804 production cooperatives with 2.5 million ha agricultural land — 20 per cent of the total area — which existed in 1951 were reduced to 688 with 233.000 ha by 1955 and then dwindled to insignificance (58, p. 111).

The 1950 Conclusions also referred to the need for 'better planning discipline' in labour recruitment. Kidric, however, revealed that the 'extensive increase in the labour force' in manufacturing and administration had led to labour shortages in agriculture and overstaffing elsewhere. Possibly under the influence of a mistaken interpretation of Marx's labour theory of value, the Yugoslav communist leaders considered any increase in the industrial labour force as a step forward. Agricultural workers were lured to factories by appeals to their patriotic feelings (LP 23.8.48) but also by withdrawal of their ration cards (LP 8.5.48), much was done to induce women 'into production', to persuade Yugoslav emigrées all over the world to come home, to recruit voluntary labour and to lengthen and intensify regular working hours.

The numbers employed were growing, yet as labour was inefficiently used, 'the most difficult problem was that there was not enough manpower' (Tito, LP 8.12.48). Kidric described (LP 25.4.48) how there were unnecessary reserves of labour everywhere, the pseudo-plans asking for seven times more than actually needed, with a 'wild struggle' for workers among enterprises and institutions leading to ever greater chaos in wages policy.

The Yugoslav non-agricultural labour force rose from 1,167,000 in 1947 (920,000 in 1939) to 1,990,000 in 1949 (58, p. 58). Kidric's speech was a sign for this policy to go into reverse. In the early 1950s 250,000 manual, administrative and professional workers were dismissed (JP 58, p. 30) though 'concealed unemployment' amounting to some 15–20 per cent of non-agricultural workers remained (72, p. 16; 79, p. 138; 23, p. 116). The previous full employment in Yugoslavia was as ficticious as in other communist countries.

Some of the dismissed found their way back to agriculture which in consequence improved its performance, but many could not because the existing agricultural over-population was aggravated by communist attempts to introduce labour-saving agricultural machinery (121, p. 164). Vukmanovic admitted that the problem of unemployment was closely linked with 'the structure of investment' (SP 1.6.53) which was biased towards heavy industry providing few jobs.

The first two problems the communists tried to deal with were food shortages and excessive employment in industry, but they thought they could do it within the existing system and even again stressed the need for concentration on key heavy industry projects.

Radical changes of the economic system were perhaps not even intended when, on 26 June 1950, President Tito (K 50) laid before parliament legislation on workers' councils and decentralisation of the economy. He regretted the previous illusions and the transplant into Yugoslavia of whatever was being done in the Soviet Union, but then hailed the forthcoming administrative decentralisation and handing over of factories to the workers as the 'withering away of the State'. Tito again wondered whether Yugoslav workers, fresh from villages, would be up to the tasks of 'worker-managers', but his answer now was that they should learn on the job.

In a subsequent statement, Kidric (K 50) dealt with the re-organisation of the State economic administration. There would be a change from the lower State form to the higher form of socialist ownership, that is to the administration of the general people's property by free association of direct producers. Continued State administration remained imperative, although it would be reformed by replacing a number of economic ministries by government councils and 'general directorates', by refurbishing planning methodology and transferring most enterprises from federal to republican and from republican to local jurisdiction. These new bodies proved so unwieldy and conservative that they were all abolished in 1952 to open the way for more self-management (JP 69, p. 427).

The Yugoslav communist leaders were groping ahead as they had a very difficult task: in their reforms they had to rely entirely on themselves because they had suppressed any dissenting professional economist in their initial zeal, so that now when advice about reforms was needed, Yugoslav economists continued publishing books extolling centralist administrative planning (20, 110). Until about 1960, Yugoslav economists were very reluctant to commit any original thought to paper and under the influence of Marxism, they concentrated mainly on institutions so that they were continuously preoccupied with the search for a new economic system instead of solving problems within the given framework (53). The consequence was an endless series of reorganisations.

The economic knowledge of the communist leaders themselves was limited to Marxist-Leninist tenets and casual observation of what was going on in other countries. Therefore their discussions strike one as esoteric. When Vukmanovic returned from the United States in 1951, he attended a meeting at which Kidric was explaining the proposed changes in the economic system and said that plans would be used to oblige workers' collectives to use their capacities to the full. Basing himself on his American impressions, Vukmanovic claimed that it would be far simpler to give them an interest in full utilisation by making them pay for the use of capital. Kidric agreed, but said that this would be a return to capitalism. They each spent a sleepless night only to find that both had reversed their positions, and the problem was only solved when Tito pronounced that charging interest would not be a return to capitalism (121, p. 153).

It was particularly curious that the architect of the reforms in the 1950s was Boris Kidric who earlier as the chief planner had been responsible for forcing on Yugoslavia what he now called 'the thoughtless adoption' (*prakticisticka recepcija*) of Soviet practice. Moreover, it was he who later in 1950 produced the *Theses on the Economics of the Transitional Period in our Country* (K 50) which contained the basis for the switch to a market economy. He maintained that the abolition of 'commodity exchange' (sale and purchase of goods in the market) would take a long time and that therefore it would be advantageous to preserve independent enterprises as 'economic-legal entities'. They were, of course, an inheritance from the past together with 'commodity exchange' itself, but as 'socialist enterprises' they contained a dialectical, relative revolutionary element, which could even be described as a qualitative jump because of (1) social ownership, (2) the framework of a social plan of basic proportions, and (3) social accumulation. In its socialist form 'commodity exchange' was a 'dialectical contradiction', which gave birth to conflicting interests but not necessarily to class antagonisms. Although couched in this Marxist-Leninist jargon, Kidric's *Theses* opened the way to economic relaxation in Yugoslavia.

2.2 THE NEW PLANNING

At the end of 1950 the Act On Planned Management of the National Economy replaced the Act on General State Economic Planning and State Planning Organs, adopted at the end of 1946. In his *On the New Economic Draft Laws* (K 51), Kidric announced that, unlike the previous *state* plans which stifled the initiative of workers' collectives and rendered self-management impossible, the new *social* plans would deal only with 'basic proportions'. These proportions were 'those, and only those, provisions of social plans which prevented innate capitalist anarchy from appearing in social production and distribution'.

In Kidric's words, the new planning was to remove 'not only exploitation by former economic, social and political ruling classes, but also by internal parasites on the socialist revolution' and Kardelj insisted that 'industry should be freed so that it could develop without interference by the bureaucracy' (B 16.7.1952).

The three fundamental planned proportions were to be: (1) compulsory minimum utilisation of capacity; (2) basic investment; and (3) average rates of 'accumulation and funds' (savings for investment and collective consumption) shown as a percentage of wages. Other proportions would then be derived from these three; in fact, the first plans determined what was to be paid out of 'accumulation and funds' to the state authorities at federal, republican and local levels and what retained by enterprises and also what part of their share was to be used for investment.

Previously plans pushed for a maximum, now merely a prescribed minimum was obligatory. Enterprises could increase their output and also their wages fund, but if they did they had to pay the same accumulation rates on the increased wages as on the minimum wages fund. If, on the contrary, they succeeded in producing more without increasing wages and, hence, also without additional accumulation rates, they achieved profits which were to be divided in a prescribed way.

Only the social plans of 1952 and 1953 were worked out on the basis of the 1951 Planning Act even though this Act remained formally valid till 1970. From 1954 on, planning was not based on any legal rules but evolved pragmatically in accordance with ever new ideological and theoretical perceptions (JP 70, p. 310).

Some Yugoslavs (16, p. 76) considered the 1951 planning to be 'in fact the old economic system', but it did loosen the central grip on the economy, in practice if not in legal terms, and enterprises could fix their level of output and product mix more freely. The dependence of workers' earnings on revenue per man also made it possible to achieve the same output with a reduced workforce (121, p. 169).

The awkward features of the first attempt at a new type of planning were the rates of accumulation and funds which were 'a ratio analogous to the rate of surplus labour and surplus product as known to Marxist political economy' (K 4–5/51, p. 109). Just as there is no way of calculating the surplus value of labour in individual cases, so there was no way to decide what the rate of accumulation and funds should be. All that could be done was to 'photograph' (Kidric's word quoted in JP 61, p. 357) the existing situation and define the rate of accumulation as the ratio of wages to 1952 revenue minus wages and input costs (B 26.7.52, Ep 7.8.52).

The results were absurd and as arbitrary as the previous 'planned' prices. No account was taken of the capital cooperating with labour in different enterprises; on the contrary, often very capital intensive branches were charged lower rates of accumulation because much of the new investment yielded very low returns on capital or even losses. The first set of rates in the 1952 plan, for instance, charged an accumulation rate of 110 per cent on agricultural machinery production, 3200 per cent on the production of ordinary nails at Jesenice, and about 700 per cent on nail production elsewhere. For this reason the results of enterprises depended largely on whether they had to pay high or low accumulation rates and most enterprises kept asking for lower rates (121, p. 170).

Even these arbitrary charges on wages were deemed not to be a sufficient guarantee against excessive wage differentials: progressive taxation was introduced on wages over dinars 9000 *on average* per worker per month and on profits. Obviously this reduced the incentives which were intended to play an important part in the working of the new system and prompted enterprises to cheat by employing extra workers with low qualifications and low wages, so as to make it possible for others to earn more (121, p. 170).

At the end of 1953, a host of economic decrees was published centred on the Decree on Total Revenue of Economic Enterprises and its Distribution. The most significant innovation was the interest rate which was to replace the rate of accumulation and was to be paid on all 'means of production' (capital) used by enterprises. Supplemented by a series of taxes, accounting wages and social security contributions, all fixed by the plans, this interest rate was to constrain enterprise profit.

The net profit was distributed according to a plan drawn up by the district people's committee. This committee was entitled to take a part for itself and a part for the municipal committee. Then the district committee determined the amount for yearly repayments of long-term loans, the amount allotted to the enterprise's reserve fund and the amount at the free disposal of the enterprise. This last amount had to be divided between supplementary wages, investment fund and other funds. But the allocation to wages was restricted by federal provisions.

The Decree on Distribution apparently stressed the role of local committees so much because, at that time, the intention was to make them the basic unit, the 'commune' (see p. 40). But it was soon felt that the powers of local committees had become excessive and the Decree on Distribution was recast in 1956.

One of the changes was the introduction of 'by-laws on wage rates' in place of 'accounting wages' which were thought to favour the worst enterprises because they were based on the results of the previous year. 'By-laws' were supposed to give enterprises more leeway (121, p. 225), although their freedom was limited by the Federal social plan which circumscribed the distribution of profits by partly determining and partly influencing the federal profit tax, supplementary wages paid out of profits, payments to social investment funds and contributions to budgets. Some profits were left to enterprises for their independent disposal.

The 1956 Decrees met with opposition (121, pp. 223, 226) for not being sufficiently radical and in particular for uncritically continuing the capitalist category of profit. Apparently the critics feared that workers would not simply try to minimise costs like capitalists, but would minimise costs other than wages, so that high revenue would lead to an increase in employment at the expense of profits and, therefore, also of profit tax. Supervision by communes would not help because they were interested in an increase of employment on their territory too.

In consequence new legal rules were adopted in 1957 which were aimed at giving enterprises further scope to decide on the distribution not of profits now but of 'income', defined as an enterprise's revenue minus production costs including interest but excluding wages, now called 'individual incomes' so as to stress that workers were no longer in a 'wage relationship'. The 'income' thus became a concept including both profits and wages. After 'minimum individual incomes' (defined by the Federation) were deducted from 'income' the base for the 'contribution out of income' was obtained. The marginal 'contribution' rose to 72 per cent for income approaching twice the total of minimum incomes for a particular enterprise.

What remained the enterprise distributed between workers' individual incomes and its own funds (fixed capital fund, working capital fund, reserve fund, and fund for collective consumption), and the allocation could be disallowed by the local people's committee or the trade union within thirty days, whereas previously it had to be expressly approved.

From individual incomes, a progressive 'contribution' had to be paid to 'local budgets': 10 per cent on the first dinars 20,000 and 40 per cent on any income over dinars 100,000. At that time dinars 20,000 was approximately $28 and was the approximate monthly earnings of the average worker.

All in all, after 1953 economic planning in Yugoslavia mainly consisted of attempts at steering economic development by taxation (various contributions), the so-called economic instruments (interest rates, depreciation rates, minimum personal incomes, etc.), and provisions on investment, especially federal investment. This applied both to yearly plans and longer-term plans such as the Five-Year Social Plan 1957–1961 which covered only 15 pages of the Official Gazette.

Yugoslav plans no longer contained mandatory provisions, although they did state development targets. This puzzled some foreign observers (123, p. 39), while others simply concluded that plans were only forecasts and that enterprises might follow them or institute their own market research (113, p. 60). The truth was that 'economic planning in Yugoslavia had not been worked out as a systematic whole' by then (102, p. 29) in spite of all the assertions that capitalist anarchy had been replaced by 'conscious actions of associated producers' (103, p. 16).

2.3 THE SOCIALIST MARKET

Kidric's *Theses* distinguished between basic planning of economic proportions by the State and operational planning which was to be handed over to direct producers in autonomous enterprises. In fact, the planning of current production from the centre was stopped — it was up to enterprises to produce what they saw fit and sell it to anybody that wanted to buy it. In Kidric's view, if the centralist plan of proportions stifled enterprises' initiative, this would mean that the plan was excessively detailed and should be made more 'complex'.

Although the social plan and the taxes and other 'instruments' it imposed was very 'complex' indeed, so that 'the allocation of resources was not much influenced by the free play of market prices' (112, p. 118), lesser Yugoslav leaders and journalists took the hint from Kidric and 'emphasised to an almost exaggerated extent the virtues of the market mechanism' (112, p. 116). Tito thought, at some stage, that he should stress that the dominant characteristic of Yugoslavia was not the market — which also existed in capitalism — but workers' self-management (B 27.12.52).

Enterprises were initially freed of most constraints by a Decree of 1952 (Sl 40/1952) abolishing practically all rules and regulations governing their activity. However, new rules immediately began to be introduced and once again had become an impenetrable maze by 1956 (99, Introduction).

In the 1950s the various planning 'instruments' were such a burden on prices that in the economy as a whole net wages represented just under 40 per cent, and in industry less than 20 per cent of price minus material costs. The rest consisted of all sorts of taxes and charges (58, pp. 81 and 82). This severely limited the flexibility of prices and thus the responsiveness of the economy.

The planning 'instruments' and the consequences of previous development policies continued to distort prices. They displayed considerable 'disparities' if compared with relative prices either elsewhere in the world or in pre-war Yugoslavia. Table 2.1 illustrates this, although the discrepancies within the manufacturing group itself were also very important, but are not shown.

Table 2.1: Retail price indices 1952 and 1962

1939 – 100	*1952*	*1962*
General index	1852	2626
Manufactured goods	2247	2567
Agricultural goods	1497	3097
Services (including housing)	607	1818

Source: JP 63, p. 261.

The price disparities were difficult to eliminate because communist planning prevented the expansion of output of goods in high demand and prescribed investment in the production of goods whose supply turned out to be excessive. As a result indirect taxes had to be levied on some goods while others could be sold, if at all, only at prices that did not cover charges for capital and depreciation, or even current costs. This applied especially to the machine building industry which—like many others—had in the end to be given subsidies (Vukmanovic V 1.1.53).

The so-called '*regresi*' (refunds) became a part of the Yugoslav economic scenery. In addition to the wrong structure of investment, this was also due to the fact that goods could not be sold because they were of bad quality or the product mix was badly chosen. In many instances the new market pressures were insufficient to change the ways to which people had become accustomed during the centralist planning period, short as this had been. This influence is not surprising since most managers were new to the job, while experienced ones were intimidated into behaving like bureaucrats. The author knows of several cases in which people were imprisoned in the 1940s for having acted 'in a capitalist way' on behalf of their enterprises. The '*regresi*' were supplemented by reduction or abolition of interest rates, writing off taxes, etc.

The scale (58, pp. 267–8) of direct 'refunds and subsidies' in 1952 amounted to dinars 19.391 million (2.1 per cent of GSP) and rose by 1960 to dinars 174.615 million (6 per cent of GSP). But these figures include neither the various reductions in interest or taxes nor the inability of many enterprises to repay bank credits, which became another form of subsidy (79, p. 71 and 118, p. 231).

Kidric anticipated from the very beginning that there would be government control of prices of raw materials and semi-finished products and exceptionally of final goods (K 4–5/51, p. 9), but the inexorable upward drift of prices as shown in Table 2.1 eventually forced the Yugoslav leadership to introduce price controls on a wider basis. By the end of the 1950s, 'ceiling' prices were imposed on 50 per cent of the value of industrial production (JP 61, p. 358) and, according to another estimate, 'the State continued to fix the prices of some 70 % of products' (16, p. 96).

In 1959 the Secretary of State for 'commodity turnover', Marjan Brecelj, publicly wondered whether price policy had 'a clearly defined place in the (Yugoslav) system' (B 1.1.59), but the Party ideologist Kardelj affirmed that price control was not alien to the Yugoslav market: 'Our free market is a conditional term . . . It has to be understood that the free formation of prices under our conditions means that they are based on supply and demand within the general proportions of the plan' (B 21.2.61). Nevertheless, distorted prices adversely influenced both current decisions (e.g. low priced inputs were used to excess) and investment decisions as well as interfering with the functioning of foreign trade (cf. JP 61, p. 81 ff.).

As soon as enterprises were given a limited autonomy, some tried to exploit their monopolistic position in the market. This development was ironical in so far as Kidric's *Theses* had foreseen the need for a 'strong element of monopolistic price', primarily to raise social accumulation and partly to stimulate direct producers. Later *Borba* demanded that formation of monopolies for the purpose of pushing up wages funds should be prevented (B 27.7.52) although the communist leaders had been warned that it was difficult to distinguish genuine market gains by workers' collectives from monopolistic profits (121, p. 171).

To some extent monopolistic pressure on prices was fostered by the communist neglect of commerce. Private trade was abolished literally overnight in 1948 and the number of retail outlets was allowed to drop from almost 90,000 in 1939, most of which still existed after the war, to just over 33,000 in 1951 (JP 57, p. 329). Subsequently investment in commercial organisation was raised and the number increased to just over 41,000 by 1960 (SG 61, p. 208).

Price control was partly justified as a measure against monopoly and in 1956 association of enterprises for common business management was still prohibited (78, p. 109 and p. 61) but later the communist preference for bigness (see p. 37) and the need for cross-subsidisation of plants (see p. 116) prevailed and associations were even fostered. In the early 1960s the mania for mergers became detrimental to the rights of workers' councils (B 26.2.60). The Yugoslav communists seem to have exaggerated both the advantages of scale and the dangers of monopoly for welfare.

Professor Bicanic wrote of the difficulty of making the Yugoslav system work because of market imperfections and administrative entanglement (79) while Jelic denied that there was only a 'quasi-market' in Yugoslavia and claimed that it functioned freely and prices were independently formed (54, p. 93).

Whatever the shortcomings of the new Yugoslav price system in the 1950s, it was a step forward because government intervention was no longer physical but by means of price manipulation, and prices were used much more flexibly. On the other hand, the government maintained that prices could not be liberalised more because of the numerous distortions in the economy. But could further administration of prices eliminate the disproportions caused by planning? The 1948 economic reform in Federal Germany seemed to prove the contrary.

2.4 INTERNATIONAL TRADE

Under the influence of Marxist doctrines and the Soviet example, the Yugoslav communists first went for autarchy and 'equivalent exchange' which implied attempts at exporting primarily sophisticated final goods, especially machinery (100, p. 103, and 101, p. 33).

In the 1952 reform, 'commercialisation' of foreign trade (15, p. 148) was deemed to be an important ingredient because it should also have helped to reduce domestic 'discrepancies'. Nonetheless, the market in which specialised foreign trade enterprises operated—95 per cent of

Yugoslav firms were still excluded from direct international exchanges (15, p. 135)—was closely guided. Although the central planning of foreign trade was ended and the Fund for Price Equalisation abolished, new 'instruments' developed. Foreign currency was converted into dinars either at fixed rates by the National Bank or freely traded at the so-called Foreign Exchange Converting Office (*devizno obracunsko mesto*). Firms could freely trade a part of their international earnings known as their 'retention quota'. This quota was fixed at 45 per cent early in 1952, but was down to 20 per cent by October, when the free rate shot up to 6.8 times the official rate. Later the retention quota dwindled to 1 per cent, a steep tax on foreign sales was advocated and the free rate reached 12.3 times the official rate by 1960 (53, p. 125).

This happened although the official rate was raised from dinars 50 per dollar to dinars 300 in 1952 and foreign trade 'coefficients' ranging from 0.8 to 4 were introduced by which the official rate was multiplied so as to discriminate between various kinds of exports and imports. In 1954 the official rate was replaced by an accounting rate of dinars 632 per dollar with coefficients 0.6 to 2.0 for exports and 2.0 to 3.0 for imports. Further administrative allocation of foreign currency by the National Bank was restored, so that real relationships were well concealed (78, p. 318). On top of that, exports were subsidised to the tune of dinars 25 billion in 1960 and 50 billion in 1962 (Sl 1/59, 52/59).

Such entanglement was due to some persisting illusions. It was thought that the completion of heavy industry 'key projects' (see p. 15) would balance trade (Kidric, SP 30.3.52). In consequence, viable light industry was starved of funds including foreign exchange. But domestic heavy industry, especially the engineering industry, was inefficient and needed protection (B 21.2.59). *Ekonomska politika* of 25.6.62 claimed that Yugoslavia had started the production of diesel locomotives but had to import needles and nails which could easily be produced at home. Matters improved somewhat when attempts to design complicated machinery from scratch in the country were largely abandoned in favour of buying foreign licences, but this sensible change again developed into a 'mania for licences' (B 8.6.60).

The continuous wish to export complicated final products (15, p. 163) so as to avoid surplus labour being transferred abroad (80, p. 136) resulted in exports below the cost of production (27, p. 69) which was against the interests of the country (107, p. 492). In 1955 to earn one US dollar Yugoslavia had to export industrial goods costing dinars 1.054, while one dollar could also be earned with the export of dinars 655 worth of agricultural produce. Imported equipment worth one dollar cost dinars 617 (23, p. 317). Besides, machinery could only be exported to other communist countries and to developing countries while imports were mostly coming from the industrial West.

In the 1950s, Yugoslavia had constant balance of payments difficulties. Whereas during the last ten years before the Second World War the values of exports on average exceeded that of imports by 8 per cent, in 1953 the trade deficit was equal to 28 per cent of the value of imports and in 1960 it was 26 per cent. Exports did not reach the pre-war volume until 1958 (78, p. 188) despite the considerable statistical increase in net production.

3: Investment Priorities

3.1 DECENTRALISATION OF INVESTMENT

The Yugoslav communists thought investment to be central to any economic system, and actually even exaggerated its importance (see p. 31). For this reason, the absence of any discussion of investment problems in Kidric's *Theses* presumably meant that, in their view, there was no need for any investment reform at that stage. The set of new economic Acts in 1952 merely relaxed the previous far-reaching centralisation of investment in so far as it preserved State planning only for 'basic investment', while the rest was to be left to the initiative of enterprises and their associations (K 4–5/51). This change, however, made very little impression on the pattern of investment until 1956 (see p. 34).

As to jurisdiction over investment, Table 3.1 shows that on the one hand there was a shift in control of investment from the federation to enterprises and, on the other hand, from the federation first to republics and then to local authorities. What was more, investment projects were no longer executed by the authorities controlling the funds—they contributed finance to projects implemented at a lower level. The channels through which finance was forthcoming were social investment funds, budgets and enterprise investment and depreciation funds.

To some extent this system made investment executants more dependent on higher authorities because they frequently had recourse to them for part of their finance. Resources were thus spent in accordance with the plans of federal authorities because they would not contribute to projects otherwise (16, p. 84; 31, p. 63). Boris Kraigher admitted at the end of the 1950s that decentralisation was limited: 50 per cent of investment resources were allocated from the centre and, if all investment expenditure in which there was federal participation is counted, the figure rises to 80 per cent (B 24.7.62).

Central allocation of investment funds could have been replaced by freer circulation of capital between enterprises but for the Marxist view that enterprises would be indulging in 'exploitation' if they invested

Table 3.1: *Percentage share in total investment funds*

Year	Participation of economic organisations (enterprises)	Other participants					
		Municipalities	Districts	Republics	Federation	Other organisations	Bank resources
1952	21.7	–	–	–	77.9	0.4	–
1953	31.5	–	1.3	38.2	16.1	2.7	–
1954	31.1	–	8.5	14.7	41.0	4.7	–
1955	36.0	9.9	7.2	9.3	37.5	8.2	0.9
1956	38.7	4.6	9.4	8.8	30.6	6.7	1.2
1957	31.0	10.8	8.2	7.8	30.0	5.4	6.9
1958	30.6	11.6	5.0	7.0	38.5	6.4	0.9

Source: 16, p. 84.

their accumulated resources elsewhere or lent them to banks. All enterprises could do was to plough their accumulation back, which could easily turn out to be wasteful. The reformers started looking for a 'suitable' system which would enable enterprises to place their excess accumulation in banks (B 7.7.57, Vukmanovic, B 26.2.60).

3.2 INVESTMENT CRITERIA

In 1947 it was stressed that accumulation for investment was very important but that it was not 'accumulation for profits' (87, p. 46). Instead, the guiding principles for investment were that industrial production was to be predominant within total production, heavy industry within industry, and output of means of production within heavy industry (20, p. 40).

The experiment with the 'rates of accumulation and funds' in 1952/3 changed little, but the re-introduction of interest rates in 1954 both as a method of gathering accumulation and as an investment criterion promised to be a major reform. Hitherto, enterprises had been allocated capital out of budgets, free of interest and without any obligation of repayment. On the re-introduction of interest payments the first requirement was to revalue enterprises' fixed assets in 1953 prices to provide a more realistic basis for interest charges. Such revaluations of assets became a regular feature of the Yugoslav economic scene.

The interest rate was set in general at 6 per cent on the revalued capital and exceptionally at 2 per cent for power generation, agriculture and public catering. These interest charges were used for investment funds established at different levels in 1953. They were distinct from budgets, but were to be administered by banks under the direction of social plans issued by political authorities at the federal, republican and local levels.

The next year the 1954 federal social plan provided for investment allocation by free competition between interested investors on the basis of the interest rates they offered to pay. So-called investment 'auctions' were to be held. It is impossible to say how the economic leaders expected the contradiction between plans based on their initial 'principles' and the need to pay interest on fixed capital, i.e. the need for investment to produce returns, to be resolved. Maybe they had illusions about the allocative efficiency of these principles and the plans previously based on them. But if an attempt is made to calculate the differences in returns on existing capital, it is found that, in 1956, the average yield on capital in textile manufacturing was 8.55 per cent, in metal processing 0.86 per cent, and in shipbuilding 0.2 per cent (calculated from 23, pp. 205 and 318, and SG 57, p. 329). Of course, caution is necessary because *inter alia* prices on which these rates of return are calculated were themselves distorted.

It seemed impossible for these industries to compete with one another for new investment unless the authorities were prepared to abandon their drive to build heavy industry first. In fact, voices were soon heard claiming that investment credits should not be allocated according to formal criteria, and that machine-building industry should be enabled to compete for capital on 'equal terms', i.e. to pay less for capital.

Matters were complicated by the irresponsibility of enterprises which sought credit regardless of cost. The National Bank had to limit interest rates to 7.5 per cent for fear that it would otherwise have been pushed up to 30 or 40 per cent. Enterprises in the most precarious financial situation offered the highest interest rates to obtain the credit they wanted. Professor Vuckovic described how one enterprise offered 17 per cent, and when the director was asked how he could hope to repay the loan on these conditions, he said that what mattered to him was to get the credit, whilst the problem of repayment did not bother him since he would no longer be the director when it became due (118, p. 256).

As a result, the 1955 social plan accepted that marginal interest rates could not be the only criterion for the allocation of investment and subsequent plans proceeded to lay down the use of accumulation funds in more and more detail. Auctions continued but they were divided into 'auction circles' insulated from each other so that in this way investment funds were directed to those economic projects which helped to implement the Yugoslav communist economic policy (78, p. 111). On what criteria this policy was determined remains unexplained to this day and Horvat claims that no serious study of the investment problem has been undertaken in Yugoslavia as yet. There is only a general recognition that political considerations and pressures play a dominant role (53, pp. 140 and 138).

In Vukmanovic's view investment remained dominated by the bureaucracy which had moved into the banks because bureaucratic cadres always move where 'the centre of control over allocation of surplus labour is situated' (121, p. 186).

3.3 INVESTMENT FINANCE

As up till 1953 investment was financed out of budgets, no distinction was possible between sources of government revenue and investment funds. The most important item was the turnover tax, an indirect tax collected on all sales. Direct taxes were less important, especially after the abolition of all taxes on wages in 1948.

With the introduction of investment funds, separate from the budget, the turnover tax as a source of investment was replaced first by the 'rate of accumulation and funds' and then by interest charges, although it continued to be used for government revenue, albeit to a much reduced extent.

Investment funds were widely financed by borrowing straight from the central bank, which meant that the money supply could be expanding even though the government budget in the narrow sense of the word was balanced or even in surplus. In consequence, currency supply rose from dinars 6 billion in May 1945 to dinars 50 billion at the end of 1952 and dinars 193 billion at the end of 1960 (58, p. 277). Bank short-term credits, which went largely to enterprises themselves to finance working capital needs, grew from dinars 457 billion in 1952 (118, p. 261) to over dinars 1.120 billion at the end of 1956. This figure fell to just over 900 billion at the end of 1957 because the difference was written off, i.e. transferred to enterprises as their 'owned' working capital. By the end of 1960, short-term bank credits again rose to almost dinars 1.250 billion (SG 61, p. 243).

Both currency issue and credit expansion were clearly inflationary and would have been even more so if Yugoslavia had not been in receipt of considerable foreign aid and loans running at about $100 billion a year each in the 1950s (58, p. 86). In Nikola Cobeljic's judgement (23, p. 150), this foreign finance was equivalent on average to 7 per cent of national income and one third of productive investment, calculated at realistic exchange rates. As Vukmanovic pointed out, the Yugoslav communists 'would not refrain from anything and used to publish ficticious data' so as to obtain as much aid as possible (121, p. 164). The falsification of data was necessary because the Western donors objected to the further concentration on heavy industry which they considered wasteful, as indeed it turned out to be. The communists interpreted this objection as a desire on the part of their benefactors to keep Yugoslavia in 'colonial dependency' (121, pp. 120–32).

Private savings in the 1950s were of minimal importance and more than matched by hire-purchase credits to the population (58, p. 278).

On the other hand, volunteer and forced labour were originally used to support the investment effort. But volunteer labour contained 'elements of compulsion' (121, p. 103) and turned out to be irrational and wasteful (121, p. 17). After the break with Stalin, the secret police organised the so-called 'socially useful work' under appalling conditions. According to Vukmanovic, this was a compulsory mobilisation for work of townspeople and peasants (121, p. 102) which eventually had to be stopped because an open clash with workers as well as peasants was looming ahead (121, p. 120). In addition, up till 1954/5 there was a prison population of some 200,000 to 300,000 persons, providing a large part of the workforce on some construction sites; thus there was a contingent of between 30,000 and 60,000 prisoners at the New Belgrade construction site in 1949/50.

Finally, depreciation was initially used to finance new 'key' investment. Although legal provisions made depreciation very low, 55 to 80 per cent of depreciation had to be paid into central amortisation funds whence it was channelled to heavy industry (121, p. 122). The result was disinvestment in many branches: in housing alone it was estimated at dinars 200 billion between 1952 and 1955 (23, p. 146 ff.).

3.4 RATE OF INVESTMENT

The 1947 Yugoslav Five-Year Plan envisaged almost a doubling of the national income based principally on a 2.5 fold increase in investment within five years. The compound annual rate of growth was to be 14 per cent. That was more than twice the planned Soviet rate (80, p. 133) so that at least one foreign observer considered it impossible of achievement and attributed it to the Yugoslav lack of experience (73, p. 134).

Table 3.2 shows that although the growth of national income and GSP lagged behind the plan, the share of fixed investment in these two aggregates continued to be high and the slight reduction in the percentage of the national income invested in 1952 was due almost entirely to a change in depreciation rules. This impression is corroborated by the averages in Table 3.3. If anything, gross investment rose as a percentage of the GSP.

Admittedly, the investment percentages in the tables are misleadingly high because they refer to the GSP defined in Marxist terms, i.e. leaving out non-productive services, which reduced it by about 10 per cent compared with the Western definition. Furthermore, the investment share was also inflated by the relatively high prices of Yugoslav

Table 3.2: Allocation of gross social product in percentages

	GSP Indices 1952–100	Personal consumption	Public consumption	Gross fixed investment	(Depreciation)	Current trade balance	Statistical discrepancy
1947	89	47	17	32	(4)	0	4
1948	107	48	17	32	(4)	−1	4
1949	116	49	18	32	(5)	−2	3
1950	106	46	23	33	(5)	−2	0
1951	116	46	25	33	(5)	−4	0
1952	100	55	23	30	(10)	−4	−4
1953	118	53	19	32	(10)	−6	2
1954	122	51	18	33	(11)	−2	0
1955	140	52	15	29	(10)	−3	7
1956	135	54	13	29	(10)	−2	4
1957	165	52	13	28	(8)	−3	10
1958	170	55	14	30	(8)	−3	4
1959	198	52	13	31	(7)	−2	6
1960	211	52	13	32	(7)	−2	5
1961	222	52	14	35	(8)	−2	1

Source: 58, pp. 80 and 83.

Table 3.3: Share of social gross investment in the gross social product 1948–1960

Period	PERCENTAGES 'Economic' investment	'Non-economic' investment	Total investment
1948–1952	25.6	6.0	31.6
1953–1956	27.5	4.2	31.7
1957–1960	28.0	7.0	35.0

Source: quoted in JP 61, p. 158.

investment goods (JP 57, p. 431). Finally, domestic savings figures were about 7 per cent lower than investment which would account for the foreign contribution (see p. 30).

Although the burden on the domestic economy was thus lower than it appeared, a decision was taken in the mid-1950s to reduce investment (121, pp. 224ff), but it was then found that once a faulty structure exists it is very difficult to change (54, pp. 54 and 85; *Ep* 7.8.52). In consequence, there was little change in the allocation of resources and Vukmanovic, whose previous economic planning allegedly hinged on investment, rightly claimed that the 'new' policy sponsored by Mijalko Todorovic did not alter the relationship between investment and consumption (121, p. 338).

Therefore, investment which was to a considerable extent a 'gigantic and monstrous waste' (Djilas, B 4.8.52) continued. Factories were built without blueprints or knowledge of the required technical processes (121, p. 124). Had the Yugoslavs invested less, they could have achieved more because they could have done it with greater care (14, p. 134). As it was, they thought that all problems could be solved through investment which led to excess capacities, over-capitalisation and insufficient attention to current production. The main reason for this attitude seems to have been ideological: the building of socialism could apparently be measured by the spending of investment funds, on the supposition that industrial development would create a working class (14, p. 131). There was a clear connection between the disproportions in the economy and the attempts at break-neck investment and growth (80, p. 153).

3.5 INVESTMENT PATTERNS

Both communist development principles and the stress on investment in practice demand concentration on industry and on heavy industry in particular. After deducting about 20 per cent of investment funds for 'non-economic' investment (schools, hospitals, housing—see Table 3.3), the 1947 Plan allotted over 50 per cent of investment to industry and smaller percentages to other branches (Table 3.4).

Table 3.4: Sector shares in total 'economic' investment

Average	*Industry*	*Agriculture*	*Forestry*	*Construction*	*Transport*	*Trade*
Plan 1947/51	51.8	8.6	1.6	1.6	31	3.5
1947/9	50.3	8.4	3.2	3.7	28.9	4.9
1950/2	64.2	5.6	1.2	3.7	22.4	2.4
1953/6	58.7	6.4	1.7	3.3	23.7	4.9
1957/60	43.8	15.8	1.5	3.6	27.4	7.9

Sources: JP 57, p. 42 5 and JP 61, p. 406.

But the exaggerated planning targets soon began to tell and together with the additional complication of political strife with the Soviet Union, forced the Yugoslav leadership by 1949 to 'narrow' the 'broad front' of development and direct all efforts 'from less important to more important projects' (121, p. 117/18). The existing ranking of investment projects was such that this shift meant the abandoning of consumer goods projects in favour of producer goods ones (20, p. 97).

Even current production was neglected in favour of investment. Tito admitted (LP 7.1.48) that in many places workers and peasants lacked basic necessities but insisted that 'factories, foundries, open hearth furnaces, oil extraction, coke' etc. should be taken care of first.

In 1950 the Five-Year investment programme had to be cut again and once more heavy industry was favoured, so that only a skeleton 'plan of key capital construction' was left. The reduced Five-Year Plan was fulfilled a year late, in 1952 (102, p. 45).

By 1952 it was clear that there were grave 'disharmonies' in the economy, but they were preserved so that concentration on heavy industry could be continued (SP 9.7.52). In percentage terms investment in industry was pushed far above what was planned, as shown in Table 3.4. Within industrial investment, there was a marked preference for energy production (electricity, coal, oil) and basic and heavy industries (iron and steel, non-ferrous metals, engineering, shipyards, electrical equipment, chemicals and construction materials). On average in 1947–56 investment in basic and heavy industries amounted to 51.2 per cent of all industrial investment, and investment in power generation to a further 31 per cent, so that only 17.8 per cent was left for consumer goods industries. The share of basic and heavy industries was as high as 57.3 per cent in 1952. On average, 12 per cent of gross industrial investment was reserved for the engineering and metals industries (JP 57, p. 426).

In 1954 'some economists' began advocating a relaxation of the forced development of industry and more attention to agriculture (121, p. 201) and Tito ordered that most new projects be discontinued so that Yugoslavia would not have to search for bread and be blackmailed by all comers (121, p. 222). In 1955 Mijalko Todorovic suggested that all key capital projects be stopped to make room for consumer goods, to which Vukmanovic retorted that the choice was not between basic and processing industries, but between rational and irrational projects, depending on profitability (121, p. 228). But how could profitability be established without a proper price system? He also claimed that it was not easy to change investment policy because it depended on the production structure previously established (121, p. 261). It was certainly difficult to change the concentration on heavy industry which was originally carried so far that it was claimed, for instance, that the turbine plant near Ljubljana would build turbines for power stations which could then generate more power to build more turbines! (SP 11.4.52).

When the concentration of investment on key projects came to an end in 1956 the output of capital equipment (means of work) was 9.7 times greater than in 1939, but much capacity could not be utilised as the production of raw materials (reproduction material) had only risen 2.5 times (SG 61, p. 149 and Ep 9.7.60, 19.8.61). It became clear that the home market was too small to absorb the output of the engineering industry, especially as the demand for one-off equipment decreased and the industry was not ready to switch over to serial production (JP 57, p. 282). Exporting was difficult because of competition and the inefficiency of Yugoslav engineering (Ep 17.3.62). Finally, there were disproportions between different stages of the engineering industry itself too (Ep 1.1.61).

Electrical power generation, another preferred industry, had also increased substantially but was insufficient because heavy industry needed relatively more power than processing industries. To make matters worse, investment was devoted to power stations while transmission grids and urban distribution networks were neglected (JP 57, p. 125). Professor Misic rightly observed (80, p. 159) that such 'disharmonies' could only be a consequence of the absence of any coordination or serious planning.

A clear change in the structure of investment came in 1956 (JP 57, p. 423), and was reflected in the aims of the Social Plan for 1957–61. This document criticised the previous one-sidedness and stated development goals in a different order. Prominence was given to agriculture, labour productivity and the balance of payments. Personal consumption was upgraded from last place to the middle of the list, and food production, i.e. agriculture, to the very top. This change in priorities influenced the actual investment structure as shown in the last row of Table 3.4.

Investment problems in Yugoslavia were aggravated by regional differences — Slovenia was at an economic level comparable with Austria, Macedonia and Montenegro with Turkey — which the communist government sought, without much success, to narrow by transferring investment funds from more advanced regions to less prosperous ones.

Table 3.5: Regional shares of fixed capital and social product

Member Republic	Percentage of fixed capital in the Yugoslav social sector 1947	1960	Percentage of the Yugoslav social product 1947	1960
Slovenia	58.2 (Slovenia and Croatia)	41.7 (Slovenia and Croatia)	14.2	15.7
Croatia			26.0	26.5
Serbia	31.5	36.3	42.8	38.0
Bosnia and Herzogovina	6.1	15.8	11.5	13.4
Macedonia	3.4	4.1	5.0	5.0
Montenegro	0.8	2.1	1.2	1.4

Source: Ep 21.1.61

From Table 3.5 it transpires that fixed capital had been redistributed between regions without, however, having much impact on the distribution of social product by region. Yugoslav regional policy deserves a separate study and can be mentioned only peripherally in this book.

3.6 SPECIAL TENDENCIES

The 1947 Five-Year Plan postulated the speed-up of industrialisation predominantly by building '*new* industrial branches and *new* plants' with the application of the '*latest* achievements of science and technology'. These two tendencies plus the preference for very large plants aggravated the problems with which the Yugoslav economy had to contend.

The 'large projects disease' was severely criticised after the initial period (LP 13.2.54) but it continued and, combined with mergers (see p. 115), reduced the number of industrial enterprises from 3400 before the war to 2500 in 1959. The average number of employees per enterprise in 1958 was 360 (JP 61, p. 16). Cobeljic put this figure at only 260 in 1955 and thought it excessive compared with corresponding figures of 128 for Federal Germany, 122 for Great Britain and 50 for Sweden (23, p. 201).

Mirkovic believed that enterprises of this size were not economical and also tended to destroy small but profitable enterprises (79, p. 95). The decline of small enterprises was also caused by the elimination of private workshops, while socialised small enterprises could not prosper 'in the rigid, formalised, collective system' (79, p. 99). The number of small workshops fell from 166,331 in 1954 to 123,117 in 1959, their labour force was static and in private enterprises was reduced from 204,669 in 1954 to 148,761 in 1959. The overall number of apprentices was almost halved during the same period (SG 61, p. 164). This decline was blamed (EP. 31.3.62) on the hostile treatment of private artisans, especially on 'progressive taxation' aimed at reducing their incomes to less than the average wage. Towards the end of the 1950s it became clear that there was a disproportion between small and large enterprises, so that small enterprises could no longer supplement and supply the needs of large works (JP 61, p. 17).

Existing enterprises were so neglected that Tito himself had to speak out in favour of the reconstruction of obsolescent plant (B 1.6.60). Depreciation policy (see p. 31) rendered so much capacity obsolete that the general development was impeded (B 11.4.59). This had come about although Vukmanovic admitted that additional investment in old-established enterprises was very efficient. 'It is easy to build a factory', he said, 'but difficult to train new cadres' (B 28.12.58).

Finally, the Yugoslav planners failed to appreciate that the most modern technological methods were not necessarily the most economical solution for Yugoslavia. As Professor Krasovec put it, for technicians the main criterion was that somebody had something technically more perfect (68, p. 24). They disregarded the principle of least cost and thought that, under communist rule, 'decrees and political power' could change economic laws. This technical 'superconscience' was so strong that it persisted after the transition to the new economic system (68, p. 27).

Often new machinery, especially when built at home very inefficiently, meant a considerable increase in production costs at that stage of development (NR 23.10.52). In 1954, when state subsidies for machinery were discontinued for a while, machinery stocks immediately began piling up. Tractors, for instance, required a rebate of 75 per cent to bring the cost of tractor ploughing down to the cost of horse ploughing (Dn 8.9.54). In addition, the depreciation rate on tractors had to be kept abnormally low (Ep 10.9.60).

By the end of the 1950s, the lessons had not been learned. On the contrary, it was suggested that the ailing Yugoslav engineering industry could be saved by the adoption of a policy of wholesale automation (B 3.4.60, cf. Ep 15.4.61). Although the new economic chief, Boris Kraigher, came out in favour of automation of all economic branches (B 22.1.60), this policy turned out to be 'very expensive' (B 16.2.60). It was certainly odd to advocate 'factories without workers' in a country with rising unemployment and scarce capital.

4: Organisation and Working of Enterprises

4.1 WORKERS' SELF-MANAGEMENT

Under the 1950 Act (see p. 1) a Yugoslav 'economic organisation' was to be managed by a workers' council, a management board and a director. The two collective bodies were supposed to take fundamental decisions and adopt various by-laws, plans, etc., while the director was to implement them and 'administer the process of work'.

The 1957 Act on Labour Relations proclaimed that Yugoslav workers were not in a wage relationship but 'free labour' which entitled them to manage the organisation by electing and being elected to the workers' council. In turn, the council elected a management board of 3 to 11 members (mandatory till 1968, see p. 209) whose individual members could serve a maximum of 2 years. Lists of candidates could be put forward by the trade union or one-tenth of the labour force, but there had to be a prescribed majority of production workers in both organs. Members were not paid for these duties.

The director was *ex officio* a member of the management board and was, up till 1963 (see p. 183), appointed (and dismissed) by the people's committee of the commune after a public competition and on the recommendation of a commission, one-third of whose members were chosen by the workers' council. He had to see to it that the enterprise's activity remained within the law and could suspend any decision contrary to it. There was a right of appeal to the commune against his decisions. The director also hired and dismissed workers, with the exception of management personnel under the jurisdiction of the board, which also dealt with complaints against his decisions on labour matters.

The workers' council was supervised by the party organisation and its 'transmission belt', the trade union in the enterprise. The party's 'interference' in the work of the commune and enterprise was described as 'aid' which made 'independent' functioning of enterprises possible

(Veselinov, B. 5.6.59). According to Kardelj, there could not be any self-management without the party (B 27.4.60).

Simultaneously, 'ordinary people' were criticised (Ep 2.12.61) for not airing their views in public, and the communists for not encouraging free discussion and then standing up for Marxist 'scientific truth'. In reality, management sometimes looked askance at criticism (JP 57, p. 22) and even dismissed workers proferring critical remarks (Tito, B 7.5.62).

In the general design of things, the commune was initially to have been the lynchpin and to defend the public interest, especially the correct allocation of revenue between wages and accumulation (Kidric, 121, p. 175). The 'communes' officially called local, town and district people's committees, and modelled on the Paris Commune of 1871, were intended to organise economic activity on their territory and generally supervise workers' councils (JP 57, p. 65) (See pp. 19, 44, 70 and 105). As the communes also levied taxes, they were said sometimes to extort money from enterprises and, on other occasions, to conspire with them to flout the rules laid down by higher authorities (88).

The 'commune' was given its outstanding importance in the Constitutional Act of 1953. Art. 3 of this Act concentrated all constitutional rights in the people's committees of the communes, so that the federation and republics had jurisdiction only in matters expressly reserved for them. Although the Constitutional Act merely amended the 1946 Constitution, it completely revised decisive parts. Nevertheless, the change was formal because the dominance of the Party continued. The Party did try to reform itself and changed its name to League of Communists, but it remained in command because no other political organisation was allowed. The new name signified that the communist organisation would no longer directly participate in administration but be inspirers and bearers of political activity.

The Council of Nations was replaced as the second chamber of the Federal Parliament by a Council of Producers with parallel changes at other levels. This was meant to show the alleged reduction in the importance of national questions in Yugoslavia. It was even suggested that Yugoslavia would become a federation of communes instead of national republics and that socialist patriotism would replace the bourgeois nationalism of individual Yugoslav nationalities.

The Council of Producers was to consist exclusively of representatives of those citizens whose work was 'productive' in the Marxist sense. In particular, medical, educational and administrative employees were disenfranchised for the purposes of this chamber. 'Productive' workers were divided into an industrial and an agricultural group, their numbers determined in proportion to their share in the national income. As a result, in 1953, 5,350,000 odd agricultural population had 67 representatives, and 1,800,000 odd industrial population had 135 representatives. The Council was to have equal jurisdiction with the Federal Council, the first chamber, in all social and economic matters. The government of the Federal People's Republic was renamed the 'Executive Council' which, it was suggested, indicated the first step towards the withering away of the state.

The communes never quite exercised the dominant role intended for them. Soon very strong anti-communal tendencies made themselves felt. There were objections to interference by the communes in the distribution of enterprises' revenue (121, p. 185) and to their direction of investment funds which, it was claimed, should have been in the hands of enterprises instead of falling into the hands of commune bureaucracies (121, p. 185). The resolution of the First Congress of Workers' Councils in 1957 (JP 57, p. 273) also demanded that the rights of communes should be clearly defined so that they would no longer put pressure on enterprises and interfere with their proper functions.

4.2 ENTERPRISES IN A WIDER CONTEXT

From the very beginning, Djilas was afraid that self-management would be used by the Communist leaders (32, p. 157) to shift the responsibility for the economic deficiencies caused by the previous 'planning' from themselves to the workers. When the economy was at the peak of the crisis in 1952 self-managers were asked to bring about profitability although they had often taken over obsolete machinery and an empty purse (SP 29.5.53). They were prompted to develop 'mass initiative' and reject 'bureaucratic calculations' (B 27.2.52) showing that enterprises were in a dire state. The more the communists became aware that higher productivity could not be achieved solely by more machines (B 3.3.59), the louder they demanded that the workers' councils should 'become the leaders of the struggle for a better organisation' (B 14.12.58) which they previously neglected because they believed, like Lenin, that anybody who knows elementary arithmetic can run an enterprise.

The workers' councils were also enjoined to reduce employment to a rational level from the artificial 'full employment' with masses of 'concealed unemployed' (see p. 14) bestowed on them by the original policy of the communist leadership. When they went about this task seriously, they were criticised as 'anti-social' (LP 26.1.52) by precisely the same people who had brought about the situation. Unemployment was rising, but communist papers kept claiming that the problem of unemployment was not 'acute' although it was known that there was still surplus manpower in economic organisations (B 28.12.58). At the end of the 1960s, Tito again called on the collectives to throw out those who did nothing (B 1.3.60).

Despite the fear of monopolies (see p. 22), and pressure that they should be profitable, enterprises were also required to cooperate with each other. For this purpose, a Decree on the Association of Economic Organisations was adopted at the end of 1953. It was amended twice and then replaced in 1958 by the Act on Associations in the Economy which was amended in 1959.

Fundamentally, a network of chambers of industry, commerce, transport, artisan production and so forth, was introduced at various levels — district, republican, federal — to fulfil functions very similar to those of corresponding organisations in private enterprise countries. Similarly, specialist associations in various production branches were to encourage technical development (cf. JP 57, p. 413, and YS 61, pp. 325, 329). These organisations were initially not allowed to foster business cooperation, but such cooperation became fashionable in the 1960s (see p. 116).

Special problems arose with respect to the so-called large systems such as the railways, postal service and power supply. In the first enthusiasm for 'economic automatism', these systems were disaggregated into small enterprises which had separate accounts, were supposed to have market relations with each other and were only loosely linked together into 'alliances' (*zajednice*) (YS 61, p. 331). The railways, for instance, consisted of separate station enterprises, traction enterprises, permanent way enterprises, and so on.

This innovation was a typical example of how, in Yugoslavia, any new principle was applied wholesale regardless of suitability: locomotives were changed at the border between two republics with separate traction enterprises and it became more complicated to buy a ticket from Ljubljana to Zagreb than from Ljubljana to London. Eventually the 'alliances' of Yugoslav Railways, of Enterprises of Yugoslav Posts, Telegraphs and Telephones and of the Electrical Power Industry were given a much firmer control over their systems again.

Attempts were also made to extend the principle of workers' self-management from 'economic organisations' (*privredna organizacija*) to other 'working organisations' (*radna organizacija*), i.e. to educational, cultural, medical and similar institutions. The concept of 'social management' was developed (JP 57, p. 313) under which the governing bodies of public services include citizens from outside the institutions themselves, appointed by political authorities, in addition to members elected from amongst the work collective. There existed also 'institutions with independent financing' in cases when an institution has an independent source of income although it might not cover its full outlays (106, p. 318). Such institutions were allowed to grant their members additional payments from their surpluses, but were under much stricter control by the political authorities and their accounts were linked with public budgets.

4.3 WORKING OF ENTERPRISES

The Constitutional Act of 1953 expressly stated in Art. 6 that 'economic organisations' were entitled to conduct their own business although their elbow room was severely limited by taxation and other economic instruments and, at times, also by supervision through communes and trade unions.

This limited scope for independent decision-making by enterprises was mainly used by the director who, beside having a powerful position in law, was the only organ appointed for a longer period who could therefore provide continuity, have time to digest information and be advised and supported by assistant directors and other specialists. What is more, he was a political nominee (cf. JP 69, p. 430) which assured him of the support of the Party and trade unions and of smooth relations with the commune officials who had the same political background. One reason for complaints (JP 57, p. 221) was the poor quality of directors, in particular their lack of education.

The communist leaders thought that the directors had to be entrenched in this way because they were afraid (121, pp. 155–6) that otherwise the workers would try to raise the wages fund per unit of production. There was the danger that workers would spend the revenue at their disposal on their own pay and leave nothing for accumulation and that excessive wage differentials would arise between enterprises. The problem was how to give the workers control over the results of their work and simultaneously prevent anarchy (121, p. 182).

Later events showed that these fears were entirely justified. Even at the end of the 1950s, Yugoslav workers were much more preoccupied with their low pay than with the entrepreneurial function entrusted—at least formally—to their collectives (79, p. 203). The average monthly earnings of a Yugoslav worker—head of a four-member family—in 1960 was about dinars 21,000 (approximately $30) (58, p. 254). Conversion at the official rate of exchange certainly undervalues the purchasing power of this wage, but earnings were very low.

Workers' self-management required an enormous number of meetings which were frequently considered a waste of time (B 12.2.60) so that it was difficult to keep workers interested (B 11.1 and 26.6.60). The discussions soon shifted away from production—which was left to management—to the problems of people in the enterprise and their mutual relationships (Ep. 30.9.61), in other words, to the distribution of money and to working conditions. Directors had to accept this priority if they wanted the workers to remain in a cooperative mood.

In Yugoslavia, it was claimed that the workers were no longer 'wage-earners' (Tito in B 1.5.60) since they themselves determined their own wages. This meant that there were no longer any clear cut labour costs, that they were merged with the distribution of profits. A way round this had to be found, first in the shape of accounting wages (1952/3), then 'by-laws and wage schedules' approved by the commune and trade unions (1954/6) and then a combination of these and government-determined 'minimum personal incomes' (1957 on). In this last period, a substitute concept for profits was developed as 'income minus minimum personal incomes' and personal incomes were formally no longer supplemented with payments 'out of profits' but 'out of surplus labour'. In reality there was of course no difference.

Responsibility then meant that workers were rewarded for the success of the enterprise by personal incomes above the minimum level, and punished by a reduction of their pay but not to less than the minimum level, which in 1958 for instance was fixed at 80 per cent of the 1957 wage schedules (JP 58, p. 8, cf. Sl 52/58). The workers willingly accepted higher incomes but resented any drop as an injustice (B 24.12.61).

The resentment is not surprising since they must have felt that they had little to do with the management of the enterprise. Decisions on production, purchases, sales etc. requires expertise and information so that in practice they remained in the hands of the director. What was worse, most investment decisions continued to be taken or at least influenced by political authorities, that is people who had nothing to do with the subsequent operation of the enterprises or their profits or losses. The late Zagreb economist Mijo Mirkovic wrote as early as 1959 that investment decisions could be wrong and that in this area a small mistake could cause enormous losses which, however, did not fall on the decision-makers in political authorities (79, pp. 144 and 185).

Because Yugoslav communists felt—maybe subconsciously—that workers should not be held responsible for the losses caused by the original investors and directors, the question of responsibility was not resolved. The reduction in personal incomes was often not implemented and, when it was, it was kept within narrow limits. If an enterprise's current revenue was not sufficient to pay the guaranteed minimum, the enterprise could use its own reserve fund or its funds of 'basic means' (fixed capital) or 'working means' (working capital) which amounted to capital erosion. In 1958 'joint reserve funds' for groups of enterprises were introduced (91, p. 220) so that cross-subsidisation had become legal.

Understandably, the result of such manipulations was that, in the 1950s, 'free distribution of net income' was minimal (16, p. 91): the average income from profits in the total income of a worker—head of a four-member family—was 2.8 per cent in 1955, reached a peak of 5.1 per cent in 1957 and then declined to 4.9 per cent in 1960 (58, p. 254). What affects the steering of the economy is, of course, not so much the average of profits but differences from enterprise to enterprise. The additional income must be large enough to be important to those who are supposed to be stimulated to take the right decisions. In Yugoslavia, the authorities were afraid that there would be 'excessive differences amongst workers' (121, p. 156) and tried to 'equalise business conditions' which all militated against the working of the market. There were even demands for a new morality which would make people dispense with wages out of profits (B 1.5.60).

4.4 ESTABLISHMENT AND WINDING-UP OF ENTERPRISES

Art. 4 of the Constitutional Act of 1953 proclaimed that 'means of production' were 'social property', i.e. owned by society, not by the state, regardless of how they were acquired. This social ownership meant that by allowing part of the net income at their disposal to be saved workers handed this accumulation over to 'society' and it did not become their property. The outward sign of this was that they had to pay interest on capital thus saved, which accrued to various investment funds. On borrowed money enterprises had to pay additional interest to the lender also. Later on, this arrangement led to considerable complications (see p. 149).

Critics claimed that there could not be any such thing as 'social' ownership because ownership implied a subject capable of being the bearer of legal rights and obligations (70), while 'society' had no organs and, therefore, could not be a legal subject. If it has, it is a state. The Marxist answer was that ownership was not so much a relationship between a legal subject and an object, but determined relations between people, which social ownership could do.

The 1957 Act on resources of economic organisations gave enterprises the right of use of their means of production, protected by law and alterable exclusively by federal Acts, whereas under the administrative system the administrative superior could allocate resources as he wished, while the enterprise could not dispose of them. Under the new system, the enterprise could sell and buy 'resources' including machinery and buildings provided it preserve the substance in its possession. The Act enjoined it to use resources with the 'application of a good businessman'. It also made the enterprise responsible for its liabilities with all resources in its use.

The establishment and winding up of enterprises were covered by Decrees introduced in 1953, with several later amendments. These Decrees provided that enterprises could be established by state authorities including communes, by business organisations including business associations, by cooperative organisations including non-agricultural ones, by social organisations including economic chambers, and by groups of citizens. The founder had to provide the capital either from his own financial resources or by guaranteeing a loan from an investment fund or a bank. In no case was the founder entitled to more than repayment of the resources lent and the payment of interest. This applied also to groups of citizens, which means that economic initiative depended entirely on public spirit, without any material incentives. A group of citizens could also start an enterprise financed by the commune. Under no circumstances was the founder entitled to interfere with the distribution of income or management of the enterprise founded by him. There are no figures on the role of the different categories of founders in practice.

During the construction of the enterprise, a director appointed by the founder organised the work as there could not be self-management organs initially. A licence issued by the commune determined how self-management bodies were to be elected and the enterprise was then handed over to them. The workers' council then worked out the by-laws and the enterprise was entered in the register of enterprises.

The rules provided that an enterprise could be liquidated if it no longer fulfilled an economic purpose or if it became insolvent, when liquidation was compulsory. Liquidation was executed by a receiver and supervised by the district economic court if it was compulsory.

It used to be said that about 20 to 30 per cent of Yugoslav enterprises operated at a loss and should have been closed down, but nobody really knew. Very few enterprises were wound up. The first figures are available for 1964 (SG 65, p. 117) when about 5500 workers lost their jobs because of liquidations.

The local authorities did their best not to close down any enterprises because they were afraid of unemployment on their territory. They could cover losses out of joint reserve funds but also put pressure on banks to extend credits which were concealed subsidies and served to cover losses (118, p. 263). Sometimes they also 'persuaded' profitable enterprises to merge with unprofitable ones. In any case there were legal provisions making possible an agreed settlement of debts between an insolvent enterprise and its creditors and a financial reorganisation under a 'compulsory administration' which suspended self-management.

5: Results up to 1960 and Interim Conclusions

5.1 GROWTH OF OUTPUT AND CONSUMPTION

The 1947 Five-Year Plan decreed that the Yugoslav Gross Social Product should rise from about 90 per cent of the 1939 level in 1947 to 180 per cent in 1951 which implied a doubling within five years and a compound growth rate of 14 per cent. In fact GSP did not reach double the 1947 level until 1959 (see Table 3.2) and the compound yearly growth rate turned out to be 7 per cent (see p. 240) which is still a very respectable achievement.

However, between 1947 and 1952 there was hardly any growth at all since in 1952 the national income was 1 per cent higher than in 1939, lower than in 1948 and some ten points higher than in 1947 (see Table 5.1). In the period 1953–6, the growth rate of national income was 8.4 per cent (per head 6.9 per cent) and in 1957–60 13 per cent (per head 11.7 per cent). This later spurt must have been at least partly due to the commissioning of new projects started in the earlier period (JP 61, p. 157) and to the renewed use of already existing capacity. For a realistic picture one would also have to deduct disinvestment, especially in housing and agriculture (see p. 31), and consider to what extent high investment and fast growth contributed to the disproportions in the economy (see p. 4).

More important still, this growth added very little to consumption by the population. The one-sided concentration on the production of 'means of production' brought about an 18 fold increase in output of this group (see Table 5.1) by 1960, while the national income had grown by only 100 per cent which naturally had consequences for the output of necessities. Between 1948 and 1956 a 1 per cent increase in the national income raised consumption by only 0.19 per cent (89).

Yugoslav communist writers admitted that consumption had stagnated from 1948 till 1956 (JP 61, p. 61; 23, p. 295; 98, p. 59), but then claimed that in 1948 total consumption was 3 per cent and consumption

Table 5.1: Rise in output, income and consumption 1947–1960

	1939	*1947*	*1948*	*1949*	*1950*	*1951*	*1952*	*1953*	*1954*	*1955*	*1956*	*1960*
Means of production	100	241	352	462	510	534	582	757	785	917	971	1789
							Plan target approx. 500					
Industrial output	100	121	150	167	172	166	164	183	208	242	286	
							Plan target approx. 193					
National income	100	89.8	107.3	118.4	108.8	114.6	101.0	120.5	123.8	141.4	137.5	211
National income per capita	100	89.6	105.7	115.2	104.4	108.5	94.1	110.7	111.8	125.7	119.9	177
Personal consumption	–	–	100	106.8	97.0	99.0	92.2	94.2	101.4	108.7	107.7	157
Recalculation	100	–	76	81	74	75	70	72	76	82	82	119
Personal consumption per capita	–	–	100	105.3	94.8	95.8	88.8	87.6	92.9	97.5	94.9	132
Recalculation	100	–	75	79	71	72	67	66	70	73	71	99

Source: SG 61, p. 149; JP 57, pp. 465, 467; JP 57, p. 517; (110); JP 61, p. 403

per head 1.6 per cent higher than in 1939 (23, p. 296; 98, p. 59). Berislav Sefer maintained this even though he himself admitted that 'immediately after the war . . . consumption was depressed' (JP 64, p. 241).

In fact consumption cannot have been higher in 1948 than in 1939. A French observer, J. Marczewski, came very early to the conclusion that Yugoslav consumption in 1947 and 1948 must have been much inferior to the pre-war figure (73, p. 170). This conclusion also follows from the share of personal consumption in the GSP in 1948 (Table 3.2) which amounted to 48 per cent. Depreciation is given as 4 per cent of GSP. If one takes a more adequate figure of 10 per cent, it transpires that the share of personal consumption in the 1948 national income must have been about 53, say 55 per cent (cf. 23, p. 293).

The Yugoslav Statistical Yearbook for 1940 (p. 465) gave budget expenditure in the financial year 1939/40 as current dinars 12,947 million. The national income in 1939 is quoted as 1938 dinars 50,987.5 million by *Jugoslovenski pregled* (1957, p. 431), which is obviously according to the Marxist definition because it is listed in a continuous series with post-war figures for national income at 1938 prices. The 1939/40 budget expenditure must, therefore, be adapted to the Marxist usage (see p. 31). This can be done approximately by halving the figure, which reduces it to about 12.5 per cent of the 1938 national income on the Marxist definition.

To obtain personal consumption, net investment in 1939 also has to be deducted, but here figures vary. The 1947 Five-Year Plan evaluates it at 15 per cent of the national income before the war. The *Economic Survey of Europe* (quoted in 73, p. 170) assesses it as 5 per cent, while various Yugoslav authors mention, albeit as averages for longer pre-war periods, 4 per cent (YS 60, pp. 35 ff.), 4–5 per cent (80, p. 125), 5 per cent (98, p. 58) and 6–8 per cent (23, p. 94). It also has to be taken into account that the 15 per cent figure in the First Five-Year Plan included investment financed out of the budget so that it is partly included in the figure for budget expenditure. It therefore seems safe to assume that, in 1939, private investment was at the most 10 per cent of national income.

Personal consumption in 1939 must have been approximately 77.5 per cent [100 −(12.5 +10)] of national income (Marxist definition). Table 5.1 shows that the index of national income in 1948 was 107 (1939 = 100). Therefore, total personal consumption in 1948 must have been about 76 per cent of consumption in 1939, the analogous consumption per head being approximately 75 per cent.

From the figures quoted (and Table 5.1), it appears probable that in 1952 Yugoslav consumption was about 30 per cent lower than before the war and even lower if the change in population is taken into account. It then recovered and reached the 1948 level again in 1954 when it was, however, still 25 per cent below the 1939 level.

The pre-war level of total consumption was reached only in about 1958 and of consumption per head in about 1960. As Tito stated that at the lowest ebb of consumption textile capacity was only 50–60 per cent utilised (B 28.7.52) and statistics (58, p. 152) show that agricultural output in 1952 was down to 52 per cent of its 1939 level, it appears that the consumer good capacity existed all along but was neglected because of the concentration on heavy industry, which contributed very little to the satisfaction of the needs of the population. The figures in Table 5.1 also show that even after 1956 the growth rate of consumption was still only about 80 per cent of the growth rate of national income.

5.2 LOW WAGES

Understandably, the lack of progress in consumption in the 1950s was reflected in low wages, so much so that the Statistical Office was reluctant to publish the relevant data (see p. 5). In 1957, the Statistical Yearbook discontinued the publication of tables on incomes of four-member families and the Jugoslavija 1945–1964 survey (58, p. 64) had to reconstruct the data as presented in Table 5.2 because — as it pointed out — trends in net personal incomes had not been followed systematically.

Table 5.3 reproduces the last figures on incomes of four-member families published in the Statistical Yearbook.

Recalculation as on p. 5 shows that, in 1955, the average manual worker's wage amounted to 78 per cent and, if the average child allowance is included, to 102 per cent, of the pre-war average wage. For white-collar employees the percentages were 58 per cent and 72 per cent.

These percentage figures may be on the high side since the average for a head of a four-member family may not have been the average for workers in general and the cost of living index may be too low. Taking the 1955 national income at current prices, dinars 1398 billion (58, p. 77) and dividing it by the national income for the same year at 1938 prices, 72.1 billion, as published in *Jugoslovenski pregled* (1957, p. 465), one obtains a price index for 1955 of 1940 which is hardly compatible with the indices of living costs of 1119 and 1065 in Table 5.3.

Further, the indices are to some extent distorted because of the very low rents of accommodation in post-war Yugoslavia as compared with

Table 5.2: Indices of nominal and real earnings 1952–1960

	Average net personal incomes in thousand dinars			Nominal incomes			Indices	1952–1960 Real incomes		
	Total	'Economy'	'Non-economy'	Total	'Economy'	'Non-economy'	Cost of Living	Total	'Economy'	'Non-economy'
1952	9.2	8.6	12.4	100	100	100	100	100	100	100
1953	9.3	8.4	13.5	101	98	109	104	97	94	105
1954	10.4	9.2	16.3	113	107	131	102	111	105	128
1955	10.8	9.8	14.5	117	114	117	115	103	99	102
1956	11.9	10.7	17.6	129	124	142	124	105	100	115
1957	14.4	13.3	19.7	156	155	159	127	123	122	125
1958	15.1	13.5	23.0	164	157	185	134	123	117	138
1959	17.7	16.3	24.8	192	190	200	136	142	140	147
1960	20.3	19.0	27.4	220	221	221	149	148	148	148
1961	22.0	21.0	28.2	239	244	227	161	149	152	141
1962	24.2	23.0	30.3	262	267	244	177	147	151	138
1963	28.5	27.2	35.9	312	316	290	167	166	169	155
1964	36.2	34.9	43.9	394	406	354	209	188	194	169

Source: 58, p. 64.

Table 5.3: *Wages and salaries 1952–1955* (1939 = 100)

	Income of a four-member family of a production worker		
	Index of nominal wages	*Index of living costs*	*Index of real wages*
1952	1,410	957	147
1955	1,583	1,119	141
	Income of a four-member family of a white-collar worker		
	Income of nominal wages	*Index of living costs*	*Index of real wages*
1952	726	929	78
1955	921	1,065	86

Source: SG 56, p. 294
cf. Tables 1.3 and 1.4

the pre-war period. But that did not change the supply, and the living area per person after the war remained at the level of just under 9 square metres till 1960 (SG 61, p. 173). In 1960, there was also a switch to more economic rents.

Taking the figures in Table 5.3 at their face values, however, we notice that manual workers did not profit from the rise in consumption between 1952 and 1955 while white-collar employees (and the rest of the population) did. This was a consequence of the initial communist policy of maintaining the standard of living of workers when their 'planning' led to a fall in consumption and shifting the burden onto everybody else (see p. 6). When the reformers then tried to revive the economy, they had to restore incentives to employees and peasants on whom the revival depended as much as or more than on manual workers. This catching up was in danger of causing unrest, possibly fomented by orthodox communists, who accused the reformers of discrimination against workers, although workers have as much to gain from the normal working of the economy as anybody else and the economy cannot move forward without the services of peasants, nor of technologists and administrators. This problem was quite acute for instance in Czechoslovakia in 1968, while it was easier to solve in Yugoslavia where the same communist team remained in power.

Table 5.3 and the percentages derived from it, make it possible to link Table 5.2 to 1939. In the mid-1950s, the ratio of manual workers to white-collar employees was 7:3 (SG 57, p. 113) from which it follows that the index of average personal incomes in 1955 was 93 (1939 = 100), so that the pre-war average wage level must have been reached and surpassed in 1957/8.

Often it was admitted that in the 1950s Yugoslav wages were low and, particularly, lagged behind the growth of the GSP, but it was claimed that this deficiency was compensated by social wages such as child allowances, health and disablement insurance, pensions and paid holiday.

Child allowances are included in the figures above. They came to be considered a disincentive to work (23, p. 229), but inflation eroded them anyway, so that they fell from 48 per cent of the average wage in 1952 to 18 per cent in 1958 (YS 60, p. 69).

In 1939, various social insurance institutions had a membership of just under 1.1 million, which rose to about 1.4 million in 1948, and almost 3.5 million in 1960 (YS 60, p. 65). However, the expenditure before the war amounted to 18 per cent of wages, after the war to 45 per cent (B 5.4.54) and was rising fast (YS 60, p. 70) so that it was a heavy burden on the economy. Nonetheless, it was not sufficient to allow workers to enjoy their full formal entitlements under the social insurance legislation (B 16.5.59, cf. 121, pp. 326 and 368).

The number of pensioners in Yugoslavia in 1939 was 105,000, a figure which rose to 205,000 in 1948 and 580,000 in 1960 (SG 61, p. 299). This was in excess of what the economy of the country could bear so that there were constant revisions and attempts at reducing the number of those entitled to pensions (cf. Tito, B 7.5.62). It was impossible to subsidise all those without a livelihood (Dn 27.3.52) and many were in this position because the communist government had deprived them of the basis of their existence. After all, private property is a kind of old-age insurance. In 1962 beggars appeared again (B 7.6 and 9.6.62).

Because of the very low share of wages in total enterprise costs, there was not much incentive to save labour and try to improve its productivity (79, p. 201, B 3.3.59). It proved impossible, in view of the prevailing human attitudes, first to improve productivity and only later to raise individual consumption, that is wages (13).

The very low incomes forced many people to take on a second job which meant that they neglected their main employment in order to be able to go on working for another three or four hours a day (13). *Borba* of 16.12.58 described how a worker sleeping at his machine was awakened and scolded by the foreman, to whom he replied: 'But, foreman, I would rather you scold me than go home tired.'

The rise in alcoholism and crime may also be an indication of the state of mind of the population and were sometimes described as such by the communist newspapers themselves. *Borba* of 14.12.58 claimed that worsening alcoholism was a sign that the Yugoslavs had not solved their problem of social adjustment.

While before the war the total number of crimes against property amounted to 7664 cases in 1938, in 1952 the number of crimes against the national economy and against private and social property rose to almost 60,000 cases (SG 61, p. 307). The strictest measures were taken and people were even shot for theft (cf. B 1.9.52), but it was denied that the rise was due to the low standard of living (Slovene Minister of the Interior, Dn 26.3.52). It was particularly irritating to the authorities that people did not regard crimes against social property as crimes at all (B 21.6.53). The general attitude was 'What belongs to everybody, does not belong to anybody' (B 10.4.54) and 'Some time or other everybody must go to prison' (SP 21.7.53). Tito complained (B 7.5.62) that convicted thieves were given back their old jobs and announced a tightening of the criminal code.

Presumably driven by the search for better pay and working conditions, workers tended to shift constantly from enterprise to enterprise, about which there were many complaints. In 1959, it was reported for instance that the turnover of unskilled workers in the mining industry amounted to 45 per cent per year (B 11.4.59).

On the whole, there was much dissatisfaction ascribed to 'petty bourgeois influences' (SP 23.6.53, *Mladina* 6.5.52). One of the manifestations was the constant stream of refugees from Yugoslavia into Italy, Austria and Greece. Data are available for 1957, when the urge to leave had subsided to some extent: in that year almost 26,000 mainly young Yugoslav workers and peasants escaped. In 1958, the number was reduced to 12,000 (126) and then almost ceased because legal emigration became possible. Another outlet for discontent were the occasional strikes, which were the more significant as the authorities took a very dim view of the strikers. A strike occurred as early as 1947 in one of the textile factories at Kranj and the strikers were dealt with very ruthlessly. Apparently quite a few disappeared. In 1958 the coal miners at Trbovlje struck and tried to spread their action to other enterprises, but their messengers were intercepted (121, p. 318). The communists were particularly worried because communists amongst the miners were kept in the dark about the action as the strike organisers did not trust them. Were the communists really to become the 'policemen of socialism'? (121, p. 189). Later on, Tito attacked those threatening strikes: 'Against whom do they want to strike? Against themselves! Such things must not be allowed!' (B 7.5.62).

5.3 EFFICIENCY OF LABOUR AND CAPITAL

Table 5.4 shows that the gross output per worker had fallen to about 85 per cent of the pre-war level in 1952 and then recovered to 94 per cent in 1956 and 114 per cent in 1960. On the other hand, gross output per unit of capital sank to 75 per cent of the pre-war level in 1956 and remained at 85 per cent of that level in 1960. Taking everything into account, the 1960 result does not seem too bad, as Yugoslavia had only started industrialisation and could not be expected to go in for capital-intensive high labour-productivity techniques. However, the figures may conceal many follies of the 1950s: some useless investment would have been written off by 1960, the rest was valued at 1962 prices instead of at the original very high production costs. As mentioned by commentators sometimes even world prices were used instead of the much higher domestic prices.

Table 5.4: Total productivities of labour and capital till 1960 (1939 = 100) (extension of Table 1.2)

	1952	*1956*	*1960*
Industrial gross output	170	266	441
Industrial labour force	201	283	385
Value of capital used	212	348	518

Source: Figures for 1960 have been computed from 58, p. 142 and 116, p. 161.

Possibly a better measure for the success of investment than gross product per unit of capital in a year is the so-called marginal (M) or incremental capital–output ratio which compares the investment each year with the increase in output of the same year (i.e. simultaneously). Table 5.5 gives the appropriate figures from which it transpires that the effects of investment in the first period were disastrous; they contributed very little to output. The very much lower average capital–output ratios (A) indicate that the previously existing capital was far more productive than the new investment. The drop in the incremental capital–output ratios in the next two years can hardly be attributed to any considerable improvement in the selection and implementation of investments, but must be due, as mentioned earlier, partly to the belated contribution of the investment in the first period and partly to the renewed utilisation of capacity which existed all along.

If one averages out the marginal capital–output ratios for the three periods in Table 5.5, the figures for the whole 1947–60 period become

Table 5.5: Comparative survey of simultaneous marginal and average capital coefficients in Yugoslavia
(prices 1962)

	1947–1952		*1953–1956*		*1957–1960*	
	M	A	M	A	M	A
Gross basis (depreciation included)						
Total Economy	14.0	4.0	3.7	4.2	2.2	3.6
Industry	10.1	3.2	4.0	4.1	2.2	3.3
Net basis (depreciation excluded)						
Total Economy	9.2	2.6	2.1	2.8	1.3	2.4
Industry	8.5	2.5	2.8	3.1	1.2	2.4

Source: 116, pp. 65, 66; Cf. also JP 61, p. 158 (see p. 4)

7.2 (gross) and 4.5 (net) for the whole economy and 5.8 (gross) and 4.3 (net) for industry. This is still very high especially as the pre-war capacity was certainly not fully utilised in 1947, so that it contributed to the later increase in output.

Table 5.6: Capital–output ratios in Yugoslavia before and after the war

	Net investment as percentage of national income	*Rate of growth of national income*	*Capital output coef-ficient*	*Rate of growth of con-sumption*
1923–1939	4	2.48	1.7	
1947–1958 (from 1949 level)	23.3	4.8	4.8	2.45
1947–1958 (from 1939 = 100)	23.3	3.9	6.0	–

Source: YS 60, p. 35ff.

Table 5.6 makes it possible to compare pre-war and post-war investment results, although one has to keep in mind that the figures for pre-war investment are far from reliable (see p. 50). The picture that emerges is of a roughly doubled growth rate as a result of raising investment almost six times. The effect of investment is even less impressive if growth is calculated from the 1939 level instead of from

1947. One can speculate that, if capitalists had been allowed to operate in Yugoslavia after the war, they could have achieved the same rate of growth as the communists by increasing investment by only 60 per cent over its pre-war level instead of by 480 per cent. Before the war, Yugoslav capitalism did in fact achieve such a rate of growth, if the crisis years 1930–34 are omitted from the calculation, according to *Yugoslav Survey* (1960, p. 35, footnote).

The results of investment between 1947 and 1960 look even poorer if one relates them to the growth in personal consumption. If 1939 is taken as the base year, there was no growth in personal consumption till 1958, so that from that viewpoint investment could be considered pure waste. With 1948 as the base year, the rate of growth of consumption was about the same as before the war despite almost six times higher investment since it has to be assumed that before the war consumption rose proportionately with national income. And this does not take into account disinvestment in some branches.

5.4 CONCLUSIONS ON THE REFORM UP TO 1960

If one looks back at the first decade of reforms in Yugoslavia, the conclusion has to be that the two decisive changes were the abolition of detailed plans of current production in 1952 and the change in the structure of investment in 1956. The first change was probably more important because it defused a very tense situation with a falling standard of living and made it possible to improve the supply of consumer goods.

The second change was only half-hearted since a consistent alignment of production and investment structure would have meant closing or running down a considerable number of misconceived new enterprises. The result was the preservation of many factories working at a loss by various financial devices and thus the preservation of distortions.

As a consequence it was not possible to allow market prices to operate fully either. They had to be manipulated and controlled. This applies also to interest charges for the use of capital. All this still narrowly circumscribed Yugoslav enterprises and their entrepreneurial functions which, in so far as they were transferred to enterprises, were mainly performed by directors anyway. After the unsuccessful attempt at introducing interest rates as an investment criterion, long-term decisions were firmly back in the hands of political authorities, with banks as their instrument.

The reluctance to or political impossibility of changing the structure of production and investment perpetuated the low utilisation of capacity and the accumulation of stocks, since it was out of the question to manipulate demand sufficiently to permit the smooth disposal of output.

Part Two

In Search of an Economic Mechanism for Self-management (1961–1965)

6: False Starts

6.1 IDEOLOGICAL HESITATIONS

At the end of the 1950s, things looked much brighter in Yugoslavia mainly because of the more pragmatic approach which led the communists to stop trying to plan all the *minutiae* and to redirect investment as far as the existing production structure would allow. This structure was the sore point as to improve it would have meant running down or even closing many new enterprises, something that was apparently politically impossible. Maybe the Yugoslav leaders hoped to overcome this difficulty by reverting to the old structure of investment in the 1961–5 Social Plan, but this was hardly consistent with the simultaneous widening of the jurisdiction of workers' councils which were supposed to act on the basis of the essential harmony between the interests of society and of enterprises and their members. At the same time, possibly to placate those who thought that pragmatism was not socialist, new nationalisation measures were adopted: the last private surgeries were eliminated, most housing was taken into public ownership and long-term action to replace private smallholders was initiated.

In December 1958, the bulk of housing plus business premises and building plots were nationalised with derisory compensation. Thereafter rents for housing rose from dinars 16 to dinars 40 per square metre because low rents were deemed inconsistent with distribution according to work (Lidija Sentjurc, B 13.1.59). This was followed by the establishment of 'housing communities' of tenants who were supposed to keep buildings in good repair through 'self-contributions' and voluntary work, and also socialise domestic work, for instance, by industrial kitchens. Women were supposed to have jobs (Tito, B 10.5.59) but the appropriate institutions could take care of only 1.2 per cent of small children (Ep 7.7.62).

6.2 'COLD COLLECTIVISATION'

In 1959 there was a record harvest in Yugoslavia, as indicated in Table 6.1. The credit for this success was claimed for the Yugoslav socialist system (B 11.7.59, Bakaric, B 29.4.60), but the achievement was in fact due to the introduction of modern agronomy (JP 72, p. 93), especially Italian types of wheat, and to the massive investment in the social sector of agriculture which rose from dinars 56 billion in 1957 to dinars 115 billion in 1960 (JP 61, p. 60). The use of artificial fertiliser increased from 31,000 tons in 1939 to 448,000 tons in 1956 and to just under 2 million tons in 1960 (JP 61, p. 326). It doubled again between the early 1960s and the early 1970s and then levelled out (JP 76, p. 333).

Table 6.1: Harvest of wheat and maize (in ten-thousands of quintals)

	1930–1939	*The best pre-war year*	*1949–1958*	*1960*	*1970*	*1975*	*1976*
Wheat	2430	3060	2180	3570	3790	4404	5979
Maize	4300	5340	3510	6160	6933	9389	9106

Source: SG 62, p. 109 and SG 77, p. 161

The result of this massive injection of funds was heavy losses for the social sector farms (Ep 21.7.62) which became a permanent feature despite lower interest rates and taxes, despite special premia (discriminating against individual farms) and despite a 33 per cent rise in agricultural prices in 1965 alone (JP 72, pp. 101 ff).

One of the reasons for this state of affairs was that, under Yugoslav conditions, the capital intensity of agricultural production in the social sector was excessive. More capital was employed per worker on average than in manufacturing, while production per worker was only one third as high (Ep 27.7., 11.8.62). The explanation was that the equipment was mostly obsolete (Ep 22.12.61) and often of the wrong kind (B 24.7.62). There were too many tractors and insufficient other agricultural equipment so that more cooperating labour was needed than normally expected (B 18.6.60). The number of 'social' tractors rose from 9000 in 1955 to 30,000 in 1960 and to 40,000 in 1965, but then fell to 28,000 in 1970 and to around 25,000 in 1975 (JP 72, p. 99 and SG 76, p. 175).

The second reason was that communist policy aimed at 'large-scale socialised production' in agriculture, though the approach had changed because of the previous failure when coercion was tried. Kardelj announced (95, p. 99) that resources would be concentrated in the social sector in order to obtain very high yields and labour productivity, so that it would entirely dominate the market. In this manner, individual producers would be by-passed and it would be only a question of time before they disappeared.

In 1960, the socialised arable land amounted to about 10 per cent of the total (JP 72, pp. 96 and 99) and it rose through purchases to about 15 per cent by 1974 (JP 75, p. 231). The use of fertiliser, measured in kilos of active matter per ha, rose in the social sector from 145 in 1960 to 210 in 1968 and fell to 165 in 1974, while in the private sector it rose steadily from 14 in 1960 to 50 in 1974 (JP 76, p. 333). This one-sided allocation was bound to have untoward consequences for the profitability of the social sector because of the law of diminishing returns which made a mockery of the official policy. Following Marx, the communist leaders first denied that there was any such thing as diminishing returns (B 24.7.62) but later allowed a more equal, albeit still rather skewed, distribution of resources over both sectors.

While the success of the social sector in agriculture is thus dubious, individual peasants have thrived over the last fifteen years. After their mistrust of communist intentions (cf. Tito, B 31.5.59 and 29.5.60) had been at least partly dispelled, they profited from the high prices required to keep the social sector going, although discrimination against them continued (JP 72, p. 101). They found it easy to adjust to the market, increased their incomes and equipped their farms with machinery which they were not even allowed to buy under the original regime. The number of private tractors rose from 5000 in 1960 (JP 72, p. 100) to 200,000 in 1976 (SG 76, p. 167). By 1969, private farmers also owned 10,000 lorries and 59,000 cars and vans (JP 72, p. 61). Private investment in agriculture amounts to about 50 per cent of social investment but is much more productive (JP 75, p. 227). Because of this in the early 1970s some communists advocated the abolition of the 10 ha limit on private holdings.

In addition to by-passing them by raising production on social farms, there was also a plan to involve private peasants in 'cooperation' with the socialist sector and in cooperatives. But the number of cooperating peasants fell from the peak of 1.2 million in 1960 to 928,000 in 1970 (JP 72, p. 100). In 1974, about 20 per cent of private farms in the crop sector and about 10 per cent in the livestock sector were taking part in the cooperation scheme (JP 75, p. 232). The official figures are 498,000 and 272,000. The peasants are known to mistrust the cooperatives (B 11.8.71) organised for them by the authorities and to want to set up cooperatives by themselves (K 6.3.70). Before the war there was an elaborate and successful network of agricultural cooperatives in Yugoslavia which was disbanded by the communists and there were suggestions that this cooperative movement should be resurrected (B 13.1.71).

The leadership, however, persists in its intention to carry through a socialist transformation of agriculture, as this was again emphasised in the Social Contract on the Further Development of Agriculture adopted in 1973 (JP 75, p. 227) and in the Conclusions of the Praesidium of the CC of the Yugoslav Communist League on the Ideological-Political Questions concerning the Development of the Social-Economic Relations in the Agro-Industrial Complex (JP 77, p. 329). The peasants should be 'integrated' with social farms, while they want to preserve their independence and their own cooperatives (Ep 30.6.77).

6.3 INVESTMENT IN THE SOCIAL PLAN 1961–1965

After the switch in investment pattern in the mid-1950s, its reversal in the Social Plan 1961–5 came as a surprise: it was at least a partial attempt at restoring the pre-reform priorities. This might have been a consequence of the renewed stress on 'the conscious social process of reproduction by planned direction', as opposed to commodity production for the market (120 p. 20).

The Social Plan 1961–5 provided for a slight rise in the share of investment in the GSP, but—more importantly—the share of industrial investment in 'economic' investment was again raised from 43.3 per cent to 47.2 per cent and there was so much emphasis on investment in 'those branches which constitute the modern long-term basis of any industrial development (electricity, iron and steel, chemicals, capital equipment . . .) . . .' that the share of 'basic' industries in industrial investment jumped from 31.4 per cent in 1957/8 to 53 per cent in 1961 Kraigher, B 24.7.62). This although in the previous period there was a shortage of 'primary and secondary raw materials' rather than of machinery.

Probably because of the existing excess capacity in machine-tool production, the plan envisaged a 60 per cent increase in the capital intensity of new projects, which was hardly the course expected in a country with a tendency to rising unemployment. Another way in which the planners hoped to cope with idle capacity was the target of an 82 per cent rise in exports of industrial products, especially of machinery and final products of the metal-working industries, shipbuilding, electrical equipment and chemicals; mostly goods in which Yugoslavia had a definite comparative disadvantage.

In mid-1962, the Five-Year Social Plan came under heavy criticism. Boris Kraigher, the new economic chief, claimed (B 24.7.62) that it had made investment unprofitable, caused the capital–output ratio to rise and reduced the growth rate of industrial output from 15 per cent in 1960 to 7 per cent in 1961 and to 4 per cent in the first half of 1962. It is difficult to explain how the shortcomings of the plan could have had such immediate effects (they were more probably due to monetary policy—see p. 83) but Milos Minic (B 24.7.62) also had no doubt that the disappointing development was due to the failure of the Social Plan. Tito exclaimed: 'We should plan a little better, comrades!' In his view, it was particularly urgent to revise the entire investment policy so that only profitable investment would be allowed (K 22.6.62).

The plan was tacitly abandoned and the break-down of the plan was explained as a misconception by the head of the Planning Institute (26, p. 162) because of which the plan was inappropriate even when it was drafted (26, p. 174) and furthermore could not be adapted to the widening jurisdiction of the workers' councils, so that it became 'a brake on the development'. There was some discussion of a new seven-year plan in line with experiments elsewhere in Eastern Europe, but nothing ever came of it.

The 1961–5 Social Plan was an attempt at solving the problem of excess capacity by returning to concentration on the production of capital goods. The idea of first producing machines and at some later date using them to produce consumer goods is superficially so attractive that even a few economists found it very hard to abandon. Radmila Stojanovic (105, p. 344) returned to it at a consultation of Yugoslav economists and insisted that socialist production relations and permanent expansion of consumption both depended on the priority development of the so-called department I. Therefore, in her view, the market was all right for short-term decisions, but long-term decisions had to be centrally planned.

On closer examination, it proves impossible to embark first on large-scale production of capital goods because this entails a very long-term planning horizon fraught with uncertainties about the future and involves an excessively roundabout way which deprives workers of any immediate stimulation in the form of increased consumption in return for their efforts. Nor have the workers time to acquire the necessary skill and habits demanded for the production, let alone design, of complex capital goods (26, pp. 192, 199). Foreign trade enables a country to produce whatever it can best, sell it abroad and import what it needs. When the market develops and the technical intricacies are mastered, the country can switch to more complicated products, though a small country can never expect rationally to produce all types of equipment. Only in this manner is it possible to produce cheaply, i.e. as much as feasible with a given effort. The plan for the share of department I to rise to a predetermined percentage of GSP by a certain time, which is an essentially physical target, may well be reached at the expense of the economic principle of least cost.

Some Yugoslav leaders seem to have understood the need to abandon this aspect of Stalinist planning very early on. In 1957, Vukmanovic replied to a question by Nasser (121, p. 285) that what should be developed in a country is not any particular type of production, but the production for which the conditions are best, the cost is lowest and output saleable in domestic or foreign markets. This approach also assured maximum accumulation and the fastest growth.

When the influence of Marxist-Leninist-Stalinist tenets was thus at an ebb, new impulses to economic irrationality often came from the West. Many Western economists developed unusual theories under the influence of alleged communist economic successes and their theories later came back to Eastern Europe, where by now the communist wisdom was subject to considerable doubts, as an endorsement of communist practice by 'bourgeois' economists.

In 1963, Nikola Cobeljic (24) again propounded the old communist principle of using the most capital-intensive techniques possible, under the guise of the claim that maximising labour productivity by capital intensity was a long-term investment criterion, while maximising capital productivity was a short term one. Bajt (6) traced the origin of Cobeljic's doctrine back to Galenson and Leibenstein (45) and showed that it was due to confusion of maximisation of productivity in a single enterprise and in the entire economy. Indubitably a worker's average and marginal productivities in a single enterprise can be raised by more and more cooperating capital. But seen from the viewpoint of the whole economy, such concentration leads to diminishing returns in the particular enterprise and to disproportionately lower labour productivity in other enterprises where it causes a relative lack of capital. It can even lead to unemployment if there is no capital left to equip some workers. From a general standpoint, the target must be maximisation of productivity of all factors or minimisation of costs.

Cobeljic accused Bajt (25) of 'intolerance for the socialist method of speeded-up industrialisation', but Bajt was able to prove that his view was backed by Yugoslav practice and various pronouncements by the League of Communists (7).

The theoretical principle involved became very topical in a different context; if workers manage or influence management and obtain capital free or at very low prices, it is in their interest to amass it so as to raise their own productivity and wages at the expense of capital intensity and wages elsewhere (see p. 203).

The worrying aspect of these two examples of Yugoslav controversies was that the debate was still so much in terms of extremes: department I or department II, capital intensity and labour intensity, instead of in terms of the optimum combination of both 'departments' or the optimum intensity.

6.4 MORE POWER TO WORKERS' COUNCILS

As early as 1957 a Resolution of the First Congress of Yugoslav Workers' Councils (JP 57, p. 271) demanded that the rights of self-managers be extended. Their jurisdiction should encompass 'free distribution of income' expected to raise labour productivity, and 'enterprises' independence should also be strengthened' by giving workers' councils more influence on investment. This was in blatant contradiction to the philosophy of the later 1961–5 Social Plan which prescribed investment according to physical criteria instead of the criterion of what raises the value of output most, which was presumably what concerned the workers.

The wishes of the self-management Congress were taken up by the trade unions, led since 1957 by Svetozar Vukmanovic-Tempo, whom the executive committee of the League of Communists had moved from his economic post to the trade-union chairmanship. Vukmanovic may have advocated an increase in the jurisdiction of workers' councils so zealously because he felt that those who considered him an intruder, a party commissar, in the unions were right and he was trying to live down his intellectual past (121, p. 320). The trade unions also wanted (121, p. 327) taxation to discriminate between income resulting from work and income due to more capital, natural rent, monopolistic position, or generally better business conditions, especially if these were a result of government policy. On the other hand, they were against a progressive tax on the enterprise's 'earned' income and even objected to the exemption of 'minimum individual incomes' (see p. 19) from the tax, i.e. enterprise's 'contribution out of income'.

At the fifth Congress of the Socialist Alliance of Working People in April 1960, Tito came out strongly in support of the reforms in the system of distribution as suggested by the Congress of self-managers and the unions, stressing however that the amount of income distributed should depend not on the work of individuals alone but also on the results of an enterprise as a whole (121, p. 366). Although a commission had been working on the new system for some time, nothing was ready, so that a mixed system consisting of old elements and trade-union proposals was adopted (121, pp. 377 ff) and rushed through parliament at the beginning of 1961.

The most important change was a new article introduced by the Amendment Act to the Act on Resources of Economic Organisations. It provided that enterprises would, from then on, allocate net income between personal incomes and funds independently (without supervision by communes and trade unions) on the basis of their own by-laws. Other Acts fixed a flat rate of 15 per cent for the 'contribution out of income' of economic organisations and a 25 per cent tax on 'exceptional income'. Any income was to be considered exceptional if it exceeded the total sum of workers' incomes equal to the average worker's income the year before plus a transfer to the funds amounting to 6 per cent of an enterprise's capital.

Further, a new Act on the Establishment of Interest Rates on Capital in the Economy confirmed that enterprises were to pay 'a contribution to the social community in the form of an interest rate (interest rate on the funds in the economy)' regardless of whether the funds were their own or borrowed (in which case interest was already being paid on them). In addition, an enterprise had to pay over to the commune and republic investment funds 20 per cent of the amount it allocated to its business fund and fund for communal consumption.

Also freshly introduced was a contribution for the exploitation of mining deposits which, however, turned out to be so arbitrary that it had to be abolished, as also was the contribution out of exceptional income, this latter within a year.

Another element in the legal and taxation framework intended to limit the freedom of workers' councils was innovations in the foreign trade regime. A general customs tariff was introduced and the so-called 'settlement exchange rate' which was to be the operational rate, was established as the official exchange rate of dinars 300 = $1.00 plus 150 per cent, which worked out at dinars 750 = $1.00. It was hoped that foreign competition would prevent firms from raising prices.

After all these preparations and the implementation of the new system of free distribution, personal incomes in industry rose by 36 per cent within nine months according to a report by *Ekonomska politika* of 10.2.62, although there is not much indication of this in official statistics. This was, of course, many times greater than the rise in productivity.

That something did go wrong is shown by the Recommendation on the Distribution of Net Income in Workers' Collectives which was adopted by the Federal People's Assembly (JP 61, p. 571) at the end of 1961. It took to task those enterprises which had not sufficiently grasped the essence of the principle of income, of distribution according to work, those collectives which approached the adoption of new by-laws in a formalistic way, and continued to consider personal incomes as an amount fixed in advance regardless of the outcome of work and business activity. Some workers wanted incomes comparable to those enjoyed by other collectives without taking account of their own productivity and some also wanted to broaden the span of personal incomes without reason. Many collectives did not have a clear policy regarding future requirements for capital, so that they neglected accumulation, the basis for future development of the enterprise and betterment of the workers' living standard.

But admonitions were not enough, so that the Federal Assembly had to adopt, on 7 Apr. 1962, an Act on the Formation of Commissions for the Implementation of the Act on Net Income of Economic Organisations and Institutions, which provided that general criteria for the distribution of net incomes would be laid down by legislation and serve as guidelines to the workers' collectives. Commissions consisting of five members would 'advise' and 'help' them, but in cases of blatant irregularities the republic commission was empowered to use any measures required. That was the end of 'free distribution' for the time being.

The Yugoslav communist leaders were very disappointed with this result because it cut at the roots of their ideology which insisted that workers will act in a responsible way if given the right to manage, though without ever explaining what economic-psychological mechanism would make them behave in that way. The disappointment was expressed by Vice-President Kardelj in the Federal Assembly on 28 May 1962: 'We entered the new system with high hopes that workers' councils and communes would be capable of implementing the intentions of the new system of distribution without organised help and supervision on the part of leading social organs' (B 29.5.62).

Tito himself seems to have been perturbed. He repeatedly referred to people who said that workers' management had not lived up to expectations (B 7.5.62) or had doubts about self-management

(B 24.7.62) and reasserted his own faith: 'It is untrue that the workers' consciousness is not up to the present requirements, that they have no feeling for the community as a whole. They do have.' Mistakes, according to him, happened only in isolated cases.

Nonetheless, Tito did not feel at all at ease. In an interview for the London weekly *Queen* on 18 Sep. 1962, he was asked by Henry Fairlie whether it was more difficult to govern than he had expected. Tito answered,

> Of course, it is more difficult than I thought. And not only I but others also thought that it would be easier. I believe that it is easier to wage war than to organise the government and to direct social development, because these things are complicated matters.

Vukmanovic also testified that, at about the same time, he had for the first time left after a talk with Tito without clearly knowing what to do (121, p. 379).

During the visit of a British Trade Union delegation at the end of 1963, Vladimir Bakaric summarised what had happened:

> But the experience of 1961–2, when some restrictions were lifted and control of incomes was sought through persuasion and indirect influence, showed that too much could be attempted too quickly. Remedial action was necessary in respect of prices as well as incomes, and the League of Communists made a great effort to explain why new and apparently reactionary measures had been necessary. The public response was good and the workers accepted directives regarding limits within which income payments should fall. Restrictions of this kind were by no means desirable and the aim was to improve practice to the point where such direct measures would become unnecessary, but that was not so yet. (109, p. 31)

What the Yugoslav leaders were trying to do was to raise the workers' 'consciousness' so that they would allocate more of their firms' net income to 'expanded reproduction', or — to use Keynesian terms — to increase their collective propensity to save and invest. Because the workers did not behave in the way required, they were accused of being half-peasants, living in villages and possessing land, which made their interests clash with the interests of factories. Trade unions were told to see that such workers did not dominate decision-taking (121, p. 438). It was obviously hoped that, with time, half-peasants would become 'real' workers who would be selfless and willingly cut their own personal incomes to raise their enterprise's accumulation.

The communist leaders appear to have seriously believed that human nature changes with production relations, that the passage from private to social property will produce unselfish persons primarily interested in the common good. Experience, including Yugoslav experience, shows that that is not true, but one can always claim that more experience is needed. In reality, workers' incomes are far too low relatively for them to wish to save as much as the Yugoslav communists envisaged even for themselves, let alone for 'their' factories.

Formally, the enterprises were not theirs but social, however, it was hoped that a real nexus would be established between workers and the plant which they used even though they did not own it. For a considerable proportion of workers such a link hardly exists: they can be dismissed or may leave of their own accord. In neither case, can they take with them whatever they have helped to invest in the enterprise.

Labour turnover, the percentage of the total number of employees that leaves the enterprise within a month or a year, is far from negligible. Monthly figures exist since 1964 and show that in that year the monthly turnover was just over 3 per cent, meaning that on average just over one third of the employees of an economic organisation changed within a year. Later, the figure slowly dropped to about 1.2 per cent per month in 1974 and 1975, which is about 14 per cent per year (SG 73, p. 102, SG 76, p. 120). In spite of the improvement, the majority of workers in an enterprise on average leave within four years so that their 'use horizon' cannot be very long, which certainly influences decisions taken by majority vote. The influence of this turnover factor can hardly be eliminated.

The Yugoslav communists fell back on 'leading social organs', as Kardelj put it, hoping that it would be for the time being only. Tito blamed the difficulties mainly on subjective mistakes by 'our leading people', to the complacency of the communists who had let the leading role slip out of their hands, while all that was expected was that they would no longer bother with every detail (B 7.5.62). Too many people, including communists, also wanted to get rich, which caused 'apathy' among the workers. Tito therefore wanted 'dishonest acquisition of wealth' to be investigated, but was against *uravnilovka*, equalisation of incomes. This could be very dangerous indeed, because it would remove executives' interest in their work, as pointed out by Boris Kraigher (B 24.7.62). And they were the only ones fufilling the function of looking after the long-term interests of enterprises.

In the end, Boris Kraigher and Milos Minic took over responsibility for the economy, while Mijalko Todorovic, who had performed this function since the departure of Svetozar Vukmanovic, was shunted to a side-line.

6.5 DISPROPORTIONS IN THE ECONOMY

The considerable disproportions, about which there could no longer be any doubt in the late 1950s, were a cause for concern and it was thought necessary to combat them by 'instilling some business discipline' (53, p. 143). For that purpose the 1961 annual plan introduced very strict provisions on credit expansion and decreed that the money supply should not rise faster than the GSP and that bank credits should finance only a part of additional working capital while the finance for the rest (about 50 per cent) should come out of enterprises' own funds and social investment funds (JP 61, p. 53). The intention was possibly also to use monetary stringency to prevent excessive rises after the liberalisation of distribution.

As was to be expected, the monetary squeeze slowed down industrial growth from figures of well over 10 per cent in the 1950s and 15 per cent in 1960 to a mere 7 per cent in 1961 and 1962, as shown in Table 6.2. This led to a heated debate which will be discussed in the following chapter. The authorities felt obliged to return to monetary largesse, so that the rate of rise in the money supply fell from 27 per cent in 1960 to 14 per cent in 1961 and then rose to 27.7 per cent in 1962 and 31 per cent in 1963. The authorities were well aware of the disproportions in the economy but did not know how to cope with them. This problem has remained central ever since.

It can best be illustrated in tables which summarise data for the whole period.

Table 6.3 shows the figures for money supply and changes in inventories according to various sources which were the basis for the discussion described in the next chapter. Tito himself said: 'Last year, our storehouses were full up with enormous quantities of unsaleable goods. These are of bad quality and cannot be sold, but they are counted as national income. What this means is not difficult to understand: these frozen assets represent an enormous burden on the economy of the socialist state' (K 21.6.62). It seems that at that time statistics simply showed stockpiling as consumption. This changed when Yugoslavia

Table 6.2: Rates of growth of some components of GSP

	Cost of living	Industrial production prices	GSP	Industrial production total	Investment	Instruments of work	Intermediate goods	Consumer goods
1952								
1953	4	−2	20	11		30	8	13
1954	−1	−2	1.3	14		4	15	15
1955	12	5	14.8	16		17	18	12
1956	8	1	−6	10		6	12	11
1957	3	–	23.9	17		16	15	22
1958	5	1	1.6	11	(14.8)	13	11	10
1959	2	–	17.7	13	(14.5)	17	11	15
1960	10	2	5.8	15	(19)	20	13	17
1961	8	4	5.7	7	(10.9)	4	8	8
1962	10	–	4.2	7	(6)	1	6	11
1963	6	1	12.4	16	(8.1)	14	15	17
1964	12	5	11.5	16	(13.9)	19	15	16
1965	35	15	1.5	8	(−12)	10	7	9
1966	23	11	8.5	4	(8)	2	4	6
1967	7	2	2.6	–	(2.1)	1	–	−1
1968	5	–	4.0	6	(8.4)	7	6	6
1969	8	3	10.4	11	(7.1)	12	12	10
1970	11	9	6.1	9	(15)	8	9	10
1971	16	15	8.8	10	(7.0)	10	10	11
1972	17	11	4.6	8	(3.2)	7	6	16
1973	20	13	5.0	6	(2.5)	6	6	6
1974	21	29	8.5	11	(8.9)	12	11	10
1975	24	22	3.6	6	(9.0)	14	4	4
1976	12	6	4	3	–	4	3	4

Source: *Cost of living*: 58, p. 235; SG 77, p. 306
GSP: see Table 6.3
Investment: SG 72, p. 104; SG 77, p. 138
Industrial production prices: 58, p. 230; SG 77, p. 303
Industrial production: SG 77, p. 189

became an associated member of the OECD and that organisation produced its first economic survey of Yugoslavia in 1962. The booklet contained data on changes in stocks based on the Yugoslav submission to the OECD. National statistics did not begin to include data on the same basis until much later.

As the table shows, the inventory situation was bad and getting worse. Looking through UN Statistical Yearbooks, one finds that the normal yearly change in stocks for OECD members is about 1 per cent of the GNP, very rarely going up to 4 or 5 per cent and sometimes falling. The same is not true of communist countries where the normal

Table 6.3: Comparative growth rates of inventories

	Money supply (percentage growth)	GSP (percentage real growth)	Fixed investment (percentage real growth)	Increase in inventories (percentage of GSP)			Horvat's figures
				nominal increases	real increases		
					OECD	input-output tables	
1953		20	22.3	3.2			1.3
1954	30	1.3	7.0				1.9
1955	0	14.8	−2.8				3.2
1956	35	−6	−1.3	7.3			10.7
1957	25.6	23.9	21.2	13.3			5.9
1958	4	1.6	14.8	8.2			8.5
1959	21	17.7	14.5	13.5			5.9
1960	27	5.8	19	10.3			7.0
1961	14	5.7	10.9	7.4			5.2
1962	27.7	4.2	6	5.8		3.8	7.1
1963	31	12.4	8.1	8.1			4.7
1964	23	11.5	13.9	11.9		10.5	5.5
1965	4.1	1.5	−12	13.5			

1966	4.5	8.5	8	13.3	13.6	12.6
1967	−2	2.6	2.1	5.9	5.6	
1968	24	4.0	8.4	3.5	3.4	3.6
1969	11.9	10.4	7.1	6.3	5.3	
1970	20	6.1	15	8.7	8.6	7.8
1971	14.9	8.8	7.0	10.7	10.5	
1972	42.3	4.6	3.2	6.0	7.5	6.4
1973	36.7	5.0	2.5	10.4	8.6	
1974	26.1	8.5	8.9	14.5	10.6	
1975	32	3.6	9	8.9	10.5	
1976	52.7	4		4.2	5.0	

Sources: *Money supply* (demand deposits, currency in circulation and float) – calculated from *OECD Surveys of SFRY*, Tables I; and 26, p. 215
GSP and fixed investment – SG 73, p. 120; SG 77, p. 138
Inventories: *nominal increases*
Calculated from *OECD Surveys of SFRY*, Table A at current prices ('Change in stock' as percentage of 'Social product')
real increases
Calculated from *OECD Surveys of SFRY*, 1976, Table A at 1966 prices ('Change in stock' as percentage of 'Social product')
Calculated from input-output tables in SG 66, p. 120; SG 68, p. 118; SG 70, p. 114; SG 72, p. 114; SG 75, p. 130; SG 77, p. 134. (Total of column 18 minus total of row 22 as percentage of total of column 24)
Horvat's figures from 52, p. 60.

rise seems to be around 10 per cent of the GSP. Naturally some rise in stocks is required as economies grow, but the lower the rate of growth of inventories the better the economic performance. High rates indicate that supply is badly matched with demand and that some parts of the stocks are unsaleable in the full sense of the word.

This was certainly true of Yugoslavia. An Act on the Valuation of Inventories, passed in 1975 to prevent the concealment of losses by high valuation of unsaleable stocks, decreed that their value should be reduced by 5 per cent after a year, by 25 per cent after two years, and by 50 per cent after three years. Inventories had also been written off in a similar way before. Changes in the value of inventories also occur because of inflation, so that one has to be careful not to include inflationary rises in value in the real additions to stocks, i.e. yearly waste. The 1976 OECD survey of Yugoslavia published figures for the change in stocks on a constant prices basis, so that these real figures can be compared with nominal increases. Another set of real figures was calculated from the input–output tables published in the Yugoslav Statistical Yearbook which would not contain changes in prices.

According to Rodic (92, p. 137), in the 1960s the value of inventories was on average equal to about two thirds of the GSP of the social sector. Since during this period the real growth rate of GSP was 6.3 per cent and the nominal growth rate of the proportion of inventories in GSP was 9.6 per cent (the real growth was about the same judging by the figures for 1966–70), the difference of 3.3 per cent of GSP must have been written off on average per year. Again according to Rodic, something approaching half of the value of inventories consisted of finished goods, about two-fifths were raw materials and other inputs, and one-fifth unfinished production.

Taking Table 5 on p. 92 of *Privredni bilansi Jugoslavije 1974* (Belgrade 1976), combined with Table 5 on p. 112 of *Privredni bilansi Jugoslavije 1966–1971* (Belgrade 1973), it can be established that in the period 1966–1974, the apparent value of inventories of raw materials in industrial enterprises was rising at an average yearly rate of 7.2 per cent, those of final products in industrial enterprises at 7.7 per cent annually, and those of final products in retail trade at 23.4 per cent, which clearly shows that the problem was not the accumulation of inventories needed for production, but of final products unsuitable for use so that they constantly had to be written off. Furthermore, 20 per cent of their value was apparently ficticious (92, p. 140).

It is clear that these rises in inventories mean that 'income is melting in warehouses' (B 3.2.73). *Ekonomska politika* of 8.9.1975 reported that, in Serbia, inventories of final production were increasing at the rate of 22 per cent year and commented that this figure indicated that the largest part of the increase in production was not being used.

Table 6.4 reproduces some data on capacity utilisation which was another indication of distortions, of the impossibility of using some of the capacity which had been built because of lack of demand and inconsistency in the productive system of the country. It is very difficult to measure utilisation because it is difficult to determine what the maximum output of an item of capital equipment can be, since this to some extent depends on the subjective skill and performance of those involved. For that reason, more schematic measures have to be used.

The method of using maximum monthly production only shows what the average annual utilisation was if the highest monthly production actually achieved is in fact equal to full production capacity. If even in the best month capacity is not used to the full, the degree of underutilisation will be understated, which is certainly the case in Yugoslavia.

Using this method, *Ekonomska politika* of 4.4.1977 claims that in Yugoslavia capacity utilisation amounted to 64–68 per cent in 1966–8 and to 73–75 per cent in 1970–5, compared with 85–90 per cent in Western Germany, Austria and the United States in the 1960s.

Vrcelj (117, JP 68, p. 19) looked at utilisation in individual branches and stressed that Yugoslav producer goods industry, represented by the metal and electrical industries, used its capacity very unevenly, so that the average production was only about 57–61 per cent of peak production, while for the textile industry, as an example of consumer goods industries, the corresponding figure was 75 per cent. How little these figures mean is shown by the figures for 1973, when utilisation was much more even, but no higher than earlier.

The low utilisation of capacity can possibly be gleaned from the data on utilisation of electric motors, if 4800 hours is taken as full utilisation in a year (two shifts of eight hours for 300 days). Electric motors were in fact used at a rate of about 2300 hours a year in the textile industry, 1100–1200 hours a year in the electrical industry, and 875 hours a year in the metal industry.

The third indication of low capacity use and hence distortions are the data on shift work. A shift coefficient is the average number of shifts worked in all plants of a branch. Table 6.4 shows that the metal and electrical industries were on little more than one shift and the textile industry on two shifts, with cotton textiles even exceeding two shifts.

The three industries are not homogeneous, so that differences in

Table 6.4: Capacity utilisation and rates of growth

	Rates of growth				Capacity utilisation										
	Money supply	GSP	Fixed investment	Stock increases	Metal ind. (1)	Metal ind. (2)	Metal ind. (3)	Electr. ind. (1)	Electr. ind. (2)	Electr. ind. (3)	Textile. ind. (1)	Textile. ind. (2)	Textile. ind. (3)	of which cotton (1)	of which cotton (2)
1962	24	4.2	6.5	5.8 (3.8)	57			75			76			81	
1963	31	12.4	8.6	8.1	55	1.32	854	61	1.51	1201	76	1.80	2314	79	2.12
1964	23	11.5	14.5	11.9 (10.5)	60			68			75				2.12
1965	4.1	1.5	−11.6	13.5	55			58			63				
1966	4.5	8.5	8.3	13.3 (12.6)	57	1.34		58	1.28		74	1.83			
1970	20	6.1	15	8.7 (7.8)	65			71			55			85	
1973	36.8	5	2.7	10.4	79	1.34	909	79	1.32	1177	83	1.81	2407		
1974	26.1	8.5	8.9	14.5		1.34	867		1.33	1110		1.82	2363		
1975	32	3.6	9	8.9	65	1.34	891	71	1.29	1129	74	1.79	2262	84	

(1) Capacity utilisation measured according to the method of maximum monthly production
(2) Capacity utilisation measured by shift coefficient – the average number of shifts in the branch
(3) The average yearly utilisation of electric motors in hours

Source: Rates of growth – Table 6.3
Capacity utilisation – 117; JP 68, p. 19; Ep 11.6.73; Ep 4.4.77; SG 75, p. 181; SG 76, p. 183; SG 77, p. 185

utilisation within them have to be taken into account. *Ekonomska politika* of 4.4.1977 published data from which Table 6.5 has been put together.

Table 6.5: Capacity utilisation of industrial activities (maximum monthly production method)

	1962	*1965*	*1970*	*1975*
bricks and tiles	51	73	94	94
raw steel	87	90	94	91
cotton spinning and weaving	81	82	85	84
wool spinning and weaving	80	56	82	81
electric household appliances	58	60	74	78
road vehicles	50	51	70	71
metal household products	70	63	64	68
agricultural machinery	42	43	58	65
electrical equipment	70	56	61	63
railway rolling stock	58	58	62	56
machinery and equipment (non-electrical)	49	45	54	48

Source: *Ep* 4.4.77

In spite of the uncertainties of these data, the article in *Ekonomska politika* correctly concludes that there is an obvious excess of capacity in processing industries and a shortage in raw material supplies from both domestic and external sources. It does not however point out that there is also a marked discrepancy between the utilisation of electrical and metal industry capacity producing consumer goods and capital goods.

The communist leadership is fully aware of the problem: At a meeting of the Praesidium of the Central Committee on 30th September, 1974, it was stated for instance that the average utilisation of Yugoslav capacity was only 50–55 per cent. This figure does not seem to have been arrived at by any of the methods enumerated above, but to be 'impressionistic' which may nevertheless be more realistic in view of the shortcomings of more rigorous approaches.

In 1977, a commission of the Federal Business Chamber was told that Yugoslav development had been hampered for years by 'excess capacity in certain branches and bottlenecks in other parts of the economy, by mis-match of the selection and quality of goods with needs and demand in the market' (Ep 14.2.77). Somewhat earlier the Zagreb economist Marijan Korosic wrote pleading that production for stockpiles should be replaced by production of commodities for use (Ep 14.7.75). These are in fact the problems, and the 1961 monetary stringency was one attempt to force Yugoslav enterprises to bring about a change in the structure of production.

7: Taking Stock

7.1 CRITICISM OF MONETARY STRINGENCY

Those who objected to the 1961 monetary stringency claimed that all it did was to slow down growth, while it could not stop inflation which was cost-push anyway (see p. 129) nor did it improve the production and investment structure. The main exponent of this view was Branko Horvat, who claimed that Yugoslav monetary policy was itself a source of fluctuations and called it, therefore, '(anti-) anti-cyclical' (53, p. 141), but Bajt (NR 23. 2. 63) and others were of a very similar opinion.

In 1962 Horvat (33) was most impressed by the high rates of growth of the Yugoslav economy, according to him the fastest in the world, between 1952 and 1960. It was true that the rate was reduced to 6.6 per cent if the period 1947–1962 was taken into consideration, but nonetheless—he thought—fast rates of growth could have been resumed if the retarding policies were discontinued. Horvat stressed the improvement in the capital–output ratio and growth of consumption in the 1950s without mentioning, however, that both may have been due to the resumption of work by industries existing since before the war but initially kept idle because they were not sufficiently 'heavy'.

At the end of 1961, two-thirds of the economy was suffering from a lack of liquidity and credit, but inflation did not stop. At the same time stocks were being accumulated at twice the rate at which the revenue of manufacturing industry was rising which must have been due to a mis-match between supply and demand. The number of unemployed reached 294,000 or 9.4 per cent of the (non-agricultural) labour force by March 1962.

Horvat's prescription was to speed up production by relaxation of credit. Plans for 1961 and 1962 were mistaken because they under-rated investment needs and investment possibilities. The production of intermediate goods and machinery should have been raised, but machinery presented problems because of the small Yugolsav market. Horvat was pressing for more growth at the beginning of the 1960s, although he admitted that there were disproportions between the development of production and consumption, and break-neck growth threatened to worsen this discrepancy.

A few years later, in 1969, Horvat's ideas were further clarified in his book on economic cycles in Yugoslavia, in particular in his treatment of inventory cycles (52, p. 58 ff). Inventories in Yugoslavia were relatively much higher than in other market economies and possibly as high as in centrally planned economies. But while some capitalist economies accumulate inventories during the upswing and shed them on the downswing, in Yugoslavia, inventories do not rise proportionately during expansion, nor do they shrink during contraction.

Looking at table 6.3 which gives Horvat's figures for inventory rises, one finds that the 6 per cent fall in GSP in 1956 corresponded to an exceptional rise in inventories, equal to 10.7 per cent of the GSP and the rise of 23.9 per cent in GSP the following year to a low in inventory accumulation of 5.9 per cent of GSP with a similar pattern in other years. From this Horvat concluded: 'According to these figures, during recessions and depressions inventories absorb a part of production which cannot be sold in the market. Thus stocks in the Yugoslav economy became an economic stabiliser' (52, p. 60).

Horvat suggested that the expansion of GSP should be stepped up so that the rate of growth would be higher than the rate of inventory accumulation, thus smoothing out the cycle and relatively reducing inventory accumulation. He argued that the expansion rate of manufacturing should be 13 to 14 per cent (52, p. 66).

The source of Horvat's figures on inventories (or rather Ljubo Madzar's, whose figures he used) is not clear. They are very different from the official OECD figures: it is true that the OECD figures are nominal, i.e. they include price changes, but Horvat's figures move in the opposite direction even when there are no price changes as in 1957, 1959, and 1962. Besides, real changes in inventories as calculated from input-output tables for the years for which they were published in the *Statisticki Godisnjak* also move differently from Horvat's figures for 1962 and 1964. Inventory figures in real terms, as recently published by the OECD, closely follow the movement of nominal figures. In later years, the figures certainly do not follow Horvat's pattern: inventory increases are larger than growth in the good years 1966, 1972 and 1974, and smaller in the bad year 1968.

In general, there seems to be a tendency for inventory accumulation to rise. This may be due to the gradual return to full utilisation of pre-war capacities, presumably well geared to demand, in the 1950s which is shown by the ease with which consumer goods output grew during those years, while its growth became more halting in the 1960s and 1970s. From 1960 onward, the distortions of post-war investment began to tell.

Horvat does not mention one thing—the final fate of inventories. Stocks in market economies have the purpose of smoothing out unevenness in supply; in planned economies and in Yugoslavia, they are largely waste, goods that cannot be sold because they are either unuseable or too expensive to attract demand. Taking the OECD figures on real increases in inventories for the period for which they exist, one finds that the yearly average addition to stocks in Yugoslavia is equal to 8.2 per cent of the GSP. If one assumes that 2 per cent of GSP per year is the necessary increase in stocks, about 6 per cent represent waste (somewhat less if GNP is taken instead of GSP).

Furthermore, some output, especially output of the engineering industry, is not used for final consumption but for the formation of new production capacity, which can be so badly chosen that it remains underutilised, which is another form of waste. The two kinds of waste together may well account for some 10 per cent on average of the Yugoslav GSP. This is bad in itself, but is made worse by the import content of this waste at a time when the country has great difficulty in keeping foreign trade in equilibrium. This is one reason why this waste cannot be simply forgotten as Horvat seems to suggest, the other being that the situation may deteriorate if this waste is disregarded and the country goes for more of the growth which has brought about this wasteful production in the first place.

Again, Horvat hardly mentions the underutilised capacity. All he says is that Yugoslav growth could be even faster if capacity were used to the full. He does not dwell on the inconsistency of the demand for investment derived from the demand for final consumer goods and the investment goods production structure. Besides, the figures on underutilisation confirm that the investment goods industry is far too big for an economy the size of Yugoslavia. It would hardly be possible to step up fixed investment above the present 30 per cent of the GSP so as to use more of the present idle metal-working capacity. According to Vrcelj (see p. 79) the doubling of output would require the utilisation of only half the existing unutilised plant. Would that not require a rise in the present share of investment in the GSP to almost 50 per cent?

A surprising feature of the inventories pattern is the high level of stocks of consumer goods. The explanation may be that producer goods are very often produced to order so that the discrepancy between the capacities of department I and department II show in underutilisation rather than in stocks. Consumer goods, on the contrary, are produced for the market without knowing the customers in advance, so that excess production occurs much more easily, but even so it seems strange that the Yugoslav market should be so saturated for instance with textiles that even bad quality textiles could not find buyers—average European consumption of textiles is about 15 kg per person per year as opposed to 6 kg (Ep 16.2.70) in Yugoslavia.

Nonetheless, inventories of textiles were still rising in 1976 (Ep 26.4.76). The explanation seems to be that, year after year, millions of Yugoslavs—in 1970 2.5 million—travelled abroad, especially to Triest and Venice, to buy textiles. In 1970 they spent about dinars 1.25 billion there on textiles, while the value of Yugoslav production was about 10 billion. When questioned about why they go and buy abroad they quoted lower prices, better quality, nicer patterns and the absence of particular goods they want on the home market (this applies to other goods too) (Ep 16.7.70). Yugoslav industry is not responsive to demand even with respect to the production of such simple goods as textiles (Ep 26.4.76). It was said of one republic (Ep 11.3.74) that, applying stricter criteria, 60 per cent of its output was rejects.

Under the conditions described it is idle to expect simple release of the monetary brake to put the economy on the way to finding its own balance and growth rate, although Horvat's views were supported by the OECD Survey of Yugoslavia in 1965, the authors of which thought that the Yugoslav problems of structural reorganisation and redistribution would be much more easily solved with rapid growth (p. 31). The OECD experts may not have been aware of the full extent of distortions in the Yugoslav economy and applied Western yardsticks to a situation where they did not fit at all at a time when their validity was beginning to be questioned even in the West.

Demand management or even the 'dashes for growth' in the usual sense had very limited scope in Yugoslavia. Low utilisation of capacity was due much less to insufficient effective demand than to the inconsistencies of the production structure—which as a whole was not matched to demand and within which various parts were not matched to each other. A rise in the activity level through demand stimulation presupposes that supply and demand are in line. What is more: when credit was relaxed, new investment, as will be shown in the next section, was no better selected than in the past, so that a 'dash' ended only in more unusable stocks and underutilised capacity. The real problem in Yugoslavia is the unresponsiveness of the economy to economic signals.

On the other hand, monetary stringency was expected to achieve far more in Yugoslavia than it usually does. It was meant to put pressure on both enterprises and political authorities, so that enterprises not producing what was in demand would go out of business and political authorities would be frightened off thoughtless investment. However, in Yugoslavia, the number and size of unprofitable enterprises was such that, when it came to the crunch, the government always retreated and began intervening in the economy again.

Branko Horvat defended this reluctance to streamline the structure (22 p. 424) by saying that large enterprises were not allowed to go out of business anywhere. The difference is, of course, that unprofitable enterprises in Yugoslavia were ill-conceived from the beginning, were a consequence—as Horvat put it—of arbitrary measures 15 years ago, for which the country had to pay now, while Western enterprises mostly become unprofitable when the economic structure—world structure at that—changes. Neither is it true that sizable enterprises do not go out of business ever: the British cotton industry reduced its production from 7.4 billion metres in 1913 to 0.7 billion in 1968, the US cotton industry from 9.4 billion in 1956 to 5.6 billion metres in 1971 so as to adjust to world economic conditions.

Finally, it has to be pointed out that the Yugoslav government, in its attempts at steering the economy, had to rely entirely on monetary policy and could not use fiscal policy. First of all, the number of budgets was such that it would have been very difficult to coordinate them and run a meaningful budget deficit: there were federal, republic and commune budgets, separate investment funds and funds for education, health service, housing etc. Further, the government could not use budgetary policy because there was no adequate money and capital market (77 p. 44 ff). For this reason, it was even impossible to issue new money via the budget, let alone borrow from the market, because the money did not easily percolate through the economy. Direct lending by the National Bank to republic and commune commercial banks was considered to be the best method. The provisions on how to allocate new monetary issue were contained in the yearly plans but it was difficult to remain within their framework.

7.2 CREDITS ABUSED FOR INVESTMENT

As soon as monetary stringency was relaxed,the previous expansion resumed. Under Yugoslav conditions this meant primarily investment in fixed assets. For reasons which are not entirely clear, but which can only be described as political, such investment was considered to be the foremost task of all those who were entitled to invest and could obtain the necessary financial resources. This meant primarily political authorities (see p. 46) especially communes which were also trying to reduce unemployment on their territory. What is more, investment was often embarked on when there was no financial cover available.

Many investors were political bodies and their logic was that of politicians who have thought and still think that development is identical to investment in anything whatsoever (Pilipovic, Ep 28.3.64, JP 70, p. 1). 'Extra-economic' thinking prevailed (33, p. 670; 26, p. 273) and 'political' factories were erected (B 8.10.66). But even enterprises were exposed to non-economic arguments and pressures from outside, so that they mostly invested in fixed assets although they had insufficient working capital, increasing which could have raised the utilisation of capacity and thus of efficiency (77, p. 75). Any financial resources of their own which enterprises had were sunk in fixed assets, where they were followed by funds earmarked for working capital, as a consequence of which short-term credits had to be turned into long-term (77, p. 73) and were possibly never repaid.

There was no guidance mechanism for investment by the many investors at different levels (33, p. 686, Minic, B 24.7.62); controlled prices almost encouraged wrong decisions (33, p. 693) and led to further distortions (33, p. 684).

In 1964, when both economic and non-economic investment was again entirely out of hand (Ep 19.9.64), the government tried to bring it back into line by stopping work on 165 investment projects worth dinars 44 billion and by prosecuting enterprises which started investment without first securing the financial cover (Ep 14.11.64). But this procedure could not be entirely welcome because it implied a more or less linear curtailment while what was needed was to allow well-chosen investment to continue and to stop bad investment (Ep 9.5.64).

Such a selective procedure was, however, very difficult to institute. Investors themselves, acting mostly for political reasons, were not sufficiently interested in economic consequences. The new enterprises would in most cases not be run by investors themselves anyway, but would be handed over to workers and managers who would, henceforward, be responsible for them. As mentioned, even enterprises themselves were exposed to pressures which often led them into duplication of industrial capacities, simply in order to invest (77, p. 73, Ep 30.5.64). There were no real businessmen who would search for the best investment opportunities, while politicians and bureaucrats were pressed for time and satisfied as soon as they could say they had tried to do something.

Banks were not much help either. They were alleged to be staffed mainly by former planning bureaucrats. They acted in a formal way and did not check whether projects were excessively ambitious, whether the designers and administrators had the required organisational, technical and business experience (Ep 1.2, 21.11.64 and 3.11.68, B 17.12.67) which was in very short supply (OECD 65, p. 19). The prosperity of banks and of their employees did not depend sufficiently on their own economic success (77, p. 46) so that they were always prepared to lend regardless of security. The customers were ready to borrow to the hilt because the interest rate of 6 per cent was meaningless under Yugoslav conditions. Besides the government credit regulations kept changing (77, pp. 43, 66) but to no avail as they never produced clearcut conditions for granting short-term credits, nor succeeded in enforcing them. The role of banks became particularly important in 1964 when the institution of separate investment funds was abolished and their resources were handed over to the banks (see p. 148).

Lax credit policy fostered indiscriminate investment, and indiscriminate investment fostered growth, but growth that ended in unprofitable investment, excessive inventories, insolvency etc. Simultaneously, good projects often had difficulty in securing the necessary finance, which was mainly lavished on inefficient producers (33, p. 693).

Tito himself highlighted the problem of investment on 30 June 1963 when he opened a new session of the Federal Assembly. He pointed out that quite a few of the most modern enterprises were using hardly 50 per cent of their capacity and working only one shift while there was an excess of labour. He concluded: 'In other words, a large part of our investment not only remains sterile but is actually wasted.' (JP 63, p. 287).

Others called newly erected plants a monument to the destruction of a part of national output (Ep 9.5.64). It may make sense to run the risk of inflation if it helps to establish productive capacity which turns out usable goods, but it certainly does not if the main results are underutilised capacity and unusable inventories (Ep 19.9.64). Inflationary monetary issue can replace taxation or high profits as sources of investment and thus raise the rate of saving possibly without the population noticing it, but it is no use if the ensuing investment activity is as wasteful as it is in Yugoslavia. All along, investment had been the main contributory factor to economic growth, but also the reason for disproportions: *insufficient* production of raw materials, *inadequate* production of equipment and *insufficient* production for export (26, p. 185 ff; 33, p. 665 ff).

In spite of reforms and changing conditions, the boom in bad investment continued. Neither various Acts on the control of investment nor public rebukes for investors served any purpose. In 1971, for instance, the trade unions demanded that investment policy should be changed so that the construction of plants which then functioned badly or were insufficiently utilised would not continue (B 22.7.71). There were complaints that because it was never made clear who was responsible for bad investment, people thought all investment wrong or, at least, politically unwise (D 21.11.70). In 1975, the head of the federal Social Accountancy Service said in an interview that there was again a tremendous surge in investment without finance but that his Service could not do much about it because it was not supported by other organs, particularly political authorities, which were themselves the main culprits. More than that, the Accountancy head complained that some people tried to interfere with his Service and prevent it from taking any action against those who contravened investment regulations. The distinction between 'priority' (planned) and ordinary investment attracts the existing finance to non-priority investment because everybody expects that priority investment will somehow be financed in the end. Even the old difficulty of insufficient working capital persists. Some enterprises invest so much in fixed capital that they do not have enough working capital to maintain current production (D 19.4.75). A year later, the same head of the Accountancy Service was saying exactly the same in an interview with *Politika* (D 9.4.76).

In 1976/77 investment has again become the prominent activity supported by monetary and credit policy (Ep 21.11.77), so that critics are again saying that investment has become an end in itself rather than a means to advance the economy (Ep 23.8.76).

Not everybody was worried about the investment chaos: in 1975, a professor of economics at Ljubljana University reacted to strictures on 'uncovered' investment by denying that investment was at the expense of consumption. This prompted *Ekonomska politika* of 19.5.75 to quote from the analysis of the Economic Institute at the Ljubljana Faculty of Law which showed that investment was indeed not financed by reduced consumption but out of the foreign deficit which had been equal to 46 per cent of investment in 1973, and to 61 per cent in 1975, so that only 12 per cent of the GSP was actually used for investment and the rest was financed out of the foreign debt.

Yugoslav commentators complained that there was no systematic measurement of investment efficiency, except for some global capital–output coefficients. According to figures published by Dragomir Vojnic (116, p. 65) the incremental capital–output ratio was 2.2 in 1957–60, 5.1 in 1961–2 and 2.2 in 1963–5, the average ratio for this period being 3.5 (but see p. 239). One possible measure of inefficiency was the share of investment costs in industrial GSP, which amounted to 34.6 per cent, and in industrial value added, which amounted to 27.1 per cent (Ep 21.11.64). At the beginning of the 1970s, a conference organised by trade unions established that the Yugoslav product per worker was five to six times lower than in industrialised countries in the engineering industry, three times in the car industry and twice in the chemical industry. Yugoslavia needed twice the investment of Romania or Spain to raise the GSP by 1 per cent (B 14.6.71).

By the 1960s some Yugoslav economists and politicians were suspicious of excessively fast growth. They realised that the previous high investment/high growth strategy had led straight to disproportions. Milos Minic (B 24.7.62) said in 1962 that everybody knew where excessive plans led and that it was better to do less, but do it properly. Speeding up growth always succeeded in temporarily improving the efficiency of investment because of higher utilisation of capacity but then pushed the economy into more disproportions (33, p. 672). In 1966, the trade unions were in favour of plans which did not lay down growth rates but created conditions for producers to achieve increases in production in accordance with their abilities (B 12.10.66). *Ekonomska politika* of 25.8.1975 warned that years which appeared very successful when judged by growth rates, could appear far less successful from the point of view of working people.

In spite of this general sobering up, some commentators never tired of wanting higher and higher growth. Horvat for instance propounded the view that a growth rate of less than 10 per cent per annum meant failure and required an investigation (51, p. 32). In his view, there was nothing wrong with investment in fixed and working capital exceeding 40 per cent of the GSP, although this 40 per cent presumably included 10 per cent inventory waste and fostered further distortions. The surprising aspect of Horvat's growth enthusiasm was that he had probably developed the taste for it during his studies in the West where his prompting for ever higher rates was much admired (*Economic Journal*, December 58; 50, p. 224). Growth enthusiasts (under the influence of alleged high growth rates in communist countries) were also at work in the OECD when it chided Yugoslavia for slowing down (OECD 65, p. 40) in order to get distortions under control.

Nor could some politicians dispense with high growth rates (Grlickov, B 23.6.70), and a meeting of Yugoslav communists came to the conclusion that growth rates must be high because socialism was supposed to speed up history (D 1.3.75). Some people were even of the opinion that the external payments deficit should be simply neglected (NR 21.2.75). The Yugoslav communists had to defend themselves against the accusation that Yugoslav growth rates were lower than those of the East European socialist countries (Bajt, D 2.11.74; Samardzija, P 7.1.77). Such pressures led to the adoption of a growth rate of 'about 7 per cent' in the 1976–80 plan (JP 76, p. 268) despite warnings (Planinc, Ep 28.7.75).

7.3 EFFECTS ON ENTERPRISES

Yugoslav investment policy again and again ran into two difficulties: lack of identifiable responsibility for economic actions and, connected with this, inadequate handling of decisions under future uncertainty. As long as one person, or one small group, decides on an investment and another has to run the plant when completed, nobody can bear the responsibility for the whole operation because responsibility cannot be split. Private ownership of capital bridges this gap because the capitalist is in the end made responsible for all operations through the varying value of his capital which depends on the overall success of the enterprise. This method also makes it possible to apportion responsibility when capital passes from one hand to another because the new owner will not pay historical costs but a price on the basis of actual performance and future prospects.

The future is not known either to individuals or organisations, including governments and planning commissions. Hence, investment decisions cannot be taken on the basis of present prices (they are only the starting point) but must be based on foreseeing future developments, including trends in prices (26, p. 226). Therefore, the best performance can be achieved if individuals make informed guesses about the future and back them, if they are enterprising, with their capital. If they are wrong, they lose all or part of their possessions.

The haphazard Yugoslav investment was bound to be reflected in the financial position of enterprises on which the functioning of the system was in principle based (M. Popovic, Ep 17.10.64). If investment is misguided, enterprises by necessity end up having losses, although these losses can be made better or worse by efficient or inefficient current management.

Inflation, of course, to a considerable extent covers up losses and exaggerates profits through nominal gains because of capital appreciation and debt depreciation. But that, nonetheless, means real capital erosion because insufficient purchasing power is left to replace stocks and fixed capital.

In Yugoslavia, in the 1960s, prices were hardly the main symptom of inflation because they were widely kept in check by price controls (see p. 22). In particular in 1964, there was high overall demand coinciding with accumulation of inventories which points to the ultimate source of losses, the production of goods nobody wants at any price because they are in excess supply or are simply unusable. In such cases, losses are equal to the full costs of production.

Regardless of whether there was demand for their products or not, Yugoslav enterprises continued to function (52, p. 143). They would not dismiss workers, but carried on production and accumulated inventories when goods were not sold and the inventories were financed out of additional credits which were lent to cover losses (77, p. 73) despite the continuous stress laid on the requirement that bank credits should finance only the production and storing of those commodities which have found a buyer (77, pp. 6 and 21). Not only did the enterprises under self-management not dismiss workers if the demand for their output fell, they on the whole kept many more workers than needed. In 1964, the number of workers 'employed without justification' was estimated at between 250,000 and 420,000 (Ep 28.8.64).

According to the Yugoslav system, losses should have been largely borne by the enterprises' staff, but the workers were not prepared to accept the responsibility for losses due *inter alia* to distorted investment which could under no circumstances be blamed on workers employed at a particular time in an enterprise. The original decision to establish the enterprise had been in most instances taken by the political authority and the workers could hardly have been expected to be willing to bear its consequences. But even if the decision was taken by the employees themselves at some stage, the consequences appeared at a later stage when the composition of the staff might have changed entirely in view of the high turnover (see p. 73).

In practice workers refused the responsibility by paying themselves personal incomes regardless of the success of their enterprises. In 1964 the Social Accountancy Service (Ep. 5.6.65) reported that all producers, including bad producers, were paying themselves high personal incomes in excess of supplies of goods. In enterprises working at a loss, the increase in nominal personal incomes was 33 per cent, only 13 per cent lower than the average. The demand for parity of wages for people doing comparable work was very much stronger than any feeling that workers should be held responsible for the failure of their enterprises. Foreign observers sometimes believe (114, p. 175) that self-management precluded cost-push inflation; in Yugoslavia it certainly does not.

What is more, since legal provisions were changing continuously and the government was tampering with prices, enterprises run at a loss could claim that their losses were due to particular government provisions and demand that they be changed (Ep 31.10.64; 26, pp. 237, 256, 281). In some cases, they were right: the prices of 65 per cent of textile production were controlled or frozen at the 1957 level while the prices of textile inputs had risen by 20 to 50 per cent between then and 1964 when the textile industry was not surprisingly among those industries which had incurred heavy losses (Ep 9.5.64).

Thus, losses primarily indicated that the payment of personal incomes was entirely out of step with the actual revenue of enterprises. The Social Accountancy Service (Ep 5.6.65) claimed that 92 per cent of losses originated in this way. But since there was the tendency to comparability of wages between enterprises, personal incomes both eroded profits and concealed losses caused in other ways (see p. 159). Any economic accountancy was difficult because wages were not established independently.

The refusal of workers to accept responsibility was justifiably considered a reason for concern, so that the leaders started looking for an appropriate solution. One of the suggestions was that lack of responsibility was due to very low wages and consumption. At the 8th Congress of the League of Communists at the end of 1964, both Tito and Kraigher stressed that personal incomes and consumption per head in Yugoslavia were too low for the level of development achieved and also as an incentive for further efforts. Tito said: 'Our working people are right when they criticise us for not paying sufficient attention to the standard of living of the working man.'

Kraigher in turn thought that an improvement in the standard of living had become a decisive factor for overall economic development. The share of consumption in 1964 was in fact only 45 per cent of the GDP (OECD 67). Just as under the best capitalists, workers should be paid well and required to work hard (Ep 18.5.63).

But higher incomes were also necessary so that they could fluctuate with the success of the enterprise, which would prevent workers' interests being limited to their wages and would 'develop their production psychology and link their interests more directly to the success of the enterprise, which requires that independence be counterbalanced by responsibility and success by risk' (26, pp. 253–5). The enterprise's efficiency must be made identical with social efficiency (26, p. 237). 'Invisible hand' thinking was very much in evidence here.

To achieve such identity of interests enterprises must further be exposed to the full rigour of the market (Tripalo, Ep 1.2.64) and there must be 'negative incentives', i.e. unsuccessful enterprises must be allowed to go to the wall (26, p. 238). The Yugoslav communists should not allow their economic system to be burdened with considerations of social justice (26, p. 252), but in so far as helping individual enterprises for social and political reasons cannot be avoided, it should be made clear why it is done and grants should be spelled out in full detail (26, p. 238). Furthermore enterprises should be given a firmer material basis, which meant more resources should have remained in their hands (Tripalo, Ep 1.2.67).

The remedies suggested were valid as far as they went, but they did not touch the core problem of establishing a relationship between workers as entrepreneurs and investment and current management.

7.4 THE ROLE OF PUBLIC FINANCE

The strengthening of the 'material basis' of enterprises primarily meant reducing the part of revenue that was taken from them in various forms of taxes. Kraigher said at the 8th Congress that, in particular, it did not make sense to extract considerable resources from the economy only to return them more often than not 'via those branches that lagged behind in productivity and rational management' (cf. 66, p. 235). The reason for this fiscal flow of funds from and back into enterprises was the same as in many Western countries. Taxation both prevents high distribution of profits and leaves insufficient retained funds for investment so that the latter has to be financed from the proceeds of taxation. In Yugoslavia this procedure was intended to concentrate investment funds in the hands of the authorities and enable them to influence a large proportion of investment through conditional participation in projects (see p. 26; 26, p. 294), a power which was frequently used unwisely.

This criticism was met by the abolition of the contribution to social investment funds in 1964 and, later, the complete elimination of the contribution out of enterprises' income. The tendency was to shift taxation from enterprises' revenue to personal incomes (JP 65, p. 261). The pre-1965 reform abolition of the contribution to investment funds raised enterprises' share in value added from 43 per cent in 1963 to 50 per cent in 1964 (JP 65, p. 261). This was considered desirable, although there were fears that workers would not use resources left to enterprises for investment but distribute them among themselves. A suggestion was put forward that 'a minimum internal rate of accumulation be introduced' (26, pp. 243–4).

The taxes and subsidies system also served to circulate capital in a situation where enterprises were not allowed to deposit excess funds in the banks on a commercial basis, a new solution still under consideration in 1963 (26, pp. 239, 242, Ep 23.5, 22.8.64).

The second criticism of public finance was simply that political authorities used too large a part of the GSP and that public consumption should have been slowed down as demanded in the Resolution on preparation of the seven-year plan (JP 65, p. 419). Local authorities, the 'communes' were extracting money from enterprises in illicit ways by pressures which the latter could not resist (Ep 1.5.65). One example of this extraction by subterfuge was the so-called 'time-deposits' which were introduced so that enterprises could keep their 'free' money in banks, so as to increase the mobility of capital. Local authorities immediately put pressure on enterprises to time-deposit any money that came their way so that they themselves could then borrow more money long-term while enterprises would ask banks for more short-term credits. *Ekonomska politika* (Ep 5.9.64) reported that a group of enterprises had put dinars 82 billion on time-deposits in the five months ending May 1964, while they had dinars 225 billion long-term debts and dinars 318 billion outstanding debt to suppliers. The monetary authorities had to step in and limit long-term credits given from time-deposits, restrict bank credits and immobilise about 10 per cent of local authorities' budgetary receipts (Ep 14.11.64).

All told, collective consumption (divided into common (*zajednicka*) when merit goods are in question and general (*opsta*) for pure public goods) was rather higher in Yugoslavia than in the neighbouring countries in the 1960s. Taking the Marxist definition, in 1962 common and general consumption amounted to 9.4 per cent of GSP. The Marxist exclusion of non-productive services makes the greatest difference here: using the standard figures, calculated by the OECD, the share of collective consumption in the Yugoslav GDP in 1962 was 19.2 per cent as compared with 10.1 per cent for Austria, 12.5 per cent for Italy and 11.0 per cent for Greece. The government has been trying hard to reduce collective consumption since then. In Marxist terms, it brought it down to 8.5 per cent of GSP in 1974 (SG 76, p. 136).

But if one takes standard definitions and includes government investment, over 40 per cent of national income still passes through the government's hands in the form of taxes and contributions (JP 77, p. 128).

It was not just that public expenditure was excessive, it was often used for 'administrative and luxury buildings' (33, p. 687) while the water supply, sewage system, etc., were inadequate (Ep 12.6.65). A considerable part of public expenditure was necessary because the population was given social security rights which were out of all proportion to level of development achieved. Kiro Gligorov thought that the burden of 'non-productive' expenditure was such that it affected economic performance (B 11.6.65). In 1975, an Act on the Limitation of Excessive Growth of 'Non-Economic' Investment was still required (Ep 19.5.75).

7.5 PLANNING OR MARKET SOLUTIONS

In the mid-sixties the Yugoslav economy faced the problems of disharmony between supply and demand and of incompetent investment. The question was whether planning or the market should be used to correct these distortions.

Among public discussions of this subject one of the most prominent gatherings was a meeting in Zagreb of the Research Section of the Yugoslav Economic Association in January 1963. Two groups of leading economists produced reports known as the 'Yellow book' (33) and the 'White book' (26). Fundamentally, the deliberations elaborated on the stand taken by the Yugoslav League of Communists at its Seventh Congress in 1958 when a new programme was adopted. Chapter Six of the programme dealt with the relationship between the plan and the market in the new Yugoslav conditions. On the one hand, it stressed that, unlike capitalism, Yugoslav socialism worked directly for people's needs rather than for profits and accumulation, on the other, that workers had been transformed from wage earners into managers who fulfilled their personal interests in independent enterprises—they worked for higher earnings, for a higher personal and social standard. This must have meant that workers, by trying to manage enterprises in a way which guarantees them higher incomes, produce for people's needs, but then it is difficult to see the difference between working for people's needs through achieving maximum incomes rather than maximum profits.

The programme also said that there was no possibility of determining for ever the quantitative relationship between planning from the centre and the activity of individual enterprises and their workers. No plan could exhaust all the possibilities and initiatives stemming from spontaneous development. The financial and monetary system were part of planning and thus helped to combine socially planned guidance with the socialist free initiative of producers. As long as commodity production, that is production for the market, was an objective necessity, any disregard for the law of value weakened the socialist elements in the economy.

The Yellow book did not pay much attention to planning, while the White book devoted one chapter out of five to planning and another to the market. Plans were needed, in the authors' view, in a decentralised socialist economy, although they must not be centralist and directive because such plans had bad social and economic consequences. While the market should be left to determine the quantity produced (verification of the social character of work) and also to provide the objective measures of profitability and economic rationality, neither the market nor economic instruments can be relied on to ensure the long-term optimal distribution of resources and optimal development. The most important plans were those encompassing 10 to 15 years and dealing with investment. Short-term decisions and long-term decisions were not the same, so that micro-economic decisions could be rational only if decision-makers had a long time horizon.

Global decentralised planning should contain only very few indicators: through the provisions on distribution of national income it could determine the framework and structure of demand, and through the decisions on the global structure of investment the general framework and structure of the production apparatus. But there must not be any hierarchy of plans — 'higher' plans should only indirectly influence 'lower' plans; such polycentric planning should be based on agreements among equal partners.

Within the planned proportions, the market should be allowed to work, but it would of course be not a spontaneous, uncontrolled market, but one in which the basic proportions of production, distribution and exchange were the result of conscious action by society.

All these words were the orthodox things to say in Yugoslavia, but they were mere words. Summarising the Yellow and White books, *Ekonomska politika* (Ep 19.1.63) wrote: 'There has not been (in the past period) any clear conception of the methodology of planning. This was shown in the arbitrary determination of basic proportions, indeed in the disharmony between the plan and the economic system.' A Federal Assembly Resolution of 24 Nov. 1963 said similar things and emphasised that planning was insufficiently influenced by working organisations and social-political organisations, but remained in the hands of the Federation.

These two strictures, at least in form, referred to the past but no change had occurred to make them invalid in 1963 or later. In spite of the call for scientific research into all relevant developmental factors and for knowledge of the laws of the socialist economy, there was no way of knowing the future and thus providing a basis for planning; the future remains uncertain for both individuals and planning groups so that it involves risk, which means that there must be economic responsibility.

Nor was there any solution to the problem of the relationship between working organisations and planning organs. Either working organisations were independent and could be held responsible for what they did or they had to act according to orders and could not. In so far as they were independent, there should have been some kind of mechanism to make them do what was in the general interest; if they had to obey orders, they should have been made to conform with them (provided, of course, that the orders were rational). Possibly there should have been a large measure of independence and limited subordination. In so far as they were independent they had to conduct their own business which, as mentioned (see p. 20) was sometimes also called planning. Todorovic even coined the term 'self-planning' (108, p. 232).

The authorities went for a mixture of much independence and little subordination because they distrusted central decision-making. Federal Assembly Resolutions (*JP* 64, pp. 164–7 and 419) and the Resolution of the 8th Congress of the League of Communists (*JP* 64, p. 451), all came out in favour of more or less free markets. They also demanded that 'irrational investment' should be brought under control, primarily by depriving administrative and political organs of their influence on investment, which was to pass under the jurisdiction of working organisations. Investment funds were to be abolished and transferred to banks for allocation and foreign trade also taken out of the hands of political bodies. Coordination should be achieved through a faster elimination of administered prices.

The leaning of most Yugoslav communists towards the market was clear, but this inclination was constantly disturbed by their Marxist doctrines. Nobody quite knew how to plan, especially not without using long-term market demand as a gauge, but markets were nevertheless continuously described as bad if they were 'spontaneous' instead of 'conscious', as plans were supposed to be. This dilemma was well expressed in the White book which said of markets (economic laws) as a check on plans:

> This does not mean that the plan (economic policy) adapts to spontaneity, but it does include the recognition of spontaneity (but not anarchy) as an essential element of economic development also in socialism. Only in this way can the economic policy of society make 'use' of economic laws. (26, p. 207)

When using the market, the Yugoslav communists were not primarily worried about allocational and technical efficiency, but about distribution, which led to discussions on business conditions and distribution according to work. Equalisation of business conditions should have apportioned to enterprises the revenue they deserved, which was the precondition for the fulfilment of this principle of just distribution.

What exactly equalisation of business conditions was supposed to mean is difficult to establish. In practice enterprises seem to have considered business conditions 'not equal' as soon as they were in any kind of trouble. They would then demand that the government should intervene. This tendency could be described as a desire for 'equalisation of (economic) results' come what may and was rejected as 'conducive to low efficiency' (26 pp. 239, 281).

Theoretically, equalisation of business conditions may have been concerned with two aspects: with the elimination of the influence of different quantities of factors (i.e. nature and capital) cooperating with labour, or with the elimination of oscillation around the equilibrium price, i.e. profits from better selection of products or better choice of technology. The first kind of equalisation was legitimate and took the form of interest payments on capital used. Attempts at eliminating the natural rent of land or mining were less successful because it was well nigh impossible to calculate.

Any elimination of the second variety of 'inequality' was doomed to failure because it would eliminate the most important function of the market — to give an advantage to those who produce what people want in the cheapest way, which should also serve as an incentive to others. On the whole, the need for such incentives seems to have been well understood although sometimes explained in a contorted Marxist way as for instance by Mijalko Todorovic in his *Liberation of Labour* (108, cf. also 121, p. 367 and passim).

It was a different thing to maintain that any kind of business conditions led to distribution according to work. At best it was distribution according to the evaluation of goods and through them work by other people demanding them in the market, but perhaps even that only when the market was in equilibrium which, of course, it never is in reality. If one chooses to call this remuneration according to work, there can be no objection to the terminology although it does not change the real relationships at all. The popular understanding is that distribution according to work is different from market distribution, probably according to some kind of physical measurement, but no objective measurement of the 'quantum of labour' exists (Vukmanovic, B 5.8.60) so that distribution according to work does not mean anything either in theory or in practice. Labour is, therefore, paid either according to the population's evaluation of goods and through them work that has produced them because demand for goods leads to 'derived' demand for labour and other factors of production, or in an entirely arbitrary way which starts endless disputes about what is just and also prevents supply from adjusting to demand.

Indeed the problem is even more complicated if we are dealing with a self-managed firm, because then the market determines only the total revenue of the firm, but does not distribute the revenue among the workers because they do not get wages, i.e. remuneration established at least *grosso modo* in outside labour markets. The distribution will have to be according to some kind of makeshift system of points (108, p. 207) which may also be called distribution according to work except that then the expression does not mean much either. Feeling that such mechanistic distribution was not very satisfactory, the Yugoslav communists soon began thinking in terms of subdividing enterprises into smaller units (called 'economic working units') which would sell products to each other, so that market prices would replace arbitrary internal distribution down to the smallest unit. This approach was called 'direct self-management' and was advocated at the Fourth Plenary Session of the Central Committee in July 1962 (121, p. 384 ff.) but was not adopted till much later. The main objection was that 'working units' would cause enterprises to disintegrate and would dissipate accumulation.

In the West, the Yugoslav or Illyrian firm and its peculiarities were discussed in the usual economic concepts and terminology, but trying to take account of the fact that worker-managers will be interested not in overall profit but profit per worker, or — which is really the same — in income per worker (122, 36, 114). The conclusion was that in the short run a worker-managed enterprise will tend to produce at a lower level than under capitalism because it will only increase output as long as the additional output per worker is larger than average earnings per worker, rather than the marginal labour product.

Yugoslav commentators never thought this a particularly important consideration and assumed that Yugoslav enterprises simply tried to maximise profits (53 p. 105). One reason was that Yugoslav workers were, on the whole, loath to dismiss their mates — a move which maximising income per head would necessitate — even when dismissal was required in the general interest. The feeling of solidarity survived. The political leaders had to prompt worker-managers to dismiss surplus labour (see pp. 42 and 93). In his discussion of Jaroslav Vanek's book, James Meade (75) clearly perceived the possibility that such dismissal would not be legally permitted, but it is just one step from such an extreme rule to the moral code of solidarity among workers. Meade also mentions 'institutional problems' and Dinko Dubravcic (37) emphasises that 'social characteristics' of the suppliers of labour can be expected to overshadow the technical conclusions derived from the pure model based on labour as an entrepreneurial input.

Neither is it certain that the workers in a large firm could easily perceive the opportunity of greater profit shares if their numbers were reduced. This perception requires acquaintance not only with accountancy, but with the current situation as it emerges from on-going operations. That may not be very easy for laymen and even managers and accountants who in addition may have different interests and views.

Finally, it is not clear what the short-run, which is an expository concept, means in practice where there is hardly any situation where capital is fixed and labour changeable. In the long-run, on the other hand, there is no difference between maximising profits and maximising income per worker — profits disappear and the highest incomes for workers are equal to their marginal productivity. Of course, profits do not disappear in practice because full equilibrium is never reached, but it should be difficult to link them in a clear way to the number of workers. For a self-managed firm there is the additional difficulty that the workers who take the decisions — if it is in fact the collective that does it — may no longer be there when the results come to fruition, so that this may influence their attitudes (see p. 73; 44, p. 104).

Maybe it is possible to say that, on the whole, the Yugoslav firm will simply try to make revenue larger than costs because it is far too complicated to do anything else and the actual decisions are not taken by the body of the workers. The real danger is not that the firm will restrict output if it can sell it, but that it will try to enhance workers' incomes through amassing capital in the firm, if there is no payment for capital or if the payment is too small. That, however, will be discussed later.

In the early 1960s, this danger was not visible yet. The communist leaders and commentators were far more worried about the distorted production structure and all the bad effects it had on the economy. That was the problem they wanted to tackle in the forthcoming reform which, they hoped, would end all reforms.

8: The Decisive Reform

8.1 PRELIMINARY CHANGE IN THE CONSTITUTION

During the debates on how to get the economy and especially investment under control, a new constitution was adopted on 7 April 1963. It proclaimed general self-management, i.e. the widening of self-management from economic working units to all working units, including such institutions as schools and hospitals, and to political units, particularly communes. Accordingly it was deemed to be more than a political constitution, namely a charter of self-management, in which 'state functions were performed less and less by a separate organisation above society but were merging with the needs of working people in their work and life'. Political power was based on 'the working class and the entire working people'. Labour had been liberated — the main principle being 'from everybody according to his capabilities — to everybody according to his work' — and the final goal was a society in which the principle would be 'from everybody according to his capabilities — to everybody according to his needs' (Art VIII). The Socialist Alliance of the Working People of Yugoslavia (Art. V) and the League of Communists of Yugoslavia (Art. VI) were expressly mentioned in the Constitution, the former as the place for political activity of all comers, the latter as the 'principal initiator of political activity'.

The Federal People's Republic of Yugoslavia was renamed The Socialist Federal Republic of Yugoslavia and the order of enumeration of its constituent republics was changed from Serbia, Croatia, Slovenia, Macedonia, Montenegro and Bosnia-Herzegovina to Bosnia-Herzegovina, Montenegro, Croatia, Macedonia, Slovenia, Serbia, i.e. in Yugoslav, or rather Croat and Slovene, alphabetical order. It was stressed that the people of Yugoslavia implemented their sovereign rights within their socialist republic, while the Federation had only that jurisdiction which the Constitution expressly entrusted to it. But the territory of Yugoslavia remained a 'unified economic and customs area' (Art. 28).

The composition of the Federal Assembly was changed. While it previously consisted of a Federal Council and a Council of Producers, it was now turned into a body consisting of a Federal Council and four Councils of working communities (Economic, Cultural, Social-Health and Organisational-Political). All legislation had to pass through the Federal Council and one of the other four.

The Constitution took over the existing economic arrangements in the main. It stated that management of production and other social activities must not be allowed to distort social relations through 'either bureaucratic arbitrariness and privileges supported by monopolistic positions or private-ownership selfishness and particularism' (Art II). Innovations included the constitutional guarantee of a 42-hour maximum working week (Art. 37) and the provision that working organisations were to adopt a 'statute' (Art. 91) which determined the detailed organisation of the enterprise. This statute had to be discussed by the commune assembly as well as the enterprise itself (D 7 and 8.12.62).

The introduction of a 42-hour week seemed particularly irrelevant. It was a follow-up to the promise of shorter working hours given by Tito at the Congress of the Communist Party in 1948 when he still believed, with Engels, that the abolition of the capitalist mode of production 'would be sufficient to reduce working hours to a very low level' (41, p. 281). Since the end of the capitalism did not bring about any upsurge in productivity, the reduction of working hours was not easy for enterprises, especially as it was coupled with the provision in the Act on Labour Relations of 1965, that it must not lead to a drop in workers' incomes. It was pointed out (Ep 8.6.63, B 18.12.66) that shorter hours do not depend on anybody's good will, otherwise they could be introduced overnight, but on an economy's or an enterprise's efficiency. When productivity is still very low, it may be more desirable to raise production than to give workers more leisure. It may have been hoped that a shorter working week would alleviate unemployment but nothing of the sort happened. The clue to higher productivity and thus shorter working hours, if desired, was a better choice of investment, but in this area the Yugoslav system failed completely.

8.2 REFORM 1965

The responsible economic leaders were clear that the future courses of the Yugoslav economy and the living standard of the population depended on the elimination of disproportions and on better responsiveness to demand, which they thought could be achieved only by 'the full affirmation of the economic factor' as Kiro Gligorov, then Secretary of Finance, put it in 1965 (Ep 19.6.65). This affirmation required both that enterprises react predominantly to domestic supply and demand conditions and that a link exist with the rest of the world to provide a check on domestic prices which had been distorted by price control and the original tendency towards autarchy. The pressure of the market should bear heavily on each individual enterprise and even on each individual worker, which was to be achieved by a reform of the taxation and banking systems.

Kiro Gligorov (B 11.6.65 and RIA 20.6.65) announced in a speech before the Federal Assembly that the 1965 reform would try to achieve the following aims:

1) normal conditions for the development of the electricity industry, raw material production and services, the prices of which had been abnormally low;
2) a thorough modernisation of the engineering industry;
3) an end to inflation, thus establishing a uniform yardstick for determining the value of goods;
4) the introduction of a realistic exchange rate for the dinar;
5) reduction of investment to a realistic level, as well as a change in its structure;
6) reduction of government expenditure;
7) concentration of investment decisions in the hands of enterprises;
8) stabilisation of the market through the accumulation of materials and foreign exchange reserves and through imports.

The engineering industry had been the weak link in the Yugoslav economy since the war. Therefore, Kraigher (66 p. 63) was right when he suggested that no sector required a more urgent overhaul than the equipment industries because they would decisively influence the future efficiency of the economy, and — one could add — because they were the source of the greatest disproportions. By the time of the reform the only means of preventing them from making the situation worse was rigorously applying economic criteria to them rather than singling out the engineering industry as in particular need of modernisation.

In reality, these industries were in trouble because they were in a sense too 'modern' for Yugoslav conditions, i.e. excessively capital and know-how intensive. Further moves in the same direction could only make matters worse. Nevertheless the special treatment went so far that import duties on machinery and component parts remained high or were even raised, while other customs duties were cut. In spite of this, it was soon evident that the reform had adversely affected the engineering, electrical and ship-building industries (B 14.11.66). This was alarming because engineering alone employed 27 per cent of the Yugoslav labour force, and provided 35 per cent of exports. Government plans for this branch read more like a sermon than a realistic solution. The relevant report in *Borba* was headlined 'Engineering demands help and protection' and ended with the question whether the country needed such an industry at all. The government was trying to cut down exports of machinery and other products of the metal-working industry because they could be sold abroad only if subsidised. Refrigerators, for instance, were exported at the price of $48 (probably because of their bad quality) although the corresponding foreign price was $105 and they were sold at home for the equivalent of $112 (B 19.10.66).

Ten years after the reform, Yugoslav engineering was apparently the 14th largest engineering industry in the world (Ep 13.9.76) but was continuously demanding support through the allocation of special credits (Ep 22.8.77) and tariff protection (Ep 19.9.77). There were also complaints that domestic iron and steel were too expensive and made engineering uncompetitive. Ship-building was in an especially difficult situation, but this was partly due to the world crisis in the shipping and ship-building industries (Ep 9.5.77).

8.3 RE-ALIGNMENT OF PRICES

The re-alignment of prices started well before the reform, in July 1964, because the prices of raw materials (including agricultural products) and fuel were so out of line with, in particular, manufacturing industry prices that they caused shortages and waste of low-priced goods at the same time. About 60 per cent of industrial production was subject to price control while in agriculture there was a system of guaranteed minimum government purchase prices. The price of electricity was raised by different amounts for different consumers by government decree and so were the prices of lead (from dinars 165,000 to 200,000 per ton), tin (182,000 to 220,000) and copper (550,000 to 600,000). The guaranteed prices of wheat, sugar beat, oil seeds, milk and cattle were raised by 22 per cent on average and the price of coal was increased by on average 40 per cent through a reduction of 'refunds' and a straightforward rise (Ep 11, 18.7.64).

These alterations would have caused a considerable fall in the living standard, had the government not decided to 'recommend' (Kraigher, B 15.11.64) that personal incomes be raised so as to compensate the consumers for the rise in prices. Many enterprises were therefore caught between higher prices of inputs and higher personal incomes, so that they were tempted to push up their own prices, but this was frowned upon as a chain reaction and 'a tendency to further, often unjustified, increase in prices' (B 16.9.64). Enterprises were told to improve productivity.

According to Kraigher, one aim of the change was to foster agricultural, raw-material and fuel production, and the other that 'live labour should become a more expensive element of business which enterprises would consider seriously in their calculations, so that they would be guided towards high productivity operation'. But he admitted that there would have to be some redistribution of income between branches in spite of compensation.

Another bout of redistribution came at the beginning of 1965. Then the government decreed (Vukovic, B 10.1.65) that coal prices might be raised by another 23 per cent (ceiling price) and that miners' personal incomes might be improved by about 40 per cent to up to on average dinars 57,200 per month. This made them 35 per cent higher than the average industrial personal income. It was thought that the miners deserved this improvement because they worked between 53 and 55 hours a week but were only in 33rd place on the league table of Yugoslav workers' incomes. The second aim was to provide collieries with finance for expansion and modernisation. This time there was no compensating increase in other incomes so that the real income of an average four-member family was reduced by 0.4 per cent.

At the same time Federal Statistical Office data for February 1965 (Ep 27.3.65) showed that retail prices in general that month were up 10 per cent on the 1963 average and 16 per cent higher than in the same month in 1963 in spite of controls and price ceilings. The Federal Executive Council decided to freeze all prices as from 22 March 1965. Kriagher considered this the only way out (B 25.3.65) as the economy would not stabilise and respond to other measures. However, he stressed that this was an exceptional and temporary measure which did not signify a retreat from the Yugoslav price system in which the market and objective economic laws had the most important place. In his view the instability was due to investment, which in money terms rose by 19 per cent in the first two months of 1965, although it was planned to rise by only 1.5 per cent. *Ekonomska politika* (Ep 3.7.65) blamed the need for the measure on those who for fear of 'political repercussions' preferred attempts to redistribute income in favour of particular groups instead of basing the economy on rising productivity.

When the main reform eventually came in July 1965, the government aimed at achieving certain shifts in prices as indicated in Table 8.1 but the actual prices behaved differently.

Table 8.1: Reform of prices (1964 = 100)

Sector	*Actual prices 1965*		*Intended prices after reform*
	1st half	*2nd half*	
I Industrial products of which	108	125	117
capital goods	105	110	
interm. goods	107	127	
consumer goods		126	
iron and steel	99	138	125
non-ferr. metals	111	153	125
metal working	104	111	110
building mat.	112	137	120
textiles	113	126	114
II Agricultural products	128	152	132

Source: OECD 66

Jugoslovenski pregled (66, p. 5) published a table, reproduced here as Table 8.2, showing the changes in prices of various categories since 1952.

Table 8.2: Retail price indices 1962, 1964 and 1965 (1952 = 100)

			1965		
	1962	*1964*	*I-VII*	*VIII-XII*	*I-XII*
General index	142	161	184	242	209
manufactured goods	114	124	138	180	155
agricultural goods	206	271	342	455	393
services (incl. housing)	299	342	386	533	446

Source: JP 66, p. 5

If this table is combined with Table 2.1, we obtain the following indices for 1965 (1939 = 100): general prices 4482, manufactured goods 4045, agricultural goods 6811 and services 3235. In other words, by 1965 agricultural prices had far exceeded their pre-war parity and even their world market parity. However, in all probability the figures for 1952 in Table 2.1 are wrong because the authorities then were still trying to conceal the injustice inflicted on the peasants after the war. It is probably true that the relationship between industrial prices and agricultural prices in 1952 as compared with 1939 was nearer 24:10 than 20:14 as in Table 2.1. The relationship then may have been even worse, but if the revised figure is taken as the basis we obtain indices of industrial prices and agricultural prices of approximately 4320 and 4550 for the second half of 1965 (1939 = 100). This is more probable and also makes more sense because the purpose of the 1965 price changes was to re-establish the old parity. *Jugoslovenski pregled* (66, p. 5) said that after the price reform the prices of final industrial goods could be kept at the existing level only with tariff protection while the prices of agricultural goods were on a par with world prices.

On the other hand, it was true of course that the prices of agricultural goods were rising fast because of the inefficiency of socialised farms. Although these farms were paid higher prices for the same products — according to *Ekonomska politika* (Ep 15.5.65) the price for milk was dinars 85 litre for socialised producers and dinars 50 a litre for private producers — the socialised farms inexorably pulled up the whole set of agricultural prices because their costs of production were so high.

All in all, prices had risen so steeply by 1965 that a new 'heavy' dinar worth 100 previous dinars had to be introduced for practical reasons. A similar operation had taken place in 1945, so that the new conversion was due entirely to inflation under communist rule.

A logical consequence of the levelling up of prices was an alteration of the accounting exchange rate from old dinars 750 to old dinars 1250 per dollar and also the abolition of the premia which contributed in practice a system of multiple exchange rates. However, as a result of various subsidies, the real accounting rate was much higher than 750 dinars and may have been as high as dinars 2000 per dollar, so the new unified rate was an appreciation instead of a devaluation for many exporters (Ep 11.9.65).

The aim was to reduce disparities from 100:140 to 100:120 (66) with new customs tariff reducing the average value tariff from the previous 23.3 per cent to 11.8 per cent while the highest tariff for capital goods was reduced to about 23 per cent. Some people feared that this might be too ambitious (Ep 11.9.65) and that various subsidies would reappear as after other reforms. This tendency to give in to the pressure of the inefficient was called the 'monopoly of the backward'.

Kraigher (B 5.8.65) explained that the 1965 reform was more than a reform of foreign exchange, but that this was the basis of it, the hope being that opening up the economy to the world would also help to put the domestic house in order.

8.4 TAXATION AND STABILISATION

Linked to price re-alignment was a tax reform which abolished the contribution out of income of economic organisations, considerably reduced the contribution out of personal income from employment, reduced the rate of contribution for social insurance, and altered the turnover tax (JP 65, pp. 261, 299).

The turnover tax was unified and abolished for intermediate goods and capital goods. The general rate was fixed at 12 per cent with a few exceptions, while the payment was to be effected when the final product was sold to the consumer—it became a sales tax. 20 per cent of the revenue from the turnover tax was to be handed over by the Federation to republics and the republics and communes were entitled to introduce their own turnover taxes.

The rate of contribution out of personal income from employment was reduced from 17.5 per cent to 10.5 per cent and it was calculated that about 2 per cent of this 7 per cent reduction was offset by the rise in the turnover tax while government revenue was reduced by the equivalent of the other 5 per cent.

The purpose of this reform was to make the price relationships within enterprises and between enterprises more transparent. The turnover tax could now also be used as a policy instrument with clear effects when it was required to cut consumption or introduce other similar policies (cf. Ep 14.11.64). Further tax changes aimed at stabilisation in addition to shifting 'material funds' from political authorities to enterprises. The shift was supposed to give enterprises a greater say in investment and give more stress to personal incomes as a reward for efficiency. But as Boris Kraigher put it (66, p. 58), what was required for stabilisation was to 'bring all kinds of expenditure within realistic limits', which meant that investment and both private and public consumption should have been kept down to a level where no inflationary finance was necessary. It is not immediately clear why a shift of resources away from political authorities was expected to achieve that.

The only tax on enterprise production remained a charge on capital and this was consolidated at a unified rate of 4 per cent, while before it was 6 per cent but with many exceptions. It was also announced that after another revaluation of enterprises' capital the charge would be further reduced. The contribution of enterprises to social insurance was limited to 20.5 per cent of distributed personal incomes. These changes meant that the share of enterprises in the Gross Social Product was again increased (see p. 96) from 54.4 per cent in 1964 to 62 per cent in 1966 (value added to 56 per cent) while the share of political authorities was accordingly reduced.

Kraigher thought that in this way investment would be brought under control (presumably because enterprises would invest more responsibly) and he claimed that the investment rush had been subsiding in 1965 anyway. The Federal Assembly adopted a Resolution on the Distribution of Income and Personal Income in Working Organisations (Suppl. B 25.7.65) which suggested that the price reform had caused a rise in the cost of living of 22 per cent and admonished enterprises to keep within this limit when compensating workers; otherwise they were to adhere to their by-laws and give pay rises in line with increases in efficiency. The communes were invited to check that no unwarranted distribution occurred.

A second Recommendation (Suppl. B 25.7.65) by the Federal Assembly tried to impress on both political authorities and working organisations 'the need for a reduction in budgetary expenditure and in unproductive outlays of working organisations'. Kraigher immediately pointed out that there was no scope for saving in federal expenditure because 75 per cent of that was earmarked for defence, pensions to invalids and veterans and foreign debt service. Furthermore, grants to less developed socialist republics in South-Eastern Yugoslavia would have to be increased.

The main burden would have to fall onto the 'communes' which, however, were not very keen on cutting their spending in spite of appeals to their 'political responsibility'. In addition they abused the changes in prices, 'going wild' (Markovic, B 5.8.65) with prices of communal services, rents, domestic electricity tariffs and meat. Boris Kraigher (B 5.8.65) had to announce in a press interview the extension of price controls to all these items.

8.5 THE WILL TO REFORM

After the reform measures had been announced, the Swiss journalist Victor Meier commented: 'If one reads the statements by Yugoslav leaders on the plans for reform, one has the impression of having read the same ten or even more years ago.' (NZZ 2.8.65.) Indeed, similar reforms were discussed in the past but were never consistently implemented because the leaders shrank from their consequences. One exception after another completely undermined the original intentions.

The early destabilising communist economic policy had made it very difficult to restore normal proportions in the economy. Boris Kraigher himself warned at the 8th Congress that 'our productive capacity was oriented towards investment and any large reduction in investment, as an isolated measure, was bound to create serious trouble in placing investment goods and to endanger existing levels of employment, utilisation of capacity and the like.' This was the problem stated very succinctly, but—if Yugoslavia was not to go on producing for production's sake—the structure of production had to be changed.

It would have required much political courage to carry a reform fraught with such dangers to a successful conclusion (Ep 5.12.64). Kraigher himself was aware of the 'need for a firm political determination' (66, p. 70) to implement the reform. He himself might have been the man to push it through, but he died in a car accident on 3 January 1967.

One of the difficulties was that previous unsuccessful attempts had made the population very sceptical. Because of too many forecasts of better times and stability in the past people no longer believed anything. Pasko Romac, a member of the Federal Assembly, complained in a speech: 'We have become masters of manipulation of indices and figures. But I am very worried about what finally becomes of what we say, conclude and decide in this Chamber and in other chambers . . . I believe that people are losing confidence in what we are promising' (Ep 19.7.64).

This was hardly surprising because of the extravagant promises by the communists before and after their take-over of power, about what they would do and how life would be easy once they abolished private ownership of capital and obtained full control over the country. After the start of reforms in 1952, they repeated all the same promises, this time making them dependent on full self-management, and every new turn on the winding road from one reform to another was announced as the final answer to all woes. They seemed to be looking for an institutional change, for a formula which would turn stone into gold (Ep. 9.5.64). In the mid-1960s it was finally admitted that it was unrealistic to hope that Yugoslavia could 'achieve in a few years what normally takes long decades' (Ep 1.1.65) and that 'wishes were not reality' (Ep 5.6.65). Eventually people were almost blamed for expecting too much of socialism, for having 'idealised it', and for having misunderstood the nature of society (Crvenkovski, B 25.12.66).

The main, if not the only, culprits were naturally the communists themselves. They not only aroused impossible expectations but also made their achievement more difficult by their mistaken policies. The distorted structure of production was entirely their fault and the correction of it — the aim of the 1965 reform — was 'an almost superhuman task' as Boris Kraigher put it in his last speech.

The director of the Federal Institute of Economic Planning, Rikard Stajner, after stressing in a statement on 26 December 1966 that 40 per cent of the industrial production structure was geared to investment, which was indubitably excessive, expressed the hope that the change required could be implemented gradually by cutting the revenue of producers of unwanted goods, thus depressing their incomes and preventing them from expanding or even maintaining their capacities.

The first panic reaction to the reform were claims that up to 50 per cent of enterprises would not be able to adjust (Ep 12.6.65). *Ekonomska politika* accused the opponents of the reform of spreading such rumours and asked them whether they were afraid of their own incompetence. Later estimates reported in the *Economist* (London, 3 and 31.12.66) put the percentage of enterprises that should be closed down to achieve consistency in the economy at 30 per cent. This sounded realistic in view of a report by the Social Accountancy Service in 1965, when there were still many subsidies, that one enterprise out of seven was working at a loss and that these enterprises employed 584,000 workers (about 20 per cent of the industrial labour force) (Vukovic, B 23.6.65).

Ekonomska politika (Ep 15.10.66) stressed that there could not be a new structure without bankruptcies and disappearance of organisations, but nothing much happened so that the paper repeated the same request for liquidations almost a year later (Ep 29.7.67). Between July 1964 and July 1966 a total of 150,000 people lost their jobs in business organisations (Ep 22.10.65) but of these only about 8300 in 1965 and 4600 in 1966 were because of the liquidation of their enterprises (SG 68, p. 104). Later on, the number of workers losing jobs because of liquidations dwindled to about 2000 in 1975 and 1976 (SG 77, p. 127). Mijalko Todorovic warned (B 18.6.65) that in order to achieve distribution according to work it was also necessary 'to stop finally the practice of adjusting policy and economic instruments to particular conditions and thus saving everything and everybody from failure, including the most irrational production.' His admonitions went unheeded.

8.6 REORGANISATION AND INTEGRATION

It was suggested that enterprises in a difficult but not hopeless situation should either a) merge (*spajanje*) or be taken over (*pripajanje*) or b) be offered financial or technical help for re-organisation (26, pp. 225, 271).

The reform measures included an Act which allowed the republic temporarily to raise the rate of the contribution out of personal income by two percentage points and feed the resulting revenue into the republic's joint reserve fund (see p. 45). The total revenue from this tax rise was expected to be about 1 billion new dinars or 1 per cent of the GSP.

The drive for integration was explained as imperative because of technical progress so that they could bring about considerable scale economies of technology, management and research (26, pp. 265, 268). The implications of the development of production forces for workers' self-management were discussed at great length (60, 83).

The number of workers per industrial enterprise rose from 260 in 1955, already high (see p. 37), to 559 in 1965 and 634 in 1972, but then fell to 430 in 1974 (JP 67, p. 480, SG 73, p. 132, SG 76, p. 146). This fall was entirely due to a sudden rise in the number of working organisations from 2398 in 1971 (SG 73, p. 128) to 4100 in 1974 (SG 76, p. 146) which indicated that there were not only integrations as expressly shown in statistics but also 'disintegrations'. In fact this term was used in an article in *Borba* of 16.7.1971 to describe the falling apart of some large integrational systems. Disregarding the disintegrations, the number of mergers and take-overs between 1965 and 1975 amounted to 5635 (SG 76, p. 143). In 1965, of all integrated organisations 67.5 per cent belonged to the same branch or group, 10.1 per cent were in the same line of production, and 22.4 per cent embraced different kinds of activity; in 1975, the corresponding figures were 52.7 per cent, 10.3 per cent and 37 per cent (SG 76, p. 143) which showed a marked tendency to conglomerates. They were apparently badly organised and generally chaotic, especially as they prevented the links between similar enterprises which were also fostered in the hope of gaining through specialisation (cf. Ep 20.12.76). In 1965, enterprises integrated predominantly within the same commune (81.5 per cent), mostly by takeovers, and hardly at all between republics (1.2 per cent), while in 1975, 66.2 per cent integrated within the same commune, 12.6 per cent within neighbouring communes, 18.9 within the same republic and 2.3 per cent between republics.

The initiative for integration came from political authorities (Ep 26.6.65) and the purpose was largely cross-subsidisation (82, p. 218, B 2.8.70, Ep 12.4.76) so that the original technical aim was on the whole not achieved (Ep 26.6.65, B 2.8.70). Integration was turned from a device for technological progress into a method, used by communes and republics, for concealing losses by combining successful and bad enterprises. The special role of associations among enterprises in the 1970s will be discussed later (see p. 212).

Business associations (JP 67, p. 479) (see p. 42) did change to commercial and production cooperation and prospered; there were 22 in 1959, 290 in 1967. Almost all metal-working enterprises were members of such associations. A new form, the so-called 'associated enterprise' (*zdruzena preduzeca*) developed, under which enterprises were independent but some common principles for their activity were established. The principal shortcoming of this looser form was that it did not have much influence on the production activity of enterprises, but was largely limited to cooperation in purchasing and marketing (82, p. 217). In the end, the new Act on Associated Labour of 1976 required a complete transformation of all such associations within two years (Ep 15.11.76).

The intention was also to use integrated enterprises for establishing a system of planning based on agreements. Such agreements were supposed to facilitate the working of the market (Suppl. B 2.8.70). One of the things that the Yugoslav leaders were trying to prevent in this way was the very frequent duplication of capacity—in particular, political authorities acting as investors were apt to build new enterprises on their territory while the capacity of similar plant elsewhere was not fully utilised (26, p. 275). It was thought that business chambers could be used for this purpose and that they could help enterprises to achieve 'direct planning cooperation (ex ante) instead of by means of the market (ex post)' (26, p. 160). The danger of such cooperation in advance is that it can easily turn into 'monopolistic collusion' (Ep 20.8.66). Indeed for a while the role of business chambers was considered so important that President Tito specially met representatives of the Federal Business

Chamber on 17 January 1966. But nothing came of this because there were so many changes in the legislation that they could not perform their functions (Ep 1.7.67). Besides, the interests of business chambers and their members in different branches and in different regions clashed. Also, when the trade unions proposed in 1965 that groups of enterprises within chambers and trade unions should negotiate on personal incomes, the Federal Assembly rejected such proposals as 'corporativist' (121, p. 475).

8.7 COOPERATION ESPECIALLY WITH FOREIGN ENTERPRISES

In spite of the communist criticism of pre-war foreign investment in Yugoslavia, it became clear in the end that foreign risk capital had advantages over simple credits because foreigners added their technical and organisational expertise to capital and also bore part of the responsibility for the success or failure of the enterprise. For Yugoslavia this turned out especially desirable as this might be a way of rescuing enterprises which on their own could not hope to prosper.

But under the conditions of self-management, it was difficult to find a procedure for the involvement of foreign risk capital as (1) capital invested in an enterprise could not belong to an outsider since all means of production were social property; and (2) nobody outside the enterprise could be allowed to interfere with self-management. The problem did not arise only with foreign participation but also with the investment of domestic capital 'belonging' to another enterprise. 'One self-manager could exploit another self-manager' or 'group ownership' could emerge (Ep 21.1 to 4.2.67). However, life required answers even if they had to be sought outside the dominating ideology as the efficiency of the system was in danger. In January 1967, the Economic Chamber of the Federal Assembly adopted a Resolution on the Further Development of Associations and Business Co-operation in the Economy which demanded that 'adequate solutions should be built (into the existing system) which would permit freer movement of accumulation and a freer market in money and would eliminate etatist (centralist, administrative) methods of collecting funds for expanded reproduction' (JP 67, p. 482). When the appropriate legal changes were debated, one member of the parliament said: 'Anyway, enterprises are concluding semi-legal or illegal contracts such as we are now planning because they are forced to do so by sheer necessity.'

The solution had indeed been found in the form of partnership or investment contracts (86). If the self-management bodies of an enterprise were prepared to conclude a contract with another domestic enterprise (possibly within the framework of a business association) or with any kind of foreign legal subject, with the effect of transferring a part of their management rights to the partner, Yugoslav law so to speak washed its hands. Such an arrangement was not considered to 'infringe basic self-management rights'. When foreigners are involved, there can be a joint business committee which can manage the joint business activity and the capital needed for such joint operations. These provisions seem to have been taken over into Art. 388 of the 1976 Act on Associated Labour. All contracts with foreign investors have to be registered with the Federal Secretariat of the Economy.

Foreign investment in any enterprise could not exceed or equal domestic investment and the foreign investor had to renounce his right of ownership, although he was entitled to a share in management and in profits and even the re-transfer of his investment abroad. Initially the foreign investor had to re-invest 20 per cent of his profits in Yugoslavia, but this provision was dropped in 1971 (JP 73, p. 295). A solution was also found for the tax on foreign profits (Sl 31/67) and on the incomes of the representatives of foreign investors in Yugoslavia (Ep 3.6.67).

After some uncertainty (Grlickov, Ep 17.6.67), the institution of part-foreign investment was included in the Constitutional Amendment XXII (later taken over by Art. 27 of the 1974 Constitution) and a separate Act was adopted in 1973. Nonetheless, the results of the Yugoslav invitation to foreign companies were rather modest: up till 1975 about 150 contracts were concluded concerning dinars 5.5 billion of foreign capital (Ep 31.1.77). Almost half of foreign investment went into enterprises in the metal-working industry which were most in need of foreign expertise. An International Investment Corporation of Yugoslavia exists now (Ep 8.3.76) and amendments to the Act on Foreign investment are envisaged.

8.8 'PERSONAL WORK WITH PRIVATE MEANS'

Although private workshops have not been directly involved in the financial and technical reorganisation of social enterprises, they should be considered here because they facilitate the functioning of big factories since they support their work by supplies, marketing and servicing, so that the operation of the whole economy becomes much smoother (see p. 37). In spite of the need for small workshops in private hands, there was a widespread feeling that any economic activity outside the social sector was 'embryonic capitalism' (Ep 11.11.67). This perception at the back of political minds put pressure on private enterprise so that the number of private artisan workshops fell from 155,000 with over 200,000 employees in 1954 to 105,000 with 134,000 employees in 1964 (SG 71, p. 172). During the same period the number of those employed in the social artisan workshops increased from 100,000 to 200,000, but social artisan workshops were rather unwieldly and could not cope with the demand.

The situation deteriorated so much that President Tito thought it necessary in 1963 to call representatives of artisans to visit him and *Ekonomska politika* (Ep 20.4.63) featured the speech he made to them prominently. He said that it was wrong to believe that artisan workshops should be liquidated and talked about 'leftist' excesses towards private artisans.

The results were encouraging: the number of private workshops rose to 145,000 in 1969, but then fell to 135,000 in 1975 (SG 77, p. 205), and the number of those employed (including owners) increased to just under 200,000, while the numbers in the social artisan sector had been stagnating till 1974 and jumped to 273,000 in 1975. The number of apprentices in the private sector was reduced from almost 50,000 in 1954 to just under 16,000 in 1964, recovered to over 32,000 in 1969 and then fell to 24,000 in 1973 (SG 73, p. 187, SG 76, p. 204).

The rescue of the private artisan workshops was considered essential also because they were the only producers of some goods and services, because of the employment they provided, and finally, because they could attract back Yugoslav migrants and their money from Western Europe (JP 71, p. 57). But any praise for private artisans was normally accompanied by warnings that private artisans could not be allowed to exploit their employees. To this Professor Aleksic, in his book on personal work under socialism, replied by asking how it was possible to talk about exploitation when workers earned more in private employment than in the social sector (1, p. 179, B 11.5.60).

'Personal work with private means of production' was mentioned in the Programme of the League of Communists of 1958 and all constitutional arrangements (JP 71, p. 57) and the Socialist Association of Working People devoted a long resolution to its own tasks in its development (JP 68, pp. 59, 63). Despite this official support, local authorities mainly considered private workshops as an object for heavy taxation. On the one hand they were aiming for doctrinaire reasons to reduce private artisans' earnings to the level of corresponding workers in the social sector, and on the other they simply wanted to raise revenue. *Ekonomska politika* (Ep 27.7.63) objected to the first goal because many independent artisans were working up to twelve hours a day, often with the help of their families, so that there could not be any comparison with those on fixed hours. There were also constant complaints that private workshops were concealing their actual incomes, which put them in a better position than social enterprises, although they were on the whole paying higher taxes, e.g. turnover tax on all their inputs, as witnessed the following extract.

> The lack of legal and economic security and inappropriate credit, taxation and general development policies, all contributed to the closure of many private workshops. In Belgrade only, the number of artisan workshops fell from 9,300 to 7,400 within the last two years, while at least 7,000 more would be needed just for repairs of 4.5 million domestic appliances (Ep 8.8.77).

The accusation of profiteering looked all the more plausible as independent artisans generally won in any competition with the social sector. This very efficiency often provoked the communal authorities to tax them out of existence (Ep 26.1.76).

Special battles were fought over private lorry-operators who often earned good money by running old lorries discarded by social transport enterprises (Ep 27.7.63). In 1964 there were about 4000 privately owned lorries (Ep 5.8.67); in 1976 there were 42,000, as compared with 10,000 in the social sector (SG 77, p. 32).

Over the years, there was considerable pressure to allow private workshops to expand and to lift the limits on their size (five employees) if for no other reason than to foster employment (B 14.6.70). The countermove was to suggest that, should private employment really widen, some kind of self-management or at least co-determination and participation in profits should be introduced in the private sector also (Ep 11.11.67). The Socialist Republic of Slovenia in fact provided for a combination of private entrepreneurship and self-management under the name of 'contractual organisation of associated labour', an institution adopted in Art. 67 of the 1974 Constitution. There is not much enthusiasm for this solution—so far only about thirty 'contractual organisations of associated labour' have been established (Ep 7.3.77)—partly because it severely limits the small private initiative and partly because local authorities are afraid that the change will reduce their tax revenue (Ep 12.12.77). Meanwhile, the shortage of small supporting enterprises continues; they are proportionately three times less numerous than in Italy and Austria (cf. JP 77, p. 137).

Part Three

Fundamental Problems (from 1965 on)

9: Inflationary Income Distribution

9.1 RISING PRICES

In the first few years after the 1965 reform, the annual rise in the cost of living was kept to single figures but then it began accelerating as indicated in Table 6.2. While in 1967–70, the rise in the cost of living was 7.7 per cent per annum on average, this rose to 19.6 per cent for 1971–75, although the average rate of growth dropped slightly from 6.3 per cent in 1966–70 to 6.0 per cent in 1971–75. There was some discrepancy between the rate of increase of prices of industrial and agricultural goods, but on balance not all that much. (Industrial prices rose 5.2 per cent in 1966–70 and 18.0 per cent in 1971–5; agricultural prices rose 6.6 per cent in 1966–70 and 20.4 per cent in 1971–5).

These price rises occurred in spite of price controls, which were at first preserved, as a temporary measure (66, p. 69), with the usual consequences: a flood of 'new' products requiring new prices (B 8.4.65). The aim was, however, quite clear — to abandon this regime of frozen prices and administrative price controls (66, p. 69) because prices needed to be allowed to perform their functions with respect to allocation, distribution, time preference, international division of labour etc. (JP 73, p. 253). It was even claimed that only free prices could guarantee distribution according to work (JP 73, p. 253).

Although in 1967 and 1968 prices behaved reasonably well, doubts started appearing possibly because growth rates were also very low. It was again argued that the solution of problems (apparently mainly structural) could not be left to the market (Ep 29.10.66) but that the right conditions should be created by 'organised social influence'. This was the old dilemma: price controls were necessary because of structural disproportions, but structural disproportions themselves were due to price controls.

It was easy to proclaim the principles of pricing but difficult to implement them (Ep 17.9.66). When some prices were freed in June

1966 (Ep 18.6.66) they rose by more than expected (Ep 29.10.66) and influenced future attitudes. In 1970, free prices were allowed for two-thirds of production by value but in 1974 the figure was only one-third again (JP 75, p. 100).

Legal rules proliferated. In March 1966, the Federal Assembly adopted the Theses on Prices which were transformed into an Act on Formation and Social Control of Prices in April 1967. Another Act on the Control of Prices was adopted in 1972. Both advocated free though not spontaneous prices, but provided for the use of the following control methods: reporting on price changes, freezing of prices, price ceilings, rules for price calculation, and permission for price changes (JP 72, p. 177).

All along there have been attempts to replace government controls by self-organisation of working organisations including contracts and agreements on prices, of course prohibiting monopolistic intentions (JP 72, p. 177). By 1973, these devices had not produced the results hoped for — they were of short duration, were not acted upon and sometimes simply abandoned (JP 73, pp. 256–7).

There is an inherent contradiction in social contracts and self-management agreements on prices. If the socio-political authorities do not participate, the agreements are purely amongst producers and must almost inevitably contain monopolistic elements and be at the expense of 'the third party', i.e. consumers (cf. Korosic, Ep 27.10.75). If political authorities do participate, either directly or as supervisors (agreements actually had to be submitted to them for approval), the agreements in fact become administrative measures. Full administrative control of the price system is, however, illusory, as prices for at least 500,000 items are involved (Ep 20.10.75).

Because of uncertainties and indecision on what the price system should be, prices in Yugoslavia are determined subjectively (Ep 12.4.76) or, in Marxist terms, on a 'voluntaristic' basis (Ep 15.8.77). This then leads to continuous attempts by enterprises to solve their problems by a rise in their prices. Such is the strange result of the endeavour to 'eliminate spontaneity' and make price controls a part of 'self-management planning' (cf. Ep 17.11.75).

Inflation was mainly blamed on 'unresolved problems of distribution' of which more in the next section, on the over-burdening of business by legal and contractual obligations and on imported price rises (JP 75, p. 101). The Zagreb economist Korosic tried to explain Yugoslav inflation as structural (Ep 1.11.76). Officially, prices in Yugoslavia were supposed to be based on world prices. For agriculture they were to be calculated on the basis of average costs of socialised farms which, according to some, was a reason for the fast rise in agricultural prices (see p. 65). The so-called 'development prices' for some selected priority branches, were intended to be held above the level on world markets by means of tariff protection (see p.106).

The link with world markets apparently worked in an absurd way: it only caused price rises and was always modified as soon as a world price fell (Korosic, Ep 27.10.75). From 1973 onwards imported inflation was often mentioned (JP 75, p. 101) but this could not have been a very strong contributory factor as the Yugoslav rate of inflation was more than twice as fast as in the OECD countries (JP 75, p. 99, cf. Ep 21.3.77). In no case could inflation have been due primarily to unsatisfied demand (Korosic, Ep 27.10.75) as inventories were accumulating (Ep 30.5.77).

The results of the Yugoslav price reform are disappointing if one takes into account that its main purpose was to bring about structural realignment, after the discovery that break-neck growth bred increasing chaos (JP 73, p. 256). Such realignment has not been achieved, presumably because the price system alone could not bring it about as it is only a part of a complete economic system for which there exists no clear overall concept (JP 75, p. 102). There can be little hope of change in the near future as the new Draft Act on Prices contains neither well-defined criteria for pricing nor properly defines who should participate in management agreements on prices (Ep 15.11.76, 17.10.77). The 1977 Contract on the Implementation of Price Policy obligated political authorities to keep price rises at the level of the year before which undoubtedly meant price controls (Ep 21.3.77). The Federal Secretary for the market and prices denied that the new Act on the System and Social Control of Prices could bring greater liberalisation (Ep 10.10.77).

9.2 PERSONAL INCOMES EXPLOSION

After the reform in July 1965, the Federal Assembly passed a Resolution on the Distribution of Income and Personal Incomes in Working Organisations, reminding workers' councils that there were limits to what could be distributed and enjoining the trade unions and communes to 'help' in holding incomes back. The adjustment of incomes was to be within the expected adjustment in prices of 22 per cent which was necessary to alter the price structure.

Eventually the cost of living rose by 33 per cent in 1965 and incomes

Table 9.1: Average net personal earnings and indices of money and real earnings

	Average net personal earnings in dinars			Chain indices						
				Money incomes				Real incomes		
	Total	economy	'non-economy'	Total	economy	'non-economy'	Cost of living	Total	economy	'non-economy'
1958	151	135	230	–	–	–	–	–	–	–
1959	177	163	248	109	123	107	100	109	120	107
1960	203	190	274	117	117	113	112	104	104	102
1961	220	210	283	107	107	100	106	100	100	93
1962	242	230	304	113	113	106	110	104	104	96
1963	285	272	360	118	118	122	106	110	110	115
1964	362	349	440	125	125	123	111	112	112	110
1965	501	484	596	140	140	133	133	105	105	100
1966	693	674	791	137	137	133	123	112	112	109
1967	787	759	927	115	115	117	108	107	107	108
1968	862	834	1008	109	109	109	104	104	104	105
1969	990	960	1149	115	115	113	108	106	106	104
1970	1173	1136	1366	119	119	120	110	108	108	110
1971	1432	1390	1654	122	122	120	116	105	105	103
1972	1676	1626	1937	117	117	117	117	100	100	100
1973	1938	1839	2164	116	116	111	120	98	98	93
1974	2477	2420	2766	128	128	128	121	106	106	106
1975	3060	2974	3491	124	123	126	124	99	99	101
1976	3535	3422	4091	116	115	117	112	104	103	104

Source: calculated from SG 73, p. 283; SG 77, p. 310

by 40 per cent (see Table 9.1). In the following five years, personal incomes rose by 19 per cent per annum on average, which compares badly with the average rise in the cost of living of 11 per cent even if the rise in industrial productivity of 5 per cent is taken into account. In 1971–5, incomes rose by 21.4 per cent per year but this rate has to be contrasted with price rises of 19.6 per cent per annum and industrial productivity rises of about 3 per cent (cf. Ep 29.8.77).

Strictly speaking, industrial productivity should not be compared with figures for the whole social sector, but there are no comparable productivity data for the broader sector and the industrial productivity rises seem to be in line with growth rates of 6.3 per cent for 1966–70 and 6 per cent in 1970–75, taking the rise in labour force into consideration.

The main inflationary harm, then, was done in the first five years after 1965. During that period personal incomes were rising at a rate of about 3 per cent per year in excess of productivity and price rises, and price rises themselves must have been to a large extent a feedback from personal incomes. Initially, it was possible to shift resources to incomes in the social sector from the rest of the economy (agricultural prices, for instance, were falling in 1967 and 1968) and imports, so that real personal incomes were able to rise at the rate of 7.4 per cent per annum which is more than the annual rise in industrial productivity, itself 'gross'.

The first period set the pattern for the second period, but then this pattern caused a serious upset for workers' management. Personal income distribution was no longer in excess of price rises plus productivity rises, so the average rate of real personal income rises was down to 1.6 per cent per year. Blue and white collar workers now had to compete for consumer goods with peasants whose incomes were rising faster again, with those who were receiving transfers from Yugoslav workers abroad (see p. 201) and with the requirement to export more (see JP 75, p. 101).

In view of the developments in 1966–70, the prevalence of the view that Yugoslav inflation was due to cost push (53, p. 142), i.e. to the way in which workers had distributed income in enterprises since 1965, was hardly surprising. As early as 1967, at a conference in Ljubljana, Aleksander Bajt read a paper (9) explaining inflation in Yugoslavia in this way and his views seem to have been widely accepted.

The main point made by Bajt was that, as soon as some incomes rise above the usual differentials, this is taken as a signal for all other incomes to follow suit, in other words 'the highest personal incomes also pull up the rest', since workers do not feel like entrepreneurs who accept different incomes as a consequence of different results, but remain workers for whom parity of wages for similar work is an important ingredient of justice.

Many reasons for increasing disparities of incomes (wages +profits) can be thought of and many operated in practice, so that the whole structure of personal incomes inexorably moved upwards. With some prices controlled and others not, some not only could be raised but were directly pushed up by money which could not be spent on goods with controlled prices. Personal incomes in these sectors moved up with prices and there was pressure elsewhere to follow them up. Monopolistic prices too led to higher incomes and a similar upward pull elsewhere.

If personal incomes tended to be proportionate to the gross revenue of an enterprise, as they did, then personal incomes in enterprises employing a large amount of capital tended to be higher if capital was free or if payments on capital were too low. The same thing happened in enterprises with better technology and where production was better matched with demand. Again higher personal incomes in some enterprises pulled up the rest.

Of course, not all enterprises could pay the personal incomes the best enterprises could, but the poorer enterprises tended to forgo accumulation, or eroded capital, or borrowed to maintain high incomes despite losses. In Yugoslavia, those enterprises with losses raised incomes as much as others or more (Ep 26.4, 20.9, 18.10.76, 28.3, 12.9, 10.10.77). The level of personal incomes was related neither to productivity nor to the efficiency with which social capital was used (Ep 17.11.75).

Haphazard payment of personal incomes was also partly a consequence of the difficulties inherent in an exact definition of the 'income' (gross or net) of an enterprise (JP 68, p. 365, Ep 10.3.75). One of the problems was what to include in the 'income' which could be distributed. Initially, for instance, returns of investment by one enterprise in another or interest earned in this way was not allowed to be included in the 'income' but had to be added straight to the enterprise's business fund. However, this seems to have become such an obstacle to capital mobility because it killed the enterprise's interest in such transactions, that the Fundamental Act on the Determination and Distribution of Income of 1968 had to change this arrangement and permit earnings on capital to be added to the income that could be distributed to the workers.

The more serious questions were whether to include in income goods in stock which might not be sold and goods which had been sold but not paid for yet. This problem was discussed as the distinction between 'invoiced' and 'paid for' sales (*fakturisana* and *naplacena realizacija*). In both cases, workers could receive personal incomes for something not verified by the market, for something that 'was only a fiction' (Ep 3.12.66). Worse than that, since workers could not be made to wait till production was sold, their incomes were in fact payments on account in advance. So the 'income' as enshrined in the Constitution of 1974 as the basis for distribution was not only difficult to define, but had to be guessed in advance and could genuinely be misjudged. In 1976 and 1977, there were again changes in the definition of 'income' which led to a jump of dinars 32 billion in the income of the first half of 1977 without any change in the underlying reality, and thus led to many harmful illusions (Ep 19.9.77).

Sometimes it was not beyond the 'consciousness' of enterprises to 'adjust' the books (B 12.1.65, Ep 12.1.76). According to Social Accountancy Service data in 1975 the sales shown in the books of all enterprises were exaggerated by dinars 732 million, depreciation was entered below the official minimum by 213 million and costs were illegally inflated by dinars 549 million, all of which reduced the consolidated loss by 549 million and raised 'income' by dinars 931 million. The ficticious picture thus created was for the purpose of allowing larger payment of personal incomes.

Ekonomska politika, which reported these figures, wondered why the workers stole from themselves in this way and came to the conclusion that they obviously did not identify their own interests with the interests of the enterprise. There is little doubt that this is true because there is no mechanism which could bring such identity about if there is no private ownership.

To remedy this situation attempts were made to associate workers with their enterprises by making their dismissal almost impossible, as in the Fundamental Act on Labour Relations, adopted in 1965 and then repeatedly amended. This meant that the enterprise, which is composed of the workers' workmates, was treated as an employer whose rights have to be curtailed to protect the rights of individuals (Ep 4.11.68). The Yugoslav leaders were taken in by their own words: on one hand, they were giving individuals extreme rights, while on the other they wanted to integrate them firmly in a variety of collectives: enterprises, communes, party, State, which all require the rights of individuals to be limited by the rights of others. However, while enterprises could not dismiss workers, workers themselves could freely leave and often did when enterprises were working at a loss (B 28.12.64) (see p. 133).

The Act that provided for the workers' entrenchment in enterprises was first praised for its advanced approach, but then criticised for making self-management impossible. Many workers could get away with doing nothing and the newspapers eventually turned on them. There were reports on how laziness was being protected (B 21.9.74) and demands that an end should be put to misconceived solidarity between workers (B 30.10.74, Ep 14.11.77). The trade unions were asked to defend those working hard from the work-shy (B 14.10.74). The Act on Associated Labour of 1976 loosened somewhat the rules on dismissals but preserved considerable restrictions on the right of the workers' councils to give notice (Arts 211–219).

It was very difficult to make workers supervise each other although workers' control was institutionalised in Art. 107 of the 1974 Constitution. The question also arose of whether workers could carry out supervision in their spare time, i.e. without becoming professional supervisors (Ep 3.9.73). It became clear that supervision was also required in the interests of other enterprises, which lost if an enterprise could not pay for goods it had received. Therefore, it was suggested that the accounts of all enterprises should be open to general public scrutiny (Ep 21.5.73).

The uncertainties caused by the category of 'income' as opposed to 'wages + profit', which it included, led some Yugoslav economists to question the very concept of 'amorphous income' as they called it (Bester, D 18.5.68). According to them, it was necessary to establish what production costs were, while the proponents of the new 'income' gloried in the idea that the old concept of production costs had been abolished. Without production costs there were no criteria for investment and employment. *Ekonomska politika* (Ep 5.2.68) stated that, 'with all due respect', the concept of 'income' was born out of the urge to sew the label 'socialist' on to everything. For this reason, the Yugoslavs have been inventing one unsuccessful 'specific' theory after another, only to re-discover in the end concepts that had been formulated by others long ago, such as interest rates, banks, commerce, convertibility etc. Had they taken a realistic view of things in the first place, they would perhaps have introduced reforms which would last for a while rather than need alteration every few years, with the excuse that they were 'necessary in the previous phase but now superseded'.

The opponents of 'income' suggested that there should be 'accounting personal incomes' and 'personal incomes out of profit', but this suggestion was attacked as being contrary to the decisions of the 9th Congress of the Yugoslav League of Communists (B 5.11.69). As it was, there was confusion as to whether costs were 'personal incomes paid on account' in advance on the basis of expected 'income' or 'accounting personal incomes'. In fact, the 1968 Act on the Determination of Income described a 'loss' as occurring if an enterprise could not cover its personal incomes on account or its legally fixed minimum personal incomes out of its net revenue. These minimum incomes later became 'guaranteed' incomes fixed by republics, provinces and communes in accordance with their capacity to maintain them and their appraisal of the level required (JP 76, p. 331).

In 1975, when new provisions on the definition of enterprises' incomes were discussed, the debate on 'incomes' and 'profits' flared up again (Bester, NR 25.7.75, Ep 28.6.76). It was then suggested that 'agreed personal incomes', presumably higher than the legal minimum, should constitute a floor below which personal incomes could not be depressed in order to enable an enterprise to continue working.

This suggestion was a consequence of the realisation that the distribution system, such as it was, was not only 'an important source of inflation' (Bajt, D 19.9.70) but sometimes also encouraged enterprises to carry on although they were very inefficient. In fact, some enterprises may avoid losses only because they pay very low personal incomes (Ep 28.6.76). Some enterprises survive although they have no future. The consequence is that in such enterprises the workers, especially the most skilled, minimise their efforts and if possible leave (Ep 7.6.76) so that the situation of such enterprises deteriorates more and more.

9.3 DISSAVING IN ENTERPRISES AND PRIVATE SAVING

The outcome of Yugoslav distribution policies can be interpreted in two ways: either the explosion of personal incomes took on such dimensions that, together with other outlays, they eroded enterprises' capital; alternatively such a large part of output went into inventories that fixed capital was eroded in order to finance the stockpiling (cf. *Bilansi*, 76, p. 19). The final outcome is, of course, the same in both cases: revenue does not exceed outlays sufficiently to finance the renewal of the existing fixed capital.

Ekonomska politika (11.7.77) calculated that the surplus of current receipts over current payments in the consolidated balance of all Yugoslav enterprises in the social sector was dinars 14.4 billion in 1973, dinars 22.2 billion in 1974 and dinars 36.2 billion in 1975. These figures compare with depreciation of fixed capital in the same three years amounting to dinars 30.8 billion, dinars 43.9 billion and dinars 48.6 billion in 1977 (SG 77, p. 133) so that the financial resources available for fixed investment were dinars 16.4 billion in 1973, dinars 21.7 billion in 1974 and dinars 12.4 billion in 1975 short of what was required to maintain enterprises' fixed capital. In 1973 and 1974, this was equivalent to 6.6 per cent and 6.4 per cent respectively of the gross income of social enterprises and 7.4 per cent and 7.2 per cent of net income (value added including stockpiling). For 1975 the figures are 2.9 per cent of gross income and 3.2 per cent of net income, but this reduction was due to especially low depreciation in this year, so that it had to be corrected later. When Yugoslav commentators say that the reproduction capacity of the economy is 9 per cent or 11.2 per cent of the value of capital (*Bilansi* 76, p. 18) or that the rate of internal accumulation is about 6 per cent (JP 75, p. 101), they arc simply comparing capital employed by social enterprises with total investment (i.e. including depreciation and investment in stocks) although nothing is left for new fixed investment.

If spending by an enterprise in excess of its value added is called a loss, then the loss shown by the consolidated balance of Yugoslav enterprises was equal to over 6 per cent in both the first two years under scrutiny. This means that part of the finance for the renewal of capacity and any capital expansion had to come from some source other than enterprises themselves. In fact only about one third of gross investment (including depreciation) came from enterprises while another third came from bank credits and the remaining third from political authorities (Ep 11.7.77 and *Bilansi* 76, p. 64). In so far as this implied credit creation, it was of course, the mechanism for inflation. The monetary values of everything were increased, so as to provide concealed savings for investment.

The calculations quoted here are confirmed *grosso modo* by Yugoslav sources which claim that the average overspending by Yugoslav social enterprises (= average losses) in 1970–5 amounted to 2.4 per cent of net income (JP 76, p. 330). These losses were not evenly distributed and some enterprises did not work at a loss at all, while some did so badly that they had to spend more than their gross income. Losses jumped from 1.4 per cent in 1974 to 3.6 per cent in 1975, but this was due to a change in accounting units, the number of which rose from 14,472 in 1974 to 23,182 in 1975; this gives some indication of how much cross-subsidisation there had been. For 1976 and 1977, the deputy general director of the Social Accounting Service quoted 6 per cent as the share of losses in the 'income' (Ep 19.9.77).

We have concentrated mainly on figures for 1973, 1974 and 1975 because these are the last full figures available but the situation had been similar before and has deteriorated since, though changes are very often due also to alterations in accountancy and statistical methods. All in all, Yugoslav social enterprises distribute more than they earn, to a large extent because a part of their production is never sold. The tendency to falling accumulation is often mentioned in Yugoslavia (Ep 18.10.76, Ep 20.12.76) although enterprises are already accumulating less than is necessary for the renewal of their capacities.

While enterprises failed to maintain their fixed capital out of their own financial resources, private savings surpassed hire purchase credits to the population at the beginning of the 1960s and the population began to build up savings deposits, which are lent by banks to enterprises or political authorities and social services. In 1973, the surplus of private savings over private investment was dinars 15 billion, in 1974 dinars 14 billion and in 1975 dinars 17 billion, so that a considerable part of bank credits for enterprise investment could have come out of these savings. In addition, private persons directly used dinars 15 billion, dinars 20 billion and dinars 23 billion for unproductive investment, mainly housing, and dinars 7 billion, dinars 5 billion and dinars 4 billion for productive investment. About one-third of financial resources for investment in 1973, one-fourth in 1974 and one-fifth in 1975 was in private hands. It must be mentioned, nonetheless, that the population received about dinars 25 billion in 1973 and dinars 30 billion in 1974 and in 1975 from abroad.

However, even taking this into account, private persons saved while enterprises dissaved which means—which is hardly surprising—that the propensity to save is higher, if the savings become the savers' property than if they become the property of the state or society. Of course workers in factories realise that their productivity will increase if they have better equipment, but there is no direct link between any individual and investment. Therefore, accumulation becomes a kind of tax which benefits everybody in general but nobody in particular, so people tend to behave as free riders—trying to use as much investment as possible and save for society as little as possible.

Under the circumstances, it is impossible to bring the interests of groups of workers, enterprises and the public into line, although the need for such alignment is discussed (Ep 18.10.76 and 13.6.77) and although Tito claimed that the interests of producers were identical with the interest of the entire community (Ep 12.12.64). Decision-making does not entail responsibility (see p. 92) and there is no direct link between the future standard of living of a worker and the present behaviour (present savings) of his enterprise (Ep 18.8.75). Hence everybody tries to get as much out of the enterprise as he can, and, simultaneously, minimises his efforts. Self-management turns out to lack a psychological mechanism which would align economic activity, especially entrepreneurial activity, with individuals' remuneration.

Jaroslav Vanek (114) in his very favourable book on labour-management was well aware of the difficulty although he did not even envisage that ownership should be social. For Yugoslavia he suggested that there should be a Council which would issue rules on distribution between personal incomes and accumulation. For this he was criticised at a meeting in Belgrade (private information) of specialists who were followers of the income-price doctrine and said that it was entirely wrong to base self-management theory on the selfish motives of the workers, so that no such Council was required. Income-price theoreticians maintain that workers distribute the 'income' correctly of their own accord (65).

Even Edward Kardelj, although claiming that there was a separate category of income, did not believe that the workers would by themselves properly distribute the revenue of enterprises. In his view, if the statistical data in fact showed that they did, it was proof that workers were being heavily 'leaned on' (61, p. 67), and such distribution would not last if they were left to their own devices. Similarly Bajt (8, p. 269) thought that it was difficult to distinguish what workers themselves really felt, and was therefore stable, from what was a 'social convention' imposed on them from outside by political activists.

On top of these straight economic difficulties, there were difficulties stemming from public finance. The slogan was 'defiscalisation' i.e. the abolition of taxes prescribed by the government, and their replacement by contributions to 'self-managing interest communities' providing educational, health, housing etc. services on the basis of 'free exchange of work'. This exchange was supposed to be voluntary, determined by self-management agreements, but since the goods supplied were merit goods which individuals left to themselves buy in smaller quantities than governments usually provide, the Yugoslav government had to impose the 'free exchange' by law, for which there is an escape clause in the Constitution. Apparently only 3 per cent of 'self-management interest communities' revenue in 1974 was contributed voluntarily (Ep 21.4.75), the rest was from legally prescribed contributions.

As a result, enterprises were burdened with heavy payments which were in fact taxes, although there were constant protests from business enterprises against excessive levies by socio-political authorities. In

1970–5 these legal liabilities of enterprises amounted to just under 20 per cent of their Social Product (value added plus depreciation) (JP 76, p. 26).

Because of the continuous protest against excessive burdens on enterprises, tax on business funds, which was like a legally compulsory interest change, was completely abolished at the beginning of the 1970s. This caused a problem because it put capital at the disposal of enterprises without any payment at all. But since Yugoslav enterprises in general do not accumulate but even erode their own capital so that they have to borrow from banks even to replace fixed capital, the abolition of the business funds tax was not as much of a relief as it may seem. Whereas in 1970 enterprises paid dinars 2.5 billion in tax on business funds and dinars 6.7 billion in bank interest, in 1975, bank interest amounted to dinars 22.6 billion, although as a percentage of gross social product bank interest remained at a level of about 9 per cent. Enterprises bitterly resent these interest payments, giving rise to a whole anti-bank theory (see p. 220).

9.4 PERSONAL INCOMES POLICY

Although immediately after the 1965 reform government reports to the Federal Assembly claimed considerable achievements and the OECD Survey 1966 joined in this praise, instability and inflationary tendencies soon appeared again and there was criticism that government bodies had again 'promised too much, forecast badly, and reacted slowly' (B 24.12.66).

A government spokesman said that the reason for the new imbalance was to be found 'in the enormous pressure of demagogical forces for *uravnilovka* (levelling of incomes), for a rise of personal incomes beyond the rise in labour productivity without any attention to the needs of economic organisations' (B 24.12.66, cf. B 25.12.66). The increases in personal incomes were lopsided so that they led to clashes with school teachers (Ep 1.10.66) and bank employees (Miljanic, B 28.12.66). Soon there were also complaints that capital was being syphoned into personal incomes (Gligorov, B 20.9.67). Branko Horvat wrote that the 'fundamental goals of the reform were not being attained' (B 9.3.67) and nine years later *Ekonomska politika* (16.2.76) came to the conclusion that in some branches the 'inflationary revenue', achieved by raising prices, amounted in some years to between 60 and 90 per cent of total revenue.

The trade unions refused to accept the assessment that personal incomes were responsible for inflation, blamed it on 'deficit financing by everybody from the Federation to enterprises' (B 27.12.66) and claimed that restriction of personal incomes would not help (B 10.9.70). The top leaders like, for instance, Kraigher (B 27.12.66) sometimes agreed with these judgements. Tito (B 30.12.66) did not want people to blame the workers who, according to him, did not put any pressure on the market because they did not buy cars, of which only about 20,000 were sold in Yugoslavia in 1965. Later on, the Vice-Premier, Sirotkovic, again exonerated personal incomes of any responsibility for the situation (P 5.12.69).

But eventually wiser councils had to prevail. In 1976, a report compiled by the Yugoslav Constitutional Court said that, in most working organisations, the distribution of income was not according to the results of work (D 5.4.76). There is criticism that in 1977 distribution is still not according to work (Dolanc, D 1.3.77) and that income should first be created and only then distributed (D 6.7.76). The complaints refer to distribution both between and within enterprises.

Complaints and criticism continue although it became clear as early as 1968 that full automatism in the distribution of income was impossible because there were no adequate social and psychological forces at work to keep distribution within limits. Therefore, the Fundamental Act on the Establishment and Distribution of Income (JP 68, p. 367) introduced self-management and social agreements on distribution on a voluntary basis, which was a solution discussed much earlier (8, p. 257; 62, p. 320) and even once rejected as 'corporativist' (see p. 117).

The Act further introduced what is called 'social guidance of distribution' by republics and the Federation 'to foster the general social development, the equalisation of conditions for earning incomes, the securing of a material base of work and consistent distribution according to work'. The social guidance of distribution thus became one of the basic elements of planning (JP 68, p. 368).

The Fundamental Act also contained a provision authorising socio-political organisations to introduce 'special measures' to restrain unwarranted distribution not based on labour results. The main special measure was expected to be progressive taxation of incomes in excess of those agreed or determined by law.

Ekonomska politika (5.2.68) reported on resistance to progressive taxation, which some described as 'anti-self-management'; this it found illogical because the very critics of progression thought it entirely normal that various party committees should decide the level of incomes acceptable from a moral-political viewpoint. *Ekonomska politika* (see also Ep 12.11.66) was in favour of indirect influence through taxation and monetary policy while it considered direct intervention like fixing wage ceilings or determing 'minimum accumulation' as an admission 'that the system could not reproduce itself on the basis of its own laws', i.e. could not work without constant government and party interference.

The voluntary coordination of incomes by agreement was soon considered insufficient (cf. B 9.4.71) and, led by Slovenia, one republic after another adopted acts on social guidance of income distribution (B 18.9.70 and 22.6.71). They determined the procedures for the conclusion of social contracts and self-management agreements on income distribution which were supposed to protect accumulation and foster creativity. The provisions were taken over by the 1974 Constitution so that the 1975 Social Contract on the Common Foundations of the Self-Management Regulation of Income and Distribution of Resources for Personal Income (JP 75, p. 161) was based on its Art. 124.

The figures quoted earlier show that the results are not encouraging. The arrangements are so complicated that the choice becomes either to produce the agreements too late or produce them in such a hurry that they are not of much practical value (Ep 9.2.76). Either way, the agreements are widely disregarded and in any case do not contain clear-cut criteria but are formal and generalised (Ep 13., 20.12.76, 8.4.77).

The main problem is that it is almost impossible to know how to formulate distribution criteria. The simplest approach is to make personal incomes proportionate to an enterprise's income per worker (Ep 5.4.76). This solution, however, disregards different capital intensity, market structure and other circumstances. There are attempts at 'cleansing' the income of these elements, but this is 'very difficult' (Ep 18.5.75). There is the further difficulty of the allocation of income between personal incomes and accumulation. Proportionality is one way out, but it is unsatisfactory. One rule considered again was that unearned income (earnings from money lent to other enterprises) should be allotted to accumulation. But what is 'unearned' income? (D 14.2.76). So the usual provision was to limit the total distribution of personal incomes, but a consequence of this is lack of interest on the part of workers. It would be necessary to give the workers a permanent interest in the development of the enterprise with which he 'had associated his past labour' (Ep 18.8.75) (see p. 218). But how could this be achieved?

Finally there remains the question of how to distribute the total amount allotted for personal incomes to individual workers. Monthly earnings are mostly distributed irrespective of 'the labour actually contributed' (D 21.6.77). However, it is not known how to measure 'the labour contribution of workers' although the 1975 Social Contract demands that differences not based on that should be made impossible. Formal criteria like education are the only ones that remain.

At the end of 1977, a campaign came underway to make the workers decide more directly on reproduction and personal incomes by obligating all working organisations to adopt appropriate self-management agreements under the Act of Associated Labour of 1976 (Ep 8.8.77) by means of referenda which required the mobilisation of all categories of working people in order to guarantee the democratic quality of the procedure (Ep 26.12.77). Trade unions were involved and the 'social community' helped. *Ekonomska politika* (19.9.77) was very sceptical. It expected that most of these agreements on remuneration and evaluation of work would be hardly usable because they would be either simply copied from somewhere or badly drafted for lack of knowledge and skill.

Excessive distribution has not stopped; it would be surprising if it did because, especially at the lower level of agreements, the measures to contain excesses are in the hands of producers of a particular branch or region, who themselves decide what they are to be paid. As long as they can push up prices or have their losses and investment covered from other sources, the temptation to agree on high personal incomes must be very strong.

9.5 CONDITIONS OF WORK AND SOCIAL PAYMENTS

The Constitution of 1963 proclaimed that safety at work was both the right and the duty of the self-managing worker, but the measures required could be introduced only against resistance, incomprehension and difficulties. The main reason was apparently the shortage of material resources (JP 70, p. 125). Between 1965 and 1976, the number of injuries at work was 280,000 per year or 60 per 1000 workers. The number of fatal injuries reached its peak of 820 in 1971 and fell to 622 in 1976 (SG 73, p. 291, SG 77, p. 317, JP 74, p. 347).

The theme of limited resources kept recurring. After the initial belief that socialism meant almost unlimited resources for social services, President Tito himself described the consequences:

> Immediately after the war, we introduced a series of measures beyond our material possibilities, for instance, with respect to social insurance and other social benefits, which are now causing difficulties. But we cannot go back on this so that we could start afresh in a more realistic way. We were wrong not to begin at a level in line with our material possibilities; because of that mistake we suffer now, but we have to persist. All our citizens know that. All sorts of social benefits of which nobody dreamt before are now considered by people to be their natural due. People think that our standard of living must constantly rise and I agree with them. (B 24.3.65)

A sense of proportion was lacking so that expenditure on social insurance (health, pensions and children's allowances) remained high and reached 12.5 per cent of national income (in Slovenia 15 per cent) in the late 1960s. According to critics, some enjoyed expensive treatment while others had to pay for it, so that the time had come to distinguish between solidarity and medical care at somebody else's expense (Ep 21.10.68).

In 1966, the government tried to stop the ever higher expenditure and limited social insurance contributions to 20.5 per cent of workers' incomes, which made likely a deficit of between dinars 350 million and one billion ($ 28 to 80 million, the upper figure being more than 1 per cent of the national income). The government was sharply criticised for first giving the population rights under the national insurance scheme and then restricting its financial resources by an upper limit on contributions which was claimed to be against the spirit of self-management (B 13.10.66, 25.8.73; 121, p. 178).

The government of Slovenia in particular set out to reduce the specific contributions for the health service from 7 per cent to 6 per cent of personal incomes, but was defeated in the Social-Medical Chamber of the Slovene parliament on 7 December 1966. Laudable as it may have been that the then Premier Janko Smole and his colleagues became the first communist government in the world to resign when voted down in parliament, they were in fact caught in Yugoslav doctrinairism. Insisting that the country be ruled not just by citizens but by 'direct producers', the Yugoslav communists led by the ideologist Kardelj devised the kind of corporativist state described on p. 105. 'Direct producers' from the appropriate activities sat in each of the four chambers with the right of blocking for six months any bill concerning their special field. In the Slovene case, the Social-Medical Chamber threw out the government proposal because it would obviously have adversely affected the members and their colleagues. It was as absurd as if the British Medical Association could vote out the government at Westminster over the financing of the National Health Service. In Yugoslavia, some people said this (B 10.12.66) and the government was reinstated after the rebellious chamber had been 'persuaded' to reverse its vote.

At the federal level, it was decided to cut insurance payments for sick leave, to make conditions for pensions more stringent, to means test child allowances, to shorten maternity leave from 135 to 105 days, to limit social insurance contributions to 19 per cent (plus 1 per cent for reserves) of personal incomes and to increase the federal tax on incomes from 3.5 to 4.9 per cent (B 9.12.66).

In consequence, social insurance organisations claimed that they could not remain solvent without introducing further direct participation by the insured in the cost of the health service. The prescription charge was raised from 1.5 to 2 dinars (about 17 US cents) and some medicaments were taken off the approved lists; the insured had to pay one dinar for general practitioner's treatment, 2 dinars for specialist treatment (with the exception of some contagious diseases) and 10 to 50 per cent of costs for dental treatment, while stays in spas would no longer be chargeable to social insurance.

The critics of these measures mainly insisted that health institutions should have been made to work more rationally instead. Hospitals and other institutions were accused of being in a monopolistic position and unduly raising the salaries of their staff. There were suggestions that work norms should be introduced for medical treatment (B 12.10., 15.12.66 and 29.1.67). Against this it was argued that each day 200,000 employed were on sick leave, about 6 per cent of the total number.

The 1966 austerity measures had some short term effect (SG 73, p. 291, SG 76, p. 316): the number of medicaments issued to the insured fell from almost 78 million in 1965 to just under 60 million in 1967, but then rose to over 126 million by 1976. The number of cases treated in hospitals for the same years were 1,870,000, 1,646,000 and 2,034,000. The rise was out of proportion to the numbers of directly insured (and insured family members): 1965, 4.2 million (+6.9 million), 1968, 4.2million (+7 million), 1976, 5.5 million (+8.6 million). The overall deficit of health insurance fell from dinars 84 million in 1966 and dinars 247 million in 1967, to dinars 34 million in 1968, but rose to dinars 194 million in 1970 (JP 71, p. 329).

In 1969, the Federal Assembly adopted a new Act on Health

Insurance which however was only a framework with the details left to individual republics.

The dissatisfaction with the health service both among patients and doctors was such that the debate on the merits of private surgeries was renewed in the mid-1960s although they had been abolished as late as 1958 (Ep 17.9.66). Doctors were said to be half-physicians and half-bureaucrats (B 9.10.65). In 1969, the average monthly income of a medical consultant was dinars 2560 (JP 71, p. 321) which at the official rate was just over $200. It was hardly surprising that some doctors were prepared to take 'private payments' concealed in envelopes and that many wanted the re-introduction of private patients, called self-payers (D 8–9.8.69). The trade unions came out against private treatment and, in the end, some medical associations followed this lead, apparently under outside influence (NR 20.3.70). Croatia, nonetheless, introduced private practice and the question was discussed again in 1977 (D 18.10.77).

The problems with pensions were similar to those with health service. Pension rights were introduced at a lavish level (see p. 54) and maintained only under strain. The Fundamental Act on Pension Insurance (JP 66, p. 14), amended more than once a year, did not contain all the pension rights envisaged in the 1963 Constitution. Amid protests, the Federal Constitutional Court organised a conference on its constitutionality, only to state that there could be no question of any violation of the Constitution because pensions did not move in line with personal incomes since the 'community' could not provide them, especially as the number of those working in the social sector could not keep up with the number of pensioners. In 1965, there were about four million employed and 850,000 pensioners, in 1967 the number of the employed had not risen, but the number of pensioners had reached one million (B 23.5.67).

By 1975, the number of pensioners rose to 1,353,000, of which 508,000 were old age pensioners (average pension about 74 per cent of average personal income), 467,000 invalid pensioners (48 per cent) and 365,000 family members entitled to pensions (41 per cent) (SG 77, p. 316, JP 71, p. 334). In the 1970s, legal provisions on pensions also became part of jurisdiction by republics so that they vary from region to region.

Amid long debates (see p. 54) the number of child allowances reached a peak of just under 3 million in 1966 and fell to about 1,700,000 in the 1970s. In 1973 the average allowance per child was dinars 1391 per year or dinars 116 per month which was about 6 per cent of the average personal income (SG 73, pp. 283 and 292) and then rose to dinars 2006 per year, dinars 167 per month, equal to about 5 per cent of average income in 1975 (SG 77, p. 31 and p. 317).

The reform of housing (see p. 63) was an integral part of the 1965 reform. It introduced the so-called 'housing enterprises' which were to look after accomodation and keep it in good repair (B 25.7.65). It immediately became clear that 'housing enterprises' would not have sufficient finance even to repair 'leaky roofs' (B 6.2.66), although enterprises were asked to pay subsidies, in a roundabout way, until rents for old houses caught up with those for new ones by means of 25 per cent per year rises.

In the end, the share of housing rents in average personal expenditure remained at about 4 per cent in the 1970s also (SG 76, p. 317) but the living space per person increased from 8.7 square metres in 1951 to 9.9 square metres in 1961, and to 12.2 square metres in 1971 (SG 76, p. 324). Often communal services could not keep up with construction so that for instance in 1965, 100,000 inhabitants of Belgrade were without water, sewers and tarmacadam streets (B 28.12.65).

A large proportion of the new housing was built by private citizens. In 1965, 'society' was responsible for building over 44,000 units, private owner-occupiers for over 77,000 units; in 1976, the figures were 61,000 vs. 89,000 (SG 76, p. 195, SG 77, p. 216). Enterprises tended to subsidise their employees, but *Ekonomska politika* (5.2.66) complained that in Belgrade, a leading employee was on average granted more than dinars 5000 for a mortgage, while manual workers obtained less than dinars 200. The comment was that the Yugoslav authorities had promised everybody more than they could be given in the most developed countries in the world (Ep 1.1.66) but then could not fulfil their promises so that only the best off were given privileges under the slogan of solidarity, humanism, culture and progress (Ep 5.2.66). Later on it was said that the housing problem must be tackled from 'class' positions (B 29.10.73).

Initially the communist government also promised that everybody would be able to enjoy a holiday away from home once a year. It was reported in 1974 that in Serbia only every tenth worker used government-sponsored holiday homes, 60 per cent stayed at home while the rest made their own arrangements. Manual workers went least on holidays because almost 80 per cent had incomes below 2000 dinars (about $118) per month and only 40 per cent of all employees were given a holiday bonus of dinars 500 per year. The trade-union official who revealed these data concluded: 'The view has spread that holidays and leisure are a private matter—this is a technocratic and managerial standpoint . . . ' (B 28.2.74, cf. Ep 21.1.74, D 8.4.76). He demanded a new approach also on a 'class' basis.

In the view of *Ekonomska politika*, it was surprising that there had not been a rebellion as yet. Workers were being asked to contribute for all sorts of services and very often not even told on their pay packets what the various contributions were for. Then the funds collected were used to subsidise a small group.

The workers were also led to expect society to provide for the education of their children up to the highest level. In the 1950s many students were in fact given scholarships and others were allowed to receive child allowances until the end of their studies. At universities the figures for 1959–60 were: 84,000 students, of whom 24,000 were getting scholarships of on average 6600 old dinars per month, and 28,000 were in receipt of child allowances (SG 61, p. 286). But child allowances were phased out in 1965–6 and out of 170,000 students only 21,000 were receiving scholarships (B 22.1.66). Scholarship payments should have come from economic organisations but they were very reluctant to part with the money. By 1969–70 the total number of students increased to 240,000 of whom only 11,000 were receiving scholarships of just under 300 dinars per month (SG 70, pp. 283 and 289). On the other hand, 41,000 students were in receipt of monthly credits of 100 to 400 dinars (SG 70, p. 290). For later years data on scholarships and credits to students have no longer been published. The number of students, however, rose to over 400,000 in 1976 (SG 77, p. 337).

In turn, the students were working without much enthusiasm. In 1965 one half of all students never bothered to graduate while the rest took over 6 years on average to complete their first degree (B 3.12.65). In 1975, only about 17 per cent graduated within the regular period (SG 76, p. 336) and only about 30 per cent graduated at all (D 6.11.76).

In conclusion, conditions of work and social services turned out to be much more difficult to improve than was first thought. Workers have to make do with much less than they were originally led to expect. And under self-management, they often prefer to raise their own personal incomes rather than use enterprises' revenue for the improvement of work conditions and additional benefits.

10: Financial Indiscipline

10.1 BANKING AND CREDIT

In the 1950s, when wages were closely restricted, monetary and credit policies were intended to prevent unwarranted investment and stockpiling, so that it was legitimate even then to claim that credit was one of the most important problems of the Yugoslav economy (118, p. 234). But credit was instead used to allow enterprises producing items not in demand to continue their operations so that it was turned into concealed subsidies (see p. 22). Regular repayment of credits should have been required (Mincev, Ep 4.3.61) but was not.

As if to counter this abuse of credits, banks were continually reorganised, though this could not make them function properly. Vuckovic (118, p. 246 ff.) counted seven reorganisations up till 1957, and more were to follow, with a particularly radical one in 1961. Decentralisation fostered by the 1961 and 1965 reforms further underlined the role of banking and credit policies (30, p. 50) because from then on financial stabilisation was also expected to keep enterprise and personal incomes within limits.

Until 1961 the National Bank remained—despite all the changes—the main dispenser of short-term credits, which apparently had the effect that the criteria adopted were very formal. Furthermore, credit plans based on the federal social plans often demanded the financing of unprofitable enterprises. The reform of 1961 (Sl 10/61) turned the National Bank into a normal central bank, preserved the three specialised banks—the Foreign Trade, Agricultural and Investment Banks—brought republic banks into existence and transformed the communal banks from their previous role as savings banks into local business banks, performing the main credit allocation function. The National Bank was to feed the rest of the banking system with credits through discount operations (30, p. 54) within the limits imposed by the Federal Social Plan. It could also influence their operations by varying their obligatory reserves deposited with itself up to the upper limit of 35 per cent. The business banks were to allocate both investments and short-term credits according to profitability.

Banks charged interest on credits, but the proceeds came under the jurisdiction (for practical purposes became the property) of the Federation in the case of the National Banks, in other cases they were paid into a separate credit fund which could not be distributed to bank employees. The workers' councils of the banks could only dispose of the 'net income of the bank', consisting mainly of bank charges, and could not influence banking operations. These were in the hands of boards appointed by the political authorities from among candidates nominated by outside self-management bodies. In exchange, the economic organisations had to guarantee the liabilities of communal banks in conjunction with their founders, the local political authorities.

In spite of the changes in rules (26, p. 296) — or perhaps because of them — enterprises continued to function as before. The inconsistent implementation of rules was notorious ('traditional', according to Ep 19., 26.10.63), sanctions were not applied (Ep 17.10.64) and there were always numerous exceptions.

The 1963 definition of credit policy was that sufficient money should be supplied to keep the existing factors of production employed (77, p. 74). This policy was supposed to have a neutral effect, but in fact it allowed all accumulation plus additional credit to be channelled into fixed investment (Ep 12.7.64).

The new bank arrangements prevented losses from falling on bank employees — they were met from the special reserve funds formed from interest charges. Therefore the employees had no incentive to see that credits were repaid (Ep 22.8.64). Neither had leading managers, who were appointed by political authorities. On the other hand, it would have been wrong to make employees responsible since the main decisions were taken by bank management rather than self-management bodies (Ep 14.11.64).

The banking system remained unresponsive to economic criteria and was bureaucratic or — as it was called in Yugoslavia — 'bankocratic' (Ep 21.5.64). The government continued blocking and restricting the bank deposits of enterprises and earmarking them for particular purposes (30, p. 21). Deposits of successful enterprises could thus be blocked, while unprofitable enterprises obtained funds from banks. Sometimes good enterprises lost through accumulation rather than gained (26, p. 297). Moreover, the influence of local political authorities who tried to keep the credits of 'their banks' on their territory, obstructed capital mobility (26, pp. 295–7; 30, p. 31).

A reduction of government interference with economic development, (*deetatizacija*), especially with expanded reproduction, by means of an adequate banking and credit system, became an important postulate (Milentije Popovic, Ep 17.10.64). The Federal Assembly approved a Resolution on Banking and Credit on 17 April 1964 which proposed the abolition of investment funds (see p. 89), demanded that henceforth their optimal use within the framework of social plans must be assured and enjoined the social-political communities to abandon direct allocation of resources and limit themselves to general regulations and social plans (annual social plans were, however, abolished in 1966). According to the Resolution, the responsibility for placing 'social reproduction resources' was to be entrusted to the banking system which was to have full business independence, while the National Bank was to take over the task of influencing the circulation of capital and of stabilising the economy.

At the end of March 1965 (Sl 12/65) this reform programme was implemented. Under the new rules, banks could be established, not only by political authorities but by working organisations themselves in cooperation with each other and with political authorities (and even with private citizens) (JP 65, p. 221). A new bank had to be licensed by the republic, unless a political authority was involved, and had to possess a certain minimum capital, but could operate all over Yugoslavia.

The actual management of banks passed from political appointees to nominees of the organisations which founded the bank and contributed to capital though none could have more than 10 per cent of the votes. The bank's workers' collective could also be represented on the bank's management assembly but with at the most 10 per cent of the votes. The assembly could decide to add the bank's net income to its capital (credit fund) and to the special reserve fund and even cancel the payment of interest to the contributors of capital. Political authorities had to leave their share of earnings in the bank, but enjoyed the right to determine to what use their contribution should be put. If however this particular use did not bring a normal return, they had to top it up out of their budget. The banks themselves had to publicise what principles they would follow in their lending, which was presumably an attempt at introducing some kind of planning.

But whatever was done, however the banks were reorganised, low credit expansion led to low growth, high credit expansion to stockpiling and underutilised capacities. After the 1965 reform there was also a high rate of increase of prices and personal incomes, especially in 1966. This prompted the government to take a second step in the reform (66, p. 240) by amending the Acts on Banks and Credit and on the National

Bank of Yugoslavia adopted the year before. This 'second step' was supposed to mean a transition from 'qualitative' to 'quantitative' criteria for the issue of credits (JP 67, p. 125 and p. 267), roughly speaking a change from the 'banking' to the 'currency' principle in the traditional terminology. While earlier the central bank laid down what kind of credits it was prepared to re-finance, now it only determined the level of credit to which it was ready to go. This arrangement was intended to give more freedom to commercial banks to act in an independent business-like way (66, p. 248).

In addition to a deposit with the central bank of up to 35 per cent of their own deposits, the bank had to have a 50 per cent liquidity ratio, i.e. assets with a maturity of less than 3 months, and a 6 to 8 per cent cash ratio. The National Bank would channel funds to them through discount operations (*re-eskont*), mainly of the newly introduced exchange bills. But credits could no longer rise above the total of banks' own capital and customers' deposits, so that no bank could again become 'a distributor of money obtained on credit from the National Bank' (JP 67, p. 129).

As a measure of last resort, ceilings could be imposed on credit expansion by business banks. Kraigher also advocated (66, p. 276) a rise in the interest rate from 8 to 10 per cent because he thought that it would otherwise be too low. This was despite previous complaints that interest rates were too high rather than too low because of the twofold interest which Yugoslav enterprises had to pay if they borrowed (see p. 45). Thus the cost of a loan in 1964, for instance (Ep 10.10.64), was twice 6 per cent, once to the bank and then a tax of the same amount, plus the bank charge of 1.5 per cent. This double interest rate was abolished at the beginning of 1971 when the interest-like tax was eliminated.

In 1967 the money supply fell by 2 per cent, although it is questionable whether this was due to the sophisticated controls or to the will to keep credit expansion down. At any rate, the money supply (see Table 6.3) shot up by 24 per cent in 1968, 42.3 per cent in 1972 and 52.7 per cent in 1976.

By 1966 Boris Kraigher (66, p. 247) had no illusions. In his view, the 'mass of credit and money' did not sufficiently affect the working of the economy. In spite of monetary stringency, inventories were rising and were twice to three times as high as in comparable Western economies; this was particularly true of engineering. Events seemed to repeat themselves without end.

10.2 ILLIQUIDITY

Just as in 1962 the attempt to prevent distortions in the economy by credit stringency in the mid-1960s pushed the economy into what was called *nelikvidnost* (illiquidity, moneylessness), a state described by the English terms insolvency or problems of cash-flow. It indicates that a firm has not kept a sufficient part of its assets in cash and other liquid forms to be able to honour its short-term liabilities. Insolvency does not necessarily mean that the total assets of an enterprise are worth less than its total liabilities, though it may mean that also. Insolvency does make a firm suspect, as stressed by *Ekonomska politika* (7.9.69) when it said that in a normal market economy firms may be liquidated for insolvency and not only when losses have become evident.

Banks should in principle be ready to finance any business operation that results in cash wherewith to repay the bank credit. But in the general euphoria of a boom it is easy for both banks and firms to misjudge the physical limitations of production and thus bring about a crisis. Therefore, central banks tend to impose limits on the expansion of central bank credit (high powered money) and bank credit which, however, hits both unviable and viable operations; the impact on the latter is worse the less capable the banks are of differentiating between economic activities with a prospect of success (equal to sale and recovery of cash with a gain) and those with no prospect (i.e. sale at a loss or no sale at all).

In Yugoslavia the application of monetary and credit stringency was especially difficult because the banks were particularly bad at judging the soundness of business operations and firms were very unscrupulous in taking on loans which they knew they would not be able to repay (B 16.7.70, Ep. 26.6.70, see p. 29). Moreover, there were always strong political pressures to disregard the distinction because it implied payment of only minimum personal incomes to workers, closures, unemployment etc. The price of avoiding short-term worries was not only to allow distortions to continue but to make them worse.

The government correctly explained the Yugoslav version of illiquidity as the expression of deep-seated disturbances in production and distribution and consumption which exceeded the economy's physical possibilities. The government blamed this state of affairs on an inadequate financial and monetary system, but *Ekonomska politika* (8.1.69) bluntly said the trouble was that, in Yugoslavia, anybody could order goods, invest, distribute and consume without paying for it. The guilty persons were not punished by being deprived, though bankruptcy, of the right independently to manage social property or budget revenue. The government had no real answer but to suggest that debtors should not be favoured and legal rules should not be infringed.

Other crises of illiquidity followed in 1971 and 1975. In discussing the reasons for these repeated crises, the distinction has to be stressed between genuine shortage of liquidity and business operations which ended in losses; the former imply a misjudgement in timing, the latter something far more fundamental, a misjudgement in the structure of production. While the first variety can be at least alleviated by credit expansion, the second was not caused by a lack of liquidity and could not be resolved through a larger supply of credit (JP 74, p. 320; 92, p. 88 and p. 155), but at best papered over. Nonetheless, illiquidity was, of course, worse when there was a slow-down or even reduction in monetary expansion.

The slow-down in credit expansion should in no way be fatal for enterprises, but it does require that an even larger part of enterprises' assets be kept in the form of cash than was usual.

In spite of the initial segregation of banks and their subsequent mergers (92, p. 99)—there were 351 independent banks in 1962, reduced to 67 by 1969—bank transfers took a long time so that the so-called 'float', money in transit, amounted to about one-fifth of the total money assets of business organisations (92, p. 110). The use of a large part of deposits was limited (see p. 147), so that they in fact represented only quasi-money, either for legal reasons—restricted deposits—or because of the need to accumulate money for later use, i.e. investment—time deposits. The government obliged working organisations to hold money as reserves or for investment on restricted deposits, which obviously slowed down its circulation. The same was sometimes true of money intended for international transactions. In 1966, almost 60 per cent of monetary resources were thus restricted, and this percentage rose to almost 80 per cent in 1969, to fall to 44 per cent in 1975 (calculated from SG 76, p. 291).

Cost increases and tax payments could further reduce liquid resources in the hands of business organisations (JP 74, p. 316; 92, p. 111). The payment of taxes on personal incomes was due before the commodities produced by the labour employed left the enterprises (92, p. 112) (see p. 131).

Finally, illiquidity was caused by switching short-term financial resources to the financing of investment which, even if appropriate, yields the return to repay the debts only in the longer term, so that the enterprises do not possess the necessary cash when the time for repayment falls due (92, p. 123, JP 74, p. 318). Something similar is, of course, true if goods produced are not sold immediately, but remain for some time in stock even though they may be eventually saleable (JP 74, p. 319; 92, p. 125). This was combined with insufficient depreciation and accumulation which did not cover the replacement cost of capacity, let alone expansion (92, p. 113).

But all these reasons for illiquidity are only a question of timing, of the kind of credit that is available, not of failure. Even if depreciation and accumulation are insufficient, the economy can continue functioning, if there are savings somewhere else. Of course, under the circumstances, the 'ownership' passes into different hands. Although, in Yugoslavia, this is allegedly not possible because ownership is 'social', it shows in the amount of borrowed social capital as opposed to freely available social capital, in the form of a particular Yugoslav version of high gearing, the relationship between an enterprise's 'owned' and borrowed capital.

In the period 1971–5, 31.7 per cent of fixed investment was financed out of the resources belonging to business organisations, 6.0 per cent out of the resources of non-business organisations, 46.3 per cent out of bank investment credits and 16.0 per cent out of the resources of political authorities (JP 76, p. 462) (see p. 134). With respect to working capital the proportions must have been even worse for business enterprises. Although the interest-like tax was abolished, enterprises still have to pay interest on borrowed capital so that there are now complaints that these changes overburden enterprises (Ep 28.11.77). But if enterprises do not save enough to finance their own operations, this overburdening is a necessary consequence unless the enterprises are to be allowed to have their cake and eat it.

Where the problem is no longer timing, but the production of goods that cannot be sold or the establishment of capacity to produce such goods (92 pp. 139, 151), the situation becomes intractable. It can also show in the form of unpaid claims of enterprises on each other or on other organisations, but this only means that enterprises have been selling to others that produce goods which cannot be sold or put up unutilisable plant or have no financial cover for part of their activity. In the period 1965–73 about 20 per cent of invoiced sales remained unpaid (JP 74, p. 321). Of these, 2.3 per cent were unpaid sales to non-business organisations.

The Yugoslav authorities tried to enforce both payments discipline and production discipline by the same monetary policy (JP 69, p. 347) so that, in the end, even those business operations which were legitimate could not be carried out because of lack of money. On the other hand, the production structure did not improve (Ep 4.4.77).

At times of monetary stringency enterprises could not pay their debts to each other because of their lack of liquidity and so began to grant each other more and more trade credit, either voluntarily in their eagerness to sell their goods or involuntarily because of the unexpected failure of the customer to pay (JP 66, p. 457). This network of trade credits can be considered a form of additional money, or an increase in the velocity of circulation, which to some extent neutralised monetary policy. But illiquidity and mutual indebtedness could also arise in times of expanding activity and ample money supply, if all Yugoslav institutions and citizens tried to spend more than they had earned and more than was produced (JP 69, p. 347).

If enterprises are trying to sell goods which are not particularly attractive, they pay little attention to the solvency of their customers and eventually a 'dictatorship of debtors' comes about (B 1.7.71) in an atmosphere of general irresponsibility. The debtors may well be taken to court but courts cannot make them pay any more than can the creditors, who are in turn debtors themselves. Often debtors reviled creditor enterprises and accused them of monopolism, arbitrariness, misunderstanding of the economic situation; in short, of slowing down economic development.

In an attempt to remedy illiquidity, the Federal Assembly adopted an Act on the Special Method of Compensation of Some Debts of Users of Social Resources at the end of March 1968. This improved the percentage of paid invoices to over 85 per cent in 1968, but in the first half of 1969 it was down again to 63 per cent. A large part of enterprises' assets and revenue was immobilised in unpaid claims on customers. In 1969, total claims of economic organisations on customers and suppliers (payments in advance) amounted to dinars 74 billion, their total debts to them to dinars 61 billion (1969 GSP dinars 132 billion). This means that their claims on customers outside the business community amounted to about dinars 13 billions.

In the first half of 1969, 34 per cent (within industry 68 per cent) of economic organisations could not regularly pay their liabilities and 29 per cent (within industry 60 per cent) could pay the personal incomes of their staff only by falling back on reserves, and 20 per cent of industrial organisations had their giro-accounts blocked for 30 or more days.

At the end of June 1969, construction and equipment industries had claims on investors amounting to dinars 9.3 billion of which dinars 5.5. billion were without assured financing. Probably claims without financial backing were actually higher because many investors submitted fictitious cover documents.

Organisations with insufficient reserves borrowed from whomever they could, mostly from banks. Banks, in turn, often could not provide finance which they were under contractual obligation to supply, because they were unable to recover credits from illiquid enterprises (JP 69, p. 347). From 1967 the National Bank no longer guaranteed the liquidity of banks and they frequently found themselves with insufficient liquidity (92, pp. 99 ff, 134).

'Clearings' of debts, as in 1962 and 1968, could have provided a partial solution, had the rise in the velocity of circulation been the only problem, but there was a considerable disequilibrium between enterprises, political authorities and the public. Some enterprises had losses and some political authorities insufficient revenue to pay for what they had undertaken. But the sinners were not taken over or liquidated, so that they heaped losses upon losses (Ep 2.6.69). Successful enterprises were then forced to lend to them—although they tried to hide their surpluses—(Ep 24.6.68) and the losses again froze the credits in inventories, leaving those who had no sales problems without money. Managers had to spend much of their time trying to find money for personal incomes instead of doing their job (D 26.7.71).

Under these conditions, mutual cancelling of debts could not achieve much. In fact, in 1971, illiquidity was again reaching a critical limit although it had been established earlier 'which working collectives were appropriating the resources of others — the money of their creditors', in other words, which were bad collectives exploiting good collectives (D 26.7.71). As early as 1965 it became apparent (JP 65, p. 464) that illiquidity originated in the construction, electrical and mechanical engineering industries, because they had difficulty in selling and, when they did sell, difficulty in getting payment from investors. The mutual debt cancellation of 1968 pinpointed the foci of illiquidity as the 80 largest enterprises in Yugoslavia, which owed dinars 10.5 billion more than was owed to them. It was true that these communist giants (see p. 37) were also owed much by the government, but without orders from political authorities their capacity utilisation would have been lower still. At the beginning of 1972, the 'non-economy' (non-business organisations) owed dinars 7.5 billion to enterprises.

In view of this situation, the then Vice-Chairman of the Federal Executive Council, Jakov Sirotkovic (B 10.8.71, D 28.8.71), thought that the 'clearing of debts' had been tried and had established the sources of illiquidity. In view of this, no general measures were possible since some enterprises were in a dire state because either their investment or their production were wrong. It seems that a temporary solution was again sought in credit expansion.

In 1974 signs of another wave of illiquidity became noticeable. Unpaid invoices were up to 36 per cent (Ep 7.10.74). At the end of September 1975, economic organisations had claims amounting to more than dinars 273 billion (1975 GSP dinars 497 billion) on customers and owed dinars 262 billion to banks.

This time it was hoped that the measures taken would be more lasting. At the end of 1975, an Act on the Safeguarding of Payments between Users of Social Resources was adopted, which required that deliveries be paid within ten days of receipt of the invoice and that, in many instances, payments be guaranteed by bills of exchange endorsed by banks. The 'new payments system' was preceded by a multilateral cancellation of debts. It was estimated (Ep 29.3.77) that the amount of unpaid debts was dinars 160 billion and that debts of 119 billion were reported but only dinars 18.3 billion cancelled. The remaining debts had to be covered by bills of exchange with endorsement.

Simultaneously the National Bank allowed a considerable expansion of credit; from 1975 to 1976 the money supply jumped by almost 57 per cent (see Table 6.3). The intention was obviously not to restrict anybody because of the lack of liquidity, but to prevent ficticious production at the same time.

10.3 DEBTS AND LOSSES

The root-cause of illiquidity, and its intractability, was losses (see p. 134 ff). In 1976 losses rose to dinars 17.2 billion (Ep 18.9.77) from dinars 11.2 billion in 1975 (JP 76, p. 330) calculated on the same basis, which is a nominal rise of about 54 per cent and a real rise of about 30 per cent, bringing the losses up to just under 5 per cent of enterprises' income. A later estimate for 1976 was losses of dinars 21.7 billion, which is 6 per cent of enterprises' income. When the deputy director of the Social Accountancy Service, Dr Milivoje Nikolic, announced this revised figure, he also explained how complicated it was to calculate losses because of the difficulty of properly distinguishing income vis-à-vis costs and inventories, and forecast that losses in 1977 would be even larger as a percentage of enterprises' income (Ep 19.9. and 28.11.77). In 1976 1715 organisations of associated labour in industry, mining and forestry, which comprised 34 per cent of all basic organisations of associated labour (Ep 27.6.77) incurred losses.

In this context it should not be forgotten that figures for losses are frequently too low because some enterprises carry unsaleable goods and bad debts as assets (JP 69, p. 351; 92, pp. 139 and 147) although they should be written off. The possible overvaluation of inventories has been estimated at 20 per cent, which would represent a once-for-all addition to losses of about 9 per cent of enterprises' income.

The year 1976 was particularly bad, but losses had existed for a very long time. The figures for 1970–5 were mentioned (see p. 134). *Jugoslovenski pregled* 1969 (p. 349) published data for the preceding period. In 1966 769 enterprises made losses amounting to dinars 340 million, in 1967 1577 enterprises lost dinars 1252 million (1.5 per cent of enterprises GSP) and in 1968 1724 enterprises lost dinars 1600 million (1.7 per cent of enterprises' GSP). In 1968, the number of enterprises making losses was 10.2 per cent of the total number, with 14.6 per cent of the labour force. As much as 58 per cent of all losses were concentrated in 46 working organisations (B 27.7.69). In 1976 117 enterprises (3 per cent of basic organisations) were responsible for 40 per cent of total losses (Ep 14.2.77). In addition to enterprises with losses, many were at the margin of profitability in 1968 (JP 69, p. 199) as well as later (D 3.3.77), but the financial situation of individual enterprises was considered a business secret and, therefore, not publicly discussed (Ep 9.8.71).

Of the total loss of dinars 17.2 billion (preliminary estimate) in 1976, losses amounting to dinars 15.7 billion had been covered by July 1977. The financial resources for this operation were drawn from banks to the tune of dinars 6 billion (38.2 per cent), from joint reserve funds — dinars 4.8 billion (30.4 per cent), and from funds established for this purpose by republic and province legislation — 3 billion (18.8 per cent). Losses amounting to dinars 1.2 billion (7.6 per cent) were covered by other basic organisations within the same working organisation and losses of dinars 0.78 billion were met from other sources, mainly by writing off debts (Polajnar, Ep 18.7.77). Debts of dinars 1.4 billion remained uncovered.

In the preceding period 1970–5 the cover for losses was obtained in similar ways except that a considerable role was played by the refund of taxes to the organisations with losses. The refunds covered just under 20 per cent of losses (JP 76, p. 331). The purpose was to prevent political authorities from spending money taken out of the ailing parts of the economy.

Enterprises working at a loss have to undergo a financial reorganisation (*sanacija*) (JP 70, p. 200, JP 76, p. 331). In the late 1960s there was again much discussion of receivership, bankruptcy and liquidation of enterprises (e.g. B 9.9.67, D 16.12.67), but then doubts appeared about whether these institutions were compatible with self-management (B 29.7., 4.9., 11.12.69). Very few bankruptcy procedures have actually been started: the peak was reached in 1967, with 86, mainly small, enterprises (JP 70, p. 200). In 1968, there were about 1500 enterprises with losses, but only 57 were liquidated (Kersnic, NR 16.7.69).

There were calls to make bankruptcy more frequent and also more painful for both the managers and workers concerned (Kersnic NR 16.7.69, B 26.12.69), but those opposing such developments prevailed in the end (B 2 and 24.2.71). Bankruptcy does not make sense under Yugoslav conditions; nobody loses his property, which is the main deterrent under capitalism, and the workers are deemed to have the right to work. As previously stressed, they cannot be held responsible for the working of the enterprise, as the investment decisions at least are rarely taken by those who are still in the enterprise when the losses caused by wrong decisions make themselves felt, while there can be no doubt that irrational investment is among the more important causes of losses (Ep 7.2.77).

Financial reorganisations, therefore, remain the way of dealing with losses. But these *sanacije* have become a pure formality, an 'administrative and book-keeping transaction' (D 3.3.77, Ep 11.4, 27.6.77), while enterprises continue to function in the old manner (Ep 4.7.77). Sometimes there are no real reorganisation programmes at all (Ep 26.7.76), at other times the programmes are not implemented (Ep 12.7.76). In 1977 the government was clearly aware that the elimination of losses would require the elimination of their basic causes which, however, were closely linked with the functioning of the whole Yugoslav system (Ep 7.2.77).

Losses continue and mean one of two things: the loss-making organisation must be cross-subsidised by other basic organisations within the same enterprise, or by other enterprises through the fund of joint reserves, now also called solidarity fund (Ep 29.3.77), or by political authorities using money obtained through taxes. (Ep 27.12.76).

Loss-making organisations can also obtain credits from banks. The banks act either as mediators and transfer to loss-making enterprises savings of other enterprises or persons, or fall back on credits from the central bank, which means credit expansion at the expense of everybody else holding money. Some credits are given under especially favourable conditions, i.e. with interest rates of 2 per cent and delayed repayment over a long period (Ep 23.5.77). Other credits are later converted from short-term into long-term credits, sometimes also at a reduced interest rate (Ep 30.5.77). Such conversions are a regular feature and at least two took place on the basis of special legal provisions in 1971 and 1973 (JP 74, p. 67).

These bank credits, which may never be repaid, stem to a large part from money creation. At a meeting of the Praesidium of the Communist Central Committee in May 1975 it was expressly admitted that monetary issue was used to pay for losses and communists were asked to see that this practice was stopped (D 26.5.75), but such appeals do not seem to have changed 'habits' (Ep 28.2.77). The transfer of funds from one enterprise to another was described as 'picking other people's pockets' (92, p. 7) and claims that these transfers were an expression of solidarity amongst workers were ridiculed (Ep 8.9.75, 19.4.76, 14.11.77).

The sanction which would have prevented the flow of income from one enterprise to another would have been to put loss-making enterprises on fixed minimum incomes determined by political authorities (JP 76, p. 331). This provision was used, albeit inconsistently, and in mid-1976 approximately 700,000 workers were on reduced pay (D 6.6.76). Sometimes workers also had to wait for their pay because their enterprises did not have enough cash (Ep 4.8.75). This should have forced the worker-entrepreneurs to mend their ways.

But workers did not feel themselves to be entrepreneurs (see pp. 88 and 175), so this sanction was difficult to use. Logically it should have been applied until the enterprises stopped making losses, while it was in fact used, if at all, only until the enterprise succeeded in covering the losses by borrowing etc. (cf. JP 76, p. 331). And there were always attempts at mitigating and postponing the sanction against the workers (Ep 27.17.76 and 18.4.77). The general feeling must have been that workers were not entrepreneurs and, therefore, must not suffer (V 21.11.72).

The Slovene Central Committee saw this dilemma and worked out appropriate theses which were summarised in *Delo* (11.1.71):

> If it is to be further accepted that working people in enterprises make business decisions, but are then not held responsible for the consequences, it cannot be expected that the economy will function successfully.

The then Slovene Prime Minister, Kavcic, recalled that in Balzac's time debtors were sent to prison if they could not pay (Ep 9.8.71). He overlooked the point that it is one thing to imprison a few capitalists and quite another to imprison a few workers' collectives. It was claimed that it would be a return to wage relationships if workers were to be guaranteed their incomes by society (Ep 19.4.76).

When it came to the crunch in 1968 and 1969, party committees (in Zagreb openly, elsewhere in secret) ordered enterprises to pay everybody their incomes and the banks obediently extended the credits necessary, with the connivance of the National Bank. 'Debtors continued to expropriate creditors.' *Ekonomska politika* (8.1.69) reported this and commented that such behaviour undermined the system; this was not caring about people rather than about rules, but making the whole of society pay for the mistakes of the debtors. The then finance minister, Janko Smole, complained that business risk was '*etatiziran*' (transferred to the State, nationalised), i.e. that the State reinsured all enterprises' risk so that they were not responsible for their mistakes at all (D 11.3.72).

Although the excessive payment of personal incomes was considered to be the main immediate cause of illiquidity and losses (92, p. 87, JP 74, pp. 69 and 320; JP 76, p. 131), they had a priviliged position (92, p. 143) and were paid out almost without default (92, p. 151). If this could not be done within the law, it was done by infringing it—which was 'normal' (B 11 and 12.10.72). Although the Communist League promised to support the Accountancy Service in its endeavours to enforce financial discipline against local pressures (B 25.10.73), economic offences were on the increase (B 10.7.74).

There is no hope that the Yugoslav system can be made to work if those who make decisions are not made to bear the consequences (Ep 28.3.77), but such sanctions do not exist (92, p. 68) or are insufficient (92, p. 118) and possibly cannot be imposed at all. At the moment, workers in collectives making losses sometimes have higher incomes than in those which are called upon 'out of solidarity', to help them (Polajnar, D 9.4.76, Ep 28.3.77) which makes many a worker think that it is an advantage for an enterprise to make losses, since they are covered by others anyway (Ep 30.5.77, Polajnar, Ep 6.6.77).

Losses do not necessarily mean that the whole economy is working poorly. Essentially they mean that some enterprises are functioning badly (see p. 93), but even then it has to be established what role is played by personal incomes. Excessive personal incomes can obviously turn any enterprise into a loss-maker. Disregarding this frequent reason, the loss-making enterprises are those catering worse than the rest of the economy for the existing demand, which also implies disproportions in the form of unsaleable inventories and underutilised capacities. If losses were not simply somehow covered, they would force enterprises to improve their performance to nearer the country's average and one way of doing this would be elimination of the production of waste. Comparisons between firms require that their costs, including labour costs, should be equal or similar (see p. 132).

But, on reflection, it seems to me that persistent losses also influence a country's general efficiency. The profits from disequilibrium (see p. 130) have the characteristic of disappearing when other firms catch up with the most successful ones and, therefore, force successful enterprises to be constantly on the alert. If a number of enterprises are in such a bad position that they cannot hope to catch up, the rest of the economy will not be under pressure to improve further. In Yugoslavia, the system has produced enterprises which have been in a very bad position right from the beginning, as well as financial indiscipline which makes life easier for those enterprises lagging behind the rest. In view of these systemic shortcomings one could hardly expect illiquidity to be overcome by 'more developed self-management relations', including an integral system of responsibility, as was suggested (D 10.6.72).

10.4 STABILISATION

President Tito declared that stabilisation must not take place at the expense of the working man (B 1.1.71). This attitude made stabilisation impossible: workers were supposed to take decisions, especially with respect to income distribution, but no sanctions could be applied against them, so the direct result was financial indiscipline and inflation. Tight monetary policy could be effective in bringing about stabilisation, but could not at the same time help to achieve employment and growth targets (30 p. 178).

In view of this situation, Bajt (9, p. 14) came to the conclusion that there were destabilising 'systemic elements' on the supply side in the Yugoslav economy and that it was, therefore, necessary to allow a 'certain rate of price rises' for the economy to function normally. If the choice that remained was between (1) a stabilised economy with low growth, and (2) an inflationary economy with high growth, the rational solution was to accept inflation. He repeated the same arguments in later years too, for example in 1975 in an article headed 'Rising prices are a lesser evil than falling production' (V 5.11.75). Bajt seems to have forgotten the structural problem which he himself had stressed at the end of 1964 (D 16–17.11.64) when he also demanded that the reform should make unprofitable production impossible (D 8.8.65).

The official view oscillated between optimism and pessimism. When he was a Vice-President of the federal government, Jakov Sirotkovic claimed that a further reform was unnecessary and that a more successful stabilisation was on the way (D 22.1.72). Such statements brought him the nickname 'Minister of Optimism'. On the contrary, four years later, Sirotkovic's successor as Vice-President, Berislav Sefer, admitted that hitherto only symptoms of instability had been tackled, whereas what was required was to deal with its causes (D 30.3.76). The official standpoint was that the problem could be solved by intensifying self-management (Sefer, D 24.7.74), but in reality it was self-management that was at the root of instability.

In 1976, there were complaints about the snail's pace of growth (D 10.4.76); a year later the growth rate improved but the trade deficit surpassed all expectations (see p. 168), although even in 1976 absorption exceeded production by 9 per cent (Ep 30.5.77). The stabilisation method was price control (cf. Sefer, D 25.2.77) which, in 1976, kept the rise of producer good prices down to 6 per cent and of retail prices to 9 per cent when money wages were rising at a rate of 16 per cent and investment outlays at 32 per cent (Ep 31.3.77). The result was the disappearance of internal accumulation by enterprises (Ep 4.10.76), the financing of investment out of monetary issue and, hence, pent-up excess demand. This is confirmed by Bajt (Ep 28.11.77) who believes that the actual rate of inflation is much higher than the statistics show. According to his data, the 1977 rise in wages was about 30 per cent, the rise in productivity small, and accumulation by enterprises vanishing; however, organisations of associated labour had by now become accustomed to external financing not only of investment but also of personal incomes, i.e. of losses.

11: Foreign Deficit

11.1 PROBLEMS BEFORE THE 1965 REFORM

The original trend to autarchy (in 1958 exports amounted to only 5.5 per cent of the GSP — Ep 1.1.64) posed difficult problems for foreign trade (see p. 23). Planning for sales in foreign markets is well-nigh impossible, so that there had been hardly any such planning at any level and trade was more or less accidental (33, pp. 673, 675). In 1961, there was an almost complete breakdown which was resolved by an IMF stabilisation loan (33, p. 674).

The exchange rates were altered frequently (see p. 170), but this could not help much as the performance of Yugoslav enterprises was very uneven. Multiple exchange rates were introduced in the form of premia on exports of 10, 22 and 32 per cent in combination with various quotas and other restrictions. At the beginning of the 1960s, regular customs duties were applied, *inter alia*, to satisfy the requirements for joining GATT (66, p. 73).

In 1952–62 there were three changes in the registration of enterprises allowed to trade abroad. The purpose was to reduce the competition between Yugoslav firms selling to foreigners (JP 67, p. 213). Nonetheless this led to accusations that some enterprises had a monopoly of foreign trade and made large profits without producing anything (Ep 11., 18.9.65) so that in the end any enterprise having sufficient capital and personnel was allowed to engage in foreign trade (Sl 28/66).

The real problems were, however, elsewhere. Agriculture was neglected and agricultural products were imported rather than exported as they had been before the war. Manufacturing production continued to be guided by criteria which did not include export possibilities (33, p. 703). What was required was a decisive change in the production structure in line with domestic and world demand and the country's comparative advantage, whereas in fact irrational projects continued to be implemented (Ep 3.7.65). Even Tito told the Central Committee (B 27.7.62) that 'we should encourage the production of those goods for export that can be sold'.

It was not only a question of what could be sold but at what price. There were losses in domestic currency which in themselves justified Kraigher's claim that policy had been to export at any price (8th Congress), resulting in an outflow of value (33, p. 678); moreover there were near-losses in foreign currency, even disregarding domestic costs. Branches like shipbuilding showed large apparent earnings of foreign currency which were actually quite ficticious as most of this currency had to be spent on buying their foreign inputs (33, p. 676).

Much of this trouble was due to government pressure in favour of investment-good industries, so that supply of these goods exceeded domestic demand (109, p. 3, see p. 67) and an outlet for them had to be found abroad. But foreign markets lifted the veil off distorted prices and showed up the high costs of production and the internal problems and shortcomings of the Yugoslav economy (Gligorov, RIA 20.6.65). Yugoslav producers had to export goods worth dinars 2000 to earn a dollar abroad while the accounting rate was dinars 750 to US $1.

To export even at a loss often required the extension of credits which Yugoslavia could ill afford (Tito, B 24.7.62) (see p. 169). It was expected that in 1965–70 Yugoslavia would have to grant $700 million worth of credits 'to continue the export of ships and equipment' (Ep 21.11.64). Federal assistance with credits to foster these exports became a regular feature (JP 69, p. 459). In the early 1970s, export subsidies amounted to 22 per cent of the value of industrial and mining exports and to 7 per cent of the GSP (47, pp. 345, 457).

Yugoslav manufactured exports were of such quality and price (NZZ 24.6.65) that they could be sold only to Eastern Europe and to developing countries, but these latter were often reluctant to buy from Yugoslavia. Presumably for political as well as economic reasons Tito also pressed for trade with developing countries (B 24.7.62). He thought that exporting to them on credit was necessary if Yugoslavia was to industrialise, especially as the country was inundated with some goods as it is.

Nevertheless, Kraigher praised those who were selling in difficult Western markets (B 27.7.62). *Ekonomska politika* (27.5.61) argued that it was illogical 'stubbornly to keep selling to where we do not buy from and vice-versa'. True, some imports paid for by convertible currency (lamps, paper napkins, toilet paper — Ep 15.5.62) were laughable, but on the whole the Yugoslav economy survived because it could import more from the West than it exported there (see p. 168).

The establishment of the European Economic Community was an additional reason in the early 1960s 'why it was difficult to trade' (B

14.5.59). At first the Yugoslav official line was against the EEC, saying that integration was good, but that it should be based on 'a programme of socialism' (Kardelj, B 12.4.59). In a series of articles in Borba (January 1962), Janez Stanovnik, later secretary general of the UN Economic Commission for Europe, described the EEC as 'a new partition of world markets by capitalist industrial countries', 'neo-colonialist exploitation', directed against 'the socialist East', etc. The EEC was seen as a means of pressure on the working class, which should, therefore, unite with developing countries. Somewhat later, Kraigher warned that European integration would not go away and that Yugoslavia had to adjust to the new, more difficult conditions (B 24.7.62).

Much later, Yugoslavia came to terms with the EEC, although it still complained about EEC restrictions on imports of meat and the general tendency to close the markets of the Nine (Smole, D 21.6.75). On the other hand, loans from the EEC countries oil the Yugoslav economy, although this is at least partly for political reasons (NZZ 16.11.76). Yugoslavia joined Comecon with observer status in 1966.

The 1965 reform would have changed the general picture of the country's foreign trade had it succeeded in making the production structure responsive to demand. It altered the exchange rate and the customs tariffs yet again (see p. 110) but the impact of these moves was so limited that the so-called 'retention quotas' (see p. 24) had to remain in force, supplemented as they had been since 1964 by 'import-linked export' arrangements (66, p. 73). Retention quotas (7 per cent in 1962) benefited the final exporter only, while it was felt that his suppliers should be given a part of this allocation of foreign currency. For this reason, banks were brought in to engineer complicated agreements on the distribution of the retained foreign currency (Ep 18.7.47). The idea of the present 'foreign exchange communities of interest' seem to have developed out of this (see p. 172). The linkage between exports and imports is unwarranted because there is no reason why exporting enterprises should be in particular need of imported inputs or why importing enterprises should be well placed also to export. What is required is an exchange rate which allocates foreign currency according to understandable if not always exact principles. Yugoslav sources make the same point when they speak about the need for 'unifying' income in foreign exchange and income in dinars (Ep 2.6.75).

11.2 FOREIGN INDEBTEDNESS

Table 11.1 shows the development of Yugoslav foreign transactions after 1960, where the figures show that the trade balance has been in the red throughout. On a few occasions special efforts and political campaigns succeeded in reducing the deficit, as in 1965 and 1972. In 1965 exports covered just under 85 per cent, and in 1972 just under 70 per cent, of imports, but in bad years exports as a percentage of imports fell to slightly over 50 per cent, as in 1974 and 1975 (SG 77, p. 237). On average, the exports paid for about 65 per cent of imports.

The difference has increasingly been covered by earnings from transport, tourism and remittances from workers abroad, which in 1965, 1972–3 and 1976 even produced a small surplus on current account. Transport is becoming an important item in bridging the gap between exports and imports, but workers' remittances and tourism have been decisive over the last ten years or so. Before that the communists would have considered both these sources of foreign exchange beneath the dignity of Yugoslavia since they were mere sale of services and had no link with engineering. Unilateral transfers will be discussed below (see p. 201).

As for tourism, in 1962 President Tito spoke at great length about its previous neglect and stressed that 'We cannot continue in this vein: we must take a different view of tourism . . . ' (B 24.7.62). The change was so rapid and enthusiastic that the ironical slogan 'Through tourism to socialism' was coined (Ep 6.7.63), though tourism also implied some concessions to the private sector which could provide accommodation and catering for tourists faster and cheaper than the social sector (see p. 118).

In normal years the sale of Yugoslav services to foreigners is not sufficient to compensate for the import deficit, so that there is also a deficit in the current balance which leads to increasing indebtedness. In 1962 Tito warned that the Yugoslav foreign debt amounted to $800 million (B 7.5.62) while somewhat later he spoke of 'nearly one billion dollars' (K 22.6.62) and added: 'This is a very large amount, but our country is potentially rich and we can and must pay back these liabilities.' At the end of 1969, the total foreign debt amounted to about $2,100 million (JP 70, p. 391).

Taking the net long-term loan figures from Table 11.1, Yugoslav indebtedness rose to about $4,500 million at the end of 1974. This figure, however, excludes short-term debts after 1969 and is net of Yugoslav loans to other countries, which are large, judging by the difference

Table 11.1: Yugoslav foreign balances
(in millions of US dollars)

	Trade balance	Transport (net)	Tourism (net)	Remittances	Current balance	Official transfer	Long-term loans gross	Long-term loans net
1961	− 346	56	8	48	− 217	34	106	
1962	− 199	68	22	57	− 48	25	88	
1963	− 278	81	44	102	− 80	5	88	
1964	− 433	97	55	106	− 203	20	84	
1965	− 195	118	63	59	70	30	121	
1966	− 351	140	82	98	− 32	11	120	
1967	− 454	145	95	118	− 75	12	192	
1968	− 532	144	136	149	− 106	11	390	178
1969	− 660	163	168	249	− 108	2	517	216
1970	−1194	201	146	500	− 340	1	636	190
1971	−1439	221	140	711	− 324	− 1	857	579
1972	− 990	230	219	1049	419	− 1	946	557
1973	−1658	323	589	1413	485	− 1		596
1974	−3715	396	644	1379	−1183			1500
1975	−3625	430	702	1327	−1032			1057
1976	−2489	429	725	1415	165			1477
1977 (est.)	−4830	430	720	1500	−1800			1500

Source: OECD 73, p. 70 and 78, p. 64
Due to change in coverage figures for 1973 are not fully comparable with those for earlier years.

between gross and net long-term loan figures in Table 11.1. In 1975 and 1976 (first 9 months) the net Yugoslav indebtedness increased by another $1,550 million (SG 77 p. 302) but simultaneously Yugoslav convertible reserves rose by $1,280 million. According to *Ekonomska politika* (Ep 23.10.78), Yugoslav foreign indebtedness reached $10.8 billion in mid-1978, but it is not clear whether this figure is net or gross.

This level was reached despite consideration of a moratorium for Yugoslavia in 1971 (V 14.2.70), especially as Yugoslavia had great difficulty in obtaining repayments from its own debtors such as Indonesia, Ghana, Guinea and Cambodia (D 3.7.71). Attempts at limiting foreign borrowing by enterprises were made (B 26.12.72, D 12.5.77) but seemingly failed.

In 1972 there were also over 400 firms abroad with a capital of over $100 million in Yugoslav ownership or with Yugoslav participation (NIN 9.2.72, D 14.7., 1.8.72). Little was known about their operations. Allegedly, their purpose was cooperation rather than profit (B 25.12.70).

It was admitted that foreign subsidiaries were necessary, but apprehensions arose both for ideological reasons—was not this partnership with foreigners to exploit Yugoslav workers? (B 19.4.70)—and also because of the dangers of corruption, which was rife in self-managed enterprises (see p. 189).

Corruption was often involved when individual Yugoslav citizens organised their own enterprises abroad, very often people who were originally employed by Yugoslav enterprises. They succeeded in establishing the contacts required and then branched out on their own. Frequently the capital was acquired through illicit commissions extracted from foreign firms by official Yugoslav representatives as a condition to clinch a deal. In the end Yugoslav firms were prohibited from trading with or through Yugoslav citizens employed by foreign firms or through firms owned abroad by individual Yugoslavs. This rule became most strictly applied against political exiles, although they were not its original target, after they had been welcome as commercial partners during the period of relaxation up till 1971 (JP 76, p. 161).

In 1964 the trade deficit was equal to just over 9 per cent of the GSP, the current deficit to about half this percentage, and foreign indebtedness to about 18 per cent of the GSP; in 1977, the trade deficit amounted to 13.3 per cent, the current deficit to 5.5 per cent and indebtedness was moving towards 30 per cent of the GSP (calculated from OECD figures.)

There is nothing wrong about foreign loans to pay for investment which later yields goods in line with domestic and world demand and thus pays for itself. But as early as 17 Apr. 1965 *Ekonomska politika* warned of the danger that foreign credits to Yugoslavia 'would be transformed into credits for consumption and for investment destined to produce "losses"'. Loans were used to maintain untenable rates of growth at the expense of the balance of payments, in short for 'artificial growth' (Ep 1.5.65).

After a respite in 1976, due to a radical curtailment of imports, the Yugoslav economy again produced a trade deficit of about $4.4 billion in 1977, and a current deficit of about $1.8 billion (OECD 1978). *Ekonomska politika* (21.11.77) quoted similar figures and commented that the rate of growth in 1977 might indeed have been almost 7 per cent, but that the question of the 'quality' of this growth could no longer be avoided.

11.3 PERSISTENT INCOMPREHENSION

In mid-1966, Kraigher volunteered (66, p. 243) the following statement:

> I know that the problems of foreign exchanges are rather complicated; I admit that, two years ago, I did not understand them as well as I do now and that discussions helped all of us to learn about these things.

Foreign trade seems to be a fertile ground for misunderstandings, but in Yugoslavia Marxist influences and nationalistic rivalries made them worse than elsewhere. In the 1960s a particular problem was that the Yugoslav leaders were not clear about the principle of comparative advantage in its widest application. They made statements like that by Kardelj that 'our production had to reach such a degree of labour productivity that it would be able to compete in international markets' (62, p. 143). In so far as international markets are concerned, the problem is not to increase general labour productivity but to make it more uniform over the whole span of the production structure. Exchange rates normally take care of differences in average productivity between countries, but they cannot function properly if there are big disparities in productivity performance between various branches in the same country, especially if the country wants to export the products of these industries in which its productivity is worst.

As it was, Yugoslavia lagged behind the average labour productivity of nine developed countries by only 28 per cent in shoe production, but by 668 per cent in iron ore mining. The production of 'a car' required 7167 man-hours in Yugoslavia and only 200 man-hours in the United States, a productivity lag of about 3500 per cent (B 11.4.65). Of course, gross labour productivity is a very inadequate measure of disadvantages because it does not take into account the cooperating capital and other factors, nonetheless, excessive differentials in labour productivity indicate a distorted structure.

Very little could be done by blanket attempts at increasing efficiency, since such attempts could only lead to results a few decades later. Blanket intensification of capital and modernisation could even cause more trouble, in particular as pouring capital into uncompetitive branches can make matters worse. It was obvious that there were large sections of industry which had developed only thanks to 'distorted price parities' (Ep 4.5.70), or, to put it more precisely, because of faulty planning and policies, not just under the centralist system but also later.

For this reason, there were tendencies to 'rising protectionism' (Ribicic, Ep 4.5.70), endangering the reform. Any attempt at lowering tariffs met with protest (B 29.3.71) and more protection was demanded (D 17.11.76).

Conversely, exporters wanted subsidised credits. In 1971 the Croat Institute of Economic Planning calculated that Croatia and Montenegro were the only republics to have a balance of payments surplus of $80 million and $3 million respectively (D 11.11.71). It did not consider it contradictory that simultaneously shipyards in Croatia demanded that the federal government should provide them with dinars 1.9 billion out of taxation to enable them to export ships on credit. The Slovene Premier came out strongly against the building of plants that could be kept working only if capital was exported in the form of loans (Ep 2.3.70).

Another misunderstanding was that Yugoslav industry should concentrate on the production of those goods for which raw materials were available at home. A domestic critic (D 20.5.72) described this attitude as an alibi for more 'political' investment and said that it was inevitable to import for instance cotton and wool. But others considered the export of textiles made of imported cotton an export of 'naked labour'. *Ekonomska politika* (18.5.74) pointed out that many advanced countries with only scarce natural resources imported raw materials when this was rational, and exported value added, i.e. primarily labour. Nor did advanced countries cultivate the prejudice that they were in a 'colonial situation' if they exported semi-finished goods instead of final goods. This prejudice was still alive in Yugoslavia (cf. JP 76, p. 395).

Because of continuing distortions and preconceived ideas, foreign trade came 'under the control of administration to a degree to which it has never been', claimed the Vice-Chairman of the Slovene Chamber of Business (Ep 13.10.75). In 1976 administrative measures achieved a rise of 8 per cent in exports and a cut of 9 per cent in imports (Ep 26.4.76) but these restrictions on imports immediately caused a cut in economic activity (Ep 19.4.76). It turned out that consumer goods accounted for less than 10 per cent of the total value of imports, which means that Yugoslav production is highly import dependent (Ep 10.5.76). Administration of foreign trade cannot work because it is slow and insensitive and the curtailment of essential imports can reduce production by up to 20 times its own value. The whole system is under a question mark at present (Ep 5.7.76).

The Praesidium of the Central Committee of the Yugoslav League of Communists considered it necessary to discuss foreign trade in the spring of 1976 and issued a resolution on the ideological activity of the League in this field (JP 76, p. 161). It insisted on the need for ideological knowledge and political qualities on the part of those engaged in foreign trade, as if this could help them in coping with the deficit. As an expression of failure it fell back on the old device of 'inimical elements' infiltrating foreign trade organisations. But the main preoccupation of the Central Committee was the alleged concentration of income (profits) in foreign trade to the detriment of direct producers (see p. 222), although it was sometimes claimed that profits from exporting were minimal (Ep 31.1.77).

11.4 CONVERTIBILITY OF THE DINAR

The dinar exchange rate to the US dollar evolved as follows:

1949	50 old dinars
1952	300 old dinars
1965	1250 old dinars
	12.5 new dinars
1971	
January	15 new dinars
December	17 new dinars

From 1971 on the dinar followed the dollar with respect to other currencies, so that it was for instance devalued by a further 10 per cent in gold terms in 1973 (Ep 19.2.73, see pp. 24, 70 and 110). After the devaluation of 1971 the introduction of a Yugoslav exchange market was discussed and a floating exchange rate was tentatively introduced (B 26.9.71). However this was very much a managed float since the National Bank guided it by means of an intervention exchange rate which was the basis for a 'list of foreign exchange rates' published by the Foreign exchange market run by the Association of Yugoslav Banks (B 30.10.74).

Alterations in the dinar exchange rate could do little good since 'the existing economic structure made it impossible for the Yugoslav economy to participate in a stable and satisfactory way in the international division of labour' (NR 12.3.71). In fact, after the January 1971 devaluation all those who were unfavourably affected clamoured for compensation for their losses. Such compensation was impossible, but the enterprises could not be simply told to sink or swim as business conditions continued to be rigged by administrative measures and many aspects of foreign trade were unclear because of the incomplete system (B 6.2.71). Nonetheless, the dinar savings of the population were revalued upward by 6 per cent (the banks and the federal government sharing the costs) (B 25.1.71). Furthermore, the effects of devaluation were soon eroded through the rise in domestic prices, as admitted by the Federal Institute of Statistics (B 22.7.71).

It would seem that under Yugoslav conditions the role of the exchange rate can only be very limited. In spite of this, the possible convertibility of the dinar was seriously discussed. The prevailing opinion amongst Yugoslav economists in 1970 was that it could be achieved within eight years (P 29.5.70) while Aleksandar Grlickov, a Vice-President of the federal government, obviously thought that it should come earlier because it was impossible to resolve the problems of 'class relations between producers' and 'the relations between nationalities' without a common denominator, 'namely a convertible national currency' (B 21.3.71).

The controversy about which Yugoslav constitutent republics earned how much foreign currency was rife in the early 1970s. Calculations about contributions to exports and shares of imports abounded (Ep 2.3.70). These disputes were somewhat absurd, as something imported by one republic could be finally consumed in another, or exports by one republic could have been produced to a large extent in another, not to speak about the provision of export credits (see p. 169). A convertible dinar could be a solution by unifying incomes in dinars and in foreign currency, were it not for administrative entanglement and structural distortions.

The way out of the 'foreign exchange maze' was sought by various councils (D 31.5.74) in which unanimity of the republican representatives is required. The principle agreed on demands that foreign exchange should go to those basic organisations of associated labour which participated in earning the exchange, but according to a system of developed self-management agreements and social contracts rather than according to the spontaneity of markets. How this could be achieved was, however, 'unclear, fluid and unacceptable to objectively different interests'.

In March 1977 a panoply of Acts on foreign transactions was adopted and it was expected that they would be supplemented by about 50 implementation decrees (Ep 18.7.77). The gist of the new legislation is to transfer a large part of jurisdiction on foreign operations from State organs to self-management bodies, although the State still preserves the right to determine the overall policy. From 1 January 1978 much regulatory activity was to be taken over by Self-Management Interest Communities for Foreign Economic Relations in republics and provinces, consisting of delegates of organisations of associated labour, and by an Interest Community of Yugoslavia for Foreign Economic Relations, the members of which were to be indirectly appointed by the republic and province communities. Their regulations would be issued in the form of self-management agreements and social contracts in line with the arrangements in other fields (see p. 213). The present administration of foreign exchange and foreign trade would remain, but pass partly into the hands of so-called 'direct producers'.

This continued administration is at least partly necessary because of 'the unreal dinar exchange rate' (D 20.10.77) which must also be one of the reasons why Yugoslav products are too expensive in world markets, another being 'the structure of export prices' (Ep 28.11.77). According to the Federal Secretary of Finance, Momcilo Cemovic, the government refuses to devalue because this 'would only revalue the country's foreign debts and place more money in the pockets of citizens with foreign currency deposits' (Ep 18.7.77).

The basic bodies which enjoy foreign exchange rights are the 'basic organisations of associated labour' which export. If they depend on suppliers, they have to conclude with them self-management agreements on the distribution of foreign exchange and in fact have to pay them in foreign currency. Should an agreement be impossible, the courts of associated labour can be invoked to decide the issue. This solution seems immensely complicated and very few people believed that it would solve the problems of foreign trade (Ep 14.11.77).

12: Problems of Organisational Power

12.1 DIFFICULTIES WITH SELF-MANAGEMENT

During the political relaxation in the 1960s a new breed of scholars came to the fore at Yugoslav universities: the sociologists. Originally sociology was not admitted to be a scholarly discipline by the communist countries, but later it was accepted and introduced in Yugoslavia and elsewhere (D 15.8.67). The sociologists started probing into the real attitudes of the population by polls and questionnaires. Evidence was produced of considerable disparity between the official doctrine and the real situation. The sociologists explained that the postulate that there would be no conflict in a socialist society, i.e. a society without private means of production, was 'idealistic' (95, p. 45; 127, p. 157), and that in so far as conflicts were absent in Yugoslav society, this was because they were suppressed, which was undesirable as it only made them worse. The basic point made at a conference of Yugoslav sociologists in 1972 was that conflicts should be legalised (Ep 2.2.72).

Yugoslav sociologists also embarked on research into differences arising between people in what they called 'social statification'. This brought some scathing criticism from Kardelj (61, p. 18) who objected to the term 'new class' based not on ownership of means of production, but on 'secondary characteristics' such as 'consumption, wealth, way of life, etc.' Kardelj admitted that research of this kind may have some scholarly significance, but said that it must be reactionary if 'it tries to replace the class treatment of production relations', and added that secondary non-property differences between people were 'precisely the new forms in which given elements of old class relations are being reproduced in socialist and self-managing production relations'. Sociologists obviously felt that such conflicts were real conflicts whatever they were called, which Kardelj admitted, in spite of his attempts to explain them both as 'non-class' and as 'remnants of the past'. The sociologists were accused of advancing theories which had a 'political role' and of 'passing to the position of fully equating capitalism and socialism, etatism and self-management'. Many sociologists did claim that to deal with problems essentially meant that 'democracy' was needed, so everything could be discussed and compromises reached (Jerovsek, NR 23.11.68). Moreover, direct democracy at grass root level was not sufficient because it led to manipulation of the electorate from above: what was needed also was representative democracy in the political sphere (95, pp. 226–9), obviously in order to allow the formation of several leading groups (Rus, Vojan, D 30.9.69).

This kind of sociology did not please the party leaders. When, in 1975, four scholars at the Faculty of Sociology, Politics and Journalism in Ljubljana came up with a new work on self-management based on research carried out in several factories, their conclusions were turned down as politically harmful (*The Times* 28.1.75). The four, including Veljko Rus and Janez Jerovsek, were accused of 'technocratic liberalist deviation' but the whole university supported them, including the party cell of their faculty (NZZ 15/16.2.75).

But regardless of whether Yugoslav leadership would allow open discussion, the sociologists (and others) had come up with a whole range of problems that seemed to make the application of self-management very difficult at least in the form in which it was introduced in Yugoslavia, (NR 28.5.71). The most disconcerting discovery of opinion research was that workers in fact did not show much interest in self-management. When asked about what interested them most in their enterprise (2), a sample of workers answered that their order of preference was as follows: high earnings, nice working mates, capable supervisors, interesting work, possibility of advancement, and finally, participation in self-management. Members of all levels of management and experts ordered their preferences differently, but also put self-management last. There were even some signs that workers were becoming less and less interested in self-management, possibly as the novelty wore off, and more and more interested in better earnings (57). The dominant concern of the 1971 congress of self-managers in Sarajevo was the 'trauma of low wages' (Ep 14.6.71) (cf. pp. 94–5).

But difficulties do not stop here. The source of power in an enterprise is organisation (95, p. 112). Wherever there is division of labour somebody has to coordinate separate activities for a common aim and those who are capable of doing that also have real power regardless of formal arrangements (127, p. 109; 95, p. 112). Yugoslav self-management legislation ignored this management function for ideological reasons (127, pp. 61, 140) and produced a system in which formal rules are one thing and reality quite another (127, pp. 99, 141; 55, p. 147). As a consequence, the working organisations have great difficulty in maintaining equilibrium as systems and a large amount of energy is spent on simply making them exist at all, which considerably reduces their efficiency (127, p. 93; 55, p. 143). If this problem is not resolved 'self-management will be reduced to an unrealistic ideological projection' (55, p. 8).

The technical working system is basic and the social system has to adapt to it, if it is to function (127, p. 116). The concept of 'self-management working organisation' is a *contradictio in adiecto* because self-management presupposes spontaneous behaviour, while spontaneous behaviour cannot be married with the need for a structured organisation (127, p. 117). The term 'self-management' has lost its meaning (55, p. 237) and become an incantation, so that a redefinition of the concept is urgently required (55, p. 198).

Formally, the workers in enterprises are given all power but they cannot exercise it and know that this is so. First, their expectations were fanned, only to be deceived, which led to 'disillusionment and frustration' (127, p. 188). At least half of the workers are fully aware that some individuals and smaller groups wield power which does not legally belong to them (2). The workers do not feel that the worker's council has much influence (127, p. 175) and will normally take their complaints to the factory director instead (55, p. 198). They themselves have neither the knowledge nor the time (8, p. 263) to carry out what is formally within their jurisdiction, nor can they acquire the day to day information which is necessary for the implementation of their tasks. Therefore, they are in a state of 'powerful impotence' (95, p. 102).

It is impossible to insist on the participation of everybody (95, p. 112). Collective responsibility cannot replace hierarchical responsibility which is apparently the reason why hierarchy persists in Yugoslav working organisations (95, p. 113). Not only is it almost physically impossible for everybody to participate, but workers also cannot participate in entrepreneurial activity because this would mean bearing risks, while the individual producer does not 'perceive' the link between his individual income and the income of the enterprise nor its dependence on the market (95, p. 16). Workers reason in terms of physical output and particularly of their own physical output rather than in terms of enterprises' revenue, i.e. output valued in the market (127, pp. 32–3). For this reason, they expect the 'authorities' to change the rules if market conditions hit them (127, p. 16) so that, in

Yugoslavia, the government is tacitly expected to 're-insure' each enterprise if it incurs losses (127, p. 63). This undermines the whole method of working of a decentralised economy.

Under Yugoslav self-management, the workers have the right to decide on the most technically involved questions, for example about investment worth hundreds of millions (55, pp. 195–6). However, what workers want is not participation in investment and similar decisions but participation on the shop floor (95, p. 189; 12) and in decisions which affect them as individuals, which mean those concerning working conditions and, above all, their own incomes (Kamusic in 18, p. 106; Supek in 18, p. 231; 47, pp. 378, 382). These latter matters can provoke long debates at meetings, while investment decisions are taken almost without discussion (Supek in 18, p. 231; 47, pp. 379–80).

Apparently the Yugoslav point of departure (Bilandzic in 18, pp. 165–6) is that economic efficiency grows in proportion to the involvement of labour, which means that the workers should run all aspects of the enterprise. Naturally, the individual worker cannot be made an expert in all fields, but he should have the power to make decisions on the general goals of his work and on the conditions under which he performs it. Unfortunately, these two last points are contradictory. The general goal of an enterprise, which comprises workers' work, can only be to produce goods as cheaply as possible which can be defeated if conditions of work, including wages, are excessively favourable.

Since the social goal of the enterprise is clear, its achievement requires expertise and conditions of work must be uniform over the economy (in line with productivity) if one group of workers is not to 'exploit' others (see p. 214, Kamusic in 18, p. 85). The scope for self-management is, therefore, very limited. The workers sense this: a newly elected chairman of a small enterprise workers' council said in an interview that he had no intention of interfering with things he could not understand, namely financial and managerial matters (D 4.7.78). The workers increasingly see the self-management structure as a sort of talking shop and a formality which conceals the real power relations (12, 4, Kurtovic, B 15.12.74). Some become passive and others incessantly talk and discuss and do not do anything else (Ep 21.7.75). Sometimes they are, nevertheless, also afraid to say what they think (D 11.11.76).

Information does not help much, on the contrary, it often turns into torrents of paper which the workers cannot digest because they have no time (D 4.3.78; 12; V 5.11.75). The Praesidium of the CC of the Slovene LC recognised that the real power was still in the hands of management and thus considered the launching of a campaign 'to give workers real influence' (Ep 16.6.75).

A vacuum has developed in which informal groups have taken over (127, p. 89; 55, pp. 141–2), and prospered. But this solution presents problems: the informal group has formally no power and, therefore, cannot be held responsible and does not feel responsible. It can always find a 'cover' for its actions by reference to decisions taken by self-management organs which do have formal power, but do not feel responsible because they themselves cannot exercise it (95, p. 124; 127, p. 154). If responsibility is described as the existence of sanctions for actions (55, p. 116; 127, p. 190) then in Yugoslav self-management organisations there is no responsibility because there are no sanctions; in fact there is internal anarchy (127, p. 205; 55, p. 122). The 1976 Act on Associated Labour postulates responsibility in several Articles but does not seem to have changed the situation despite attempts to turn responsibility into socialist morality (D 20.11.76).

This situation also makes it possible for managers not to be professionally qualified for their jobs, since bad results will not disqualify them (127, p. 154). Fundamentally, they can be mere manipulators (95, p. 124) or cliques (127, p. 108). Attempts to halt this development resulted in a deluge of regulations, sometimes imposed from outside and sometimes taking the form of internal by-laws, though mostly adopted under outside influence (8, p. 263; 127, p. 137) (see p. 209). But these attempts were not of much avail because it is impossible to regulate the day to day activity of a working organisation (127, p. 136). The outside provisions, of course, tended to limit the autonomy of the organisation (127, pp. 134–5) and created insecurity because they were continually changed (95, p. 199) (see p. 236) when they did not work, as they could not, since regulations cannot replace responsible action by managers. To some extent, the unpredictability of change in all sorts of legal acts, from the constitution downwards, even fostered the concentration of power as well as 'political' management (127, p. 110) (see p. 181), because only those politically well connected could take action without running into trouble with the State apparatus (8, p. 199).

Regardless of the internal distribution of power, a working self-management system would also have to find a solution for the need to take into account the interests of consumers. We have already noted that workers do not 'perceive' the link between the revenue of the enterprise and their own wage (see p. 175) which also means that they do not identify with the aims of the enterprise. This has further consequences: the enterprise broadly achieves its aims if it produces what its customers want at the cheapest prices, but this may not be what the workers want because it may involve changing jobs and exerting themselves. In other words, the supreme aim of a production organisation is efficiency, which may clash with the social interests of workers' collectives, so that a compromise between the business goals of the enterprise and the workers' interests is required (95, pp. 10, 16). If in this compromise, too much weight is given to workers' interests this, in the end, is to the detriment of customers, i.e. ultimately consumers (95, p. 109), which is the more deplorable because the consumers are the workers who thus, in fact, hurt themselves. Or, if only one group of workers imposes its will on consumers, this means then that that group is living at the expense of other groups. Therefore, it is important that in an enterprise somebody represents the aims of the enterprise and thus, ultimately, the interests of consumers, i.e. workers themselves wearing their other hat.

Self-management can disturb the balance between the population as producers and the population as consumers, if it gives workers too much power or if it simply causes inefficiency. The experience so far rather points in this direction (127, p. 124). The Yugoslav theoretical literature generally denies that self-management can perform an 'instrumental function' as a reaction to the attempts at introducing self-management in the form of collectivisation and deprofessionalisation of decision-making (95, p. 25). Self-management can only fulfil the function of social integration, i.e. establishing some kind of morale, of ethical rules, socially regulating a system of activity for all people. But the connection between this kind of 'morale' and productivity, i.e. service to consumers, is not very strong (127, p. 84), perhaps also for the simple reason that people do not know how to serve each other once society becomes more complicated and if wishes are not expressed in terms of material incentives, that is through the market.

12.2 SOLUTIONS SUGGESTED BY SOCIOLOGISTS

Yugoslav sociologists not only dismantled the 'romantic' facade of the existing system, but also put forward proposals for a more realistic new system of self-management. The starting point for such suggestions was that mere verbal proclamation of self-management in no way changed the distribution of influence and power in the organisation (127, p. 110), and that the only result if reality was ignored was anarchy or abuse of *de facto* power.

The first thing to do was to recognise the power of managers resulting from their position in the enterprise and to give it a legitimate basis (128; 95, p. 190). The 'legitimisation' of power also made it possible to define and limit it, which was of decisive importance for internal relations in the enterprise (95, p. 194). Further, legitimate power would finally allow responsibility to be placed on leading individuals who could carry it because they took decisions, and not on the participatory multitude which in practice cannot be held responsible (V 10.3.68; 95, p. 196).

Well-defined, legitimate power and responsibility would, on the other hand, enable the self-management organs to take over the function which they were capable of fulfilling: the function of control and surveillance (95, p. 112). It should be possible not to redistribute power, but to give more power to everybody by increasing both the active power of decision-making and the passive power of control (95, p. 99). Jerovsek quotes a survey (81) indicating that workers were interested in checking on the management, but not in deciding all important questions themselves. Rus wished the leadership of the country would abandon romantic illusions about eliminating power altogether (withering away of the State) and instead see to it that power was used rationally, which should also enable the government to prevent the uncontrolled exercise of power (95, p. 46).

Parallel to the provision of a legitimate basis for management power, workers should be allowed to organise themselves into real trade unions so that they could confront management both in the enterprise (workers' council) and elsewhere as an equal bargaining partner. Only an independent working class organisation could give them the required countervailing power (12; 128; 95, pp. 190–4). This change was intended to restore the unity of workers both inside and outside the enterprise, which obviously means that the workers as workers would give up the pretence that they are entrepreneurs and would again strive for the best possible wages for all workers in comparable jobs regardless of whether their enterprises work at a profit or a loss. This arrangement seems sensible as workers *en masse* do not seem to perceive the entrepreneurial risk (see p. 174) as a part of the economic scenery, and since the distribution of 'profits' does not appear to stimulate their efforts in any major way (55, p. 218) (see p. 45).

In many respects, this role of trade unions would be a return to the situation in 'pre-socialist' times. The sorely tried Yugoslav workers would probably not be very unhappy about that. But the return would also have its dangers, as active trade unions might again fan the belief that there was some surplus value somewhere to be gained, which would only lead to lethal inflation. One hopes that the Yugoslav workers have learnt a lesson from their trials and tribulations over the last 30 years, but one also has to say that nothing can replace an elementary explanation of the economic facts of life, which have been obscured by Marxist terms such as 'exploitation' and 'alienation'.

Many a Yugoslav sociologist and possibly economist wishes the mechanism of management–trade union bargaining could be revived, but many have very strong doubts about the feasibility of this reform. Rus, for instance, gives several reasons why he does not believe that real trade-unionism could be brought back. The main one appears to be the present leadership of the trade unions, which has hardly anything to do with workers. These leaders are bureaucrats, members of the 'political élite', who do a stint in the trade unions and then move on to higher things. This accusation was levelled at them even at a symposium on the role of trade unions in Belgrade in 1972 (Ep 28.2.72, NR 24.3.72) where it was also revealed that in one enquiry 41 per cent of workers answered that the trade unions did not fulfil any autonomous task. In fact, Stipe Suvar said at the gathering that the trade unions were still engaged more in explaining government policy than listening to workers' wishes.

In reality, trade-union leaders were far more interested in repressing strike leaders than in leading strikes themselves or dealing with workers' grievances (95, p. 192). The only solution would be the rise of new trade-union leaders from workers' ranks. Judging by some recent articles (NR 6.12.74), such a renewal is improbable. The 'renewal' as envisaged now consists in the repetition of old dicta on how trade unions should be under the ideological-political leadership of the League of Communists, how they are a class political organisation and the school of self-management and how there should be no candidate and no delegate without the cooperation of the trade union. In other words, it is intended that they should remain a transmission belt for the League of Communists, i.e. the political élite.

In what way should the power of managers be defined and limited? The answer to this question poses a problem which goes to the core of economic activity. What managers do or do not do depends on other groups participating in their enterprises' or the country's economic activity. Who, therefore, can limit their powers? Trade unions would be one such group but as we have seen, there seems little hope that their activity will turn in this direction. Not only that, it would seem very difficult for the trade unions which are supposed to look after the workers as producers to define and limit the power of managers which is supposed to be used to achieve the business goals of the enterprise, that is to a large extent serving the interests of workers as consumers.

The second possibility would be for professional colleagues, that is managers as a professional body, to develop some kind of ethic of management which would lay down the rules according to which this activity is to be carried out, in the same way as doctors or architects regulate their own activities. But Rus doubts that the problem could be solved in its entirety in this way, since management is a leadership activity also including the incurring of risks. There can be no rules about taking risks because they can be evaluated only on a mainly subjective basis and one person's judgement is as good as another's or, for that matter, as the judgement of a body such as a planning commission (100, p. 77). The question of risk cannot be resolved on the basis of social or State ownership. In the first case, there is no owner (there is talk of 'non-ownership') and therefore nobody to bear the risk, in the second, the risk is carried by the State, which means everybody, which again in effect means nobody. Rus concludes that the question of risk under social ownership remains unsolved (95, p. 113; Smole, B 11.3.72) (see p. 158).

The next possible way which Rus sees to define and limit the power of management is by government legislation. The government can fulfil this function by planning, i.e. telling the managers what to do. This approach turned out to be impossible of fulfilment because life at present is too differentiated and complex, so that it would require some entirely new system of information and communication (see pp. 7–9). It also has undesirable social consequences: the population is reduced to passivity and infantilism (95, p. 200).

The replacement of total planning by continual intervention by the State apparatus is even worse. In Yugoslavia the constant changes of constitutions and other legal acts and provisions (see pp. 177 and 187) destroy any long-term business policy and are responsible for the legal, economic and social uncertainty in collectives. For this reason, Yugoslav enterprises have to be even more flexible than enterprises normally, which makes for great concentration of power in individuals or small groups. These unsystematic interventions by the government led to a state where the best managers are those who care least about self-management. 'To comply with regulations means to go under', said a caption in *Ekonomska politika* (4.9.72).

The best way of defining and limiting the power of managers is by defining property relationships. Clarified property relationships could renew legal security and social stability and leave considerable leeway for personal, group and institutional initiative. Even indicative planning is best married to a system of organised property relations.

The strenuous attempts to abolish ownership altogether are a consequence of the misunderstanding that property is only a source of enjoyment, that it is based on selfishness, and not also a source of administration, preservation and increase of wealth (95, p. 107). The problem is not who uses property but how it is used, says Rus (p. 202). We should distinguish between private and individual or personal ownership, as the purpose of socialisation is deprivatisation, not collectivisation (94). The differences could be explained by means of the old Latin definition of ownership as '*ius iutendi et abutendi*', the right to use and abuse a thing. Individuals should be prevented from abusing things but not from using them. It is not even correct to define private ownership, with Marx, as that form of property which is used to satisfy one's own interests. Owners should only be prevented from using property in a way which harms others. This difference is interesting but seems very difficult to implement in practice. It probably means that the use of property should be regulated to a much greater extent than it used to be, or than the Roman law formula implies.

If the State or a workers' collective abuses property, it is as much private, albeit collective, property as if an individual abuses it. Property is being abused if an enterprise working at a loss pays high wages or if the management of a factory, which has caused its failure, is dismissed without being subject to any kind of sanctions. The means of production in Yugoslavia have been radically expropriated and etatised, but they have not been deprivatised.

Under the present conditions, it is possible to reduce such abuses only by introducing mechanisms of control, public responsibility and sanctions. Business norms are needed which should include norms on depreciation and amortisation. Only those workers' collectives that can live up to business norms, that are 'socially mature', should be allowed to self-manage. But a collective can be responsible as a whole only if its internal relationships are clear, which would require some kind of collective contracts between managers and self-management organs which would guarantee minimum wages. In parallel, there would also be contracts between 'the society' (probably government) and enterprises.

These last proposals are not so unlike what the Yugoslav government is trying to introduce in the 1970s (see pp. 213ff). Therefore, it is somewhat surprising that Rus was first attacked for wanting to 'legalise élites' and advised to pay more attention to 'historical materialism and inductive method' (NR 24.11.72), which Rus considered an attempt at political disqualification (NR 8.12.72), and that he finally ran into trouble at the university (together with Jerovsek). However, in their stress on the advantages of property relations, Rus and other came close to the views of the Yugoslav economist living in the US, Svetozar Pejovich, and his co-author Eirik Furubotn, who have written about the role of property rights in economics, to a considerable extent also on the basis of Yugoslav experience (42, 43, 84, 85).

12.3 ATTITUDE TO MANAGERS AND SPECIALISTS

Originally managers were given considerable power (see p. 43) and were also badly qualified (see p. 43). But in the 1960s this formal power was reduced and during the same period some of them became quite professional. At an international conference at Ermenonville near Paris, Aleksander Bajt (10) claimed that a rapidly growing class of managers was one of the main assets of the Yugoslav economy, although their quality was still well below Western standards. They were the main searchers for new product and market possibilities, detectors of comparative advantage, and technical innovators. Some even created and developed their enterprise more or less single-handed.

On the other hand, according to Zupanov (127, p. 209) the present educational level of Yugoslav directors is 'an incomprehensible anachronism', but professional specialists do not seem to be motivated to take on this job (127, pp. 212–65). Immediately after the war there were few managers in Yugoslavia—and some of these were sent to prison—while the long administrative period generated more bureaucrats than managers (see p. 21). Now management is still to a large extent 'political' instead of 'professional' and managers may still be ideologically considered 'social-political officials' (127, p. 210). They continue to combine the roles of bureaucrats supervising the legality of enterprises' activity, local politicians representing local interests in the enterprise, very influential advisors to workers' councils and executives of the councils' formal decisions, as well as managers in their own right (127, pp. 214–5). These various roles hamper each other and hamper the managers' general efficiency (95, p. 108).

Originally (see p. 43) directors were appointed by the commune but the 1963 Constitution transferred this right to the workers' council; however this Council elected them from among candidates selected by a mixed commission half of whose members were appointed by one or more State bodies (JP 68, p. 137). The Act on Associated Labour allows the working organisation to have either one individual director or a collegiate management body with a chairman. Both the individual director and chairman and members of the collegiate body are appointed by the workers' council from a list prepared by a commission consisting of representatives of the working organisation and the trade union on the one hand, and of the social community on the other. Its recommendations have to be by a two-thirds majority. The director is appointed for four years and then has to be reappointed, which makes his appointment less secure than the job of other members of the enterprise (Ep 6.8.73). This situation makes it necessary for directors to be primarily 'public relations' men both vis-à-vis the authorities and the party and vis-à-vis the workers who now have at least the legal possibility of refusing to appoint them. But politicians do try to unload their fellow bureaucrats on enterprises.

The place of directors in Yugoslav society is even more precarious. In the visualised future socialist society there is no place for either entrepreneurs or managers as distinct from workers. Everybody will do all jobs one after the other (74, p. 22). This is so utopian that even Kardelj said that anybody who imagined it could be introduced soon, and the contrast between intellectual and physical work abolished, was 'either an anarchist or a fool' (D 19.11.71). Yet in the background the utopian idea persists and influences present attitudes: it is contained in the idea prevailing amongst Yugoslav leaders that, while some professional knowledge and information is required, both can be acquired within a short time by a great majority of workers (10).

One consequence of this view of management is that directors are considered usurpers and their public image is negative. The fact that in practice they are irreplaceable only makes them more irritating. The spread of this image is all the easier as the Yugoslav social culture includes a general adverse view of 'businessmen' (127, pp. 223–4). Directors can be made general scapegoats as 'substitute capitalists'. Because they can be identified, they are much more usable as bogeymen than the abstract 'bureaucracy' (127, p. 225). In Yugoslavia, even more than elsewhere, any deficiency in production is always blamed on those who try to organise production while their inactive critics are themselves considered to be above criticism.

Not only do the politicians not produce anything, in Yugoslavia they constantly get in the managers' way. Social designers, the ideologists, keep dreaming up 'progressively more progressive ideas' and unsettling economic life by changing laws and programmes. As stressed in several places in this book, one day enterprises are merged, then they are split into 'economic units', then again into 'basic organisation of associated labour', in short one reorganisation follows another and makes the managers despair (10). Often they try to get back into some quieter administrative job and generally say that they do not want to continue as directors (127, p. 264).

In spite of their important role, directors are not particularly well paid. For 1972, Bajt mentions an average general manager's income of about dinars 5500 per month, as compared with the overall Yugoslav average personal income of dinars 1500. In the general atmosphere as created in Yugoslavia through constant stress on 'social' and 'equal', it has become impossible to pay even moderately well for good work. Jerovsek (55, p. 232) quotes an example when a director was awarded a bonus of dinars 25,000 (about £650) by his workers' council. He was taken to court and was given a suspended sentence of five months imprisonment and repayment of the bonus, although it was not certain whether the bonus was illegal or not – 'We do not have a consistent rule of law', adds Jerovsek. Conversely, no case is known where a director was punished for bankrupting his enterprise. Thus, under the present conditions in Yugoslavia, it is bad to be successful and be paid for it, but it is all right to be irresponsible and ruin a business. Even the Chairman of the Executive Council of Bosnia and Herzegovina commented that it was all very well to be irritated by high incomes, but wondered why it was not considered a sin to be paid and not do any work or much less than commensurate with the pay received (Ep 7.9.73). Some enterprises are trying to give incentives to their managers and professional specialists by sending them abroad on 'business trips', but experts continue to be uninterested in leading posts mainly because of low pay and the unfavourable climate (Ep 19.7.76).

The ambiguous attitude to directors—ideological depreciation and practical importance—produced curious debates in newspapers. In 1967, *Borba* published a long series of articles on the 'director problem' under the general heading 'What is a director?' (B 28.3.67). The articles came out, on the whole, in favour of directors, but soon afterwards one of the political leaders Veljko Vlahovic, felt it necessary to stress that the League of Communists was not an organisation of managers (P 15.9.69).

In this climate the degree of interest in managerial posts was low. For the re-election of directors in both 1966 and 1970 there were hardly any more candidates than posts and the candidates were mostly previous directors (B 11.5.66, K 5.11.71, Ep 10.4.74, B 7.8.74). There were resignations and one leading director said that it was impossible to manage if the rules were continually changing and the successful were punished while the lazy were protected by the government (Atelsek, D 11.8.73). The job simply was not attractive enough (55, p. 238). In 1975, there was still on average only just over one candidate per post (Ep 2.2.76) and the incumbent director usually remained in his place (47, p. 339). One quarter to one third of managing posts remains unfilled (Ep 19.7.76, 29.11.76), and the League of Communists had to put pressure on its members to accept managerial appointments (B 4.9.74). Furthermore, successful enterprises paid hardly any better than those making losses (Ep 12.9.77).

The communists vacillated between attacking directors for not giving the workers their full rights (B 21.1.65, 28.2.65) and defending them against the workers. In thc end, it was suggested, at least by the Slovene League of Communists, that the League should once again exercise stronger influence over appointments in workers' organisations, so that directors would again become less businessmen and more political workers (Ep 2.10.72). According to private information, many directors who were not members of the Communist League were eased out in the 1970s. Apparently in 1975, 15 per cent of directors of foreign trade organisations were not members of the League of Communists (Ep 14.2.77). The party renewed its control over and increased political pressure on management (47, pp. 320, 326).

Attacks on managers are mostly extended to include professional specialists, particularly engineers. They are accused of 'bureaucratic-technocratic, petty-bourgeois and civil servant practice and tendencies' because they allegedly 'undermine the power of workers and productive labour in the name of rationality and businesslike behaviour so as to protect their own interests and monopoly'. Instead of talking primarily of self-management, they apparently leave that to the representatives of the League of Communists and trade-unions, and busy themselves with the problems of economy and technology (D 12.1.72, 10.11.73, P 16.5.70).

12.4 'POLITICIANS' AND 'BUSINESSMEN'

Although there are very close links between the political hierarchy and the business leadership (fusion of party and management in 12) the communist leaders constantly felt threatened by those who were successful in running production enterprises. There are two possible explanations: one is that a manager by necessity creates a position of power for himself and thus becomes less dependent on politicians and hence dangerous to them, and the other, partly linked with the first, that life forces managers to seek practical solutions and that they, therefore, stop believing in Marxism and in this way undermine the position of political leaders. The distinction between 'politicians' and 'businessmen' caused considerable annoyance to the League leadership, which called this distinction 'artificial' (B 28.3.63).

Bajt thought that politicians distrusted managers because they were bound to compete with them for political control, and Jerovsek considered that the fear of technocracy's influence on political structures was not without foundation (55, p. 237). In Bajt's view this mistrust leads to cyclical outbursts of anti-managerialism when managers — the word itself is derogatory — are accused of technocratism, autocratism, commercialism, unlawfulness and such like (10). Attempts were made to give this accusation some kind of scientific respectability (D 15/22/29.6., 6.7.74). Technocraticism was linked with etatism, i.e. Stalinism, although it was the exact opposite of it in most respects. Both were said not to believe in 'our working class' as the main factor in 'our socialist society' (B 3.8.71). The political leaders were intent on keeping the working class atomised and not allowing it to coalesce around anybody, let alone communist managers.

The institution of re-election was apparently designed to prevent managers from staying in the same enterprise for a prolonged period, although this might seem to be one of the requirements for a business to succeed. The Belgrade local politicians, for instance, included quicker rotation in a 'self-management agreement', only to be accused of trying to browbeat the old, experienced managers. The directors reciprocated the dislike of politicians and accused them of only knowing how to talk instead of doing anything (D 9.7.72). Businessmen did not want to be just the politicians' 'long arm' (D 25.8.71). They resented the unstable legal conditions and the endless meetings and conferences (127, p. 233).

The pragmatism of managers was, of course, a thorn in the flesh of ideologists: of the three initial tenets of Marxism-Leninism — abolition of private ownership of the means of production, centralist planning, and priority for the production of the means of production — only the first one remained. The other two had not only been given up, but turned out to have been misconceived. People started doubting that private ownership was in fact the root cause of all evil. It had been abolished, but evil continued because of the concentration of power in the hands of politicians and there might even have been exploitation since attempts to work out clear rules for distribution failed.

The party ideologist Edward Kardelj tried to prevent such doubts spreading wider and wider by reasserting the 'class position of the League of Communists today' (D 19.10.69). Attempts by managers to organise the country on a down-to-earth basis were described as a 'mass invasion of petty-bourgeois mentality' which had to be countered by 'loyalty to our socialist vision' (D 14.3. 70). Topical economic questions were concealing the real class essence of the political struggle (Kraigher, S., D 22.4.72). Discussions on Marxist theory followed one another (NR 20.4., 8.6., 31.8.73). The League of Communists was the first to give up its monopoly, it was said, but this move had been misunderstood. It could not be implemented overnight and it was blurred by 'a great error conceived by Milovan Djilas' (D 8.10.71). In short, the League of Communists wanted its leading position back (P 29.2.72).

In 1968, the students' demonstrations in Belgrade were an opportunity for the political leadership to crack down on managers and technocrats (D 26.3.69). They conveniently forgot that the students were attacking primarily the politicians — the 'red aristocracy' — and only then the communist businessmen — the 'red bourgoisie' — and inaugurated a campaign against 'people getting rich'. Communist organs one after the other came out against 'riches' and ascribed them to 'abuses, non-fulfilment of social obligations, inefficient taxation policy, inadequate distribution and such like' (D 9.6.68). Small private entrepreneurs were also included in the measures taken to limit 'wealth'.

Many measures were taken and statements issued with the aim of eliminating inequalities, which all culminated in the 1972 Conclusions of the Federal Assembly on the Tasks for Preventing and Eliminating Socially Unjustified Social Differences (Sl 35/72). These conclusions came as an anticlimax because, besides various references to illegal acts, social differences were mainly blamed on the incompleteness of the economic system, unequal business conditions, difficulties about employment, and imperfectly regulated relationships in organisations of associated labour. The remedies were (more) changes in the economic system, contractual personal incomes policies, revision of property conveyancing and taxation policy, and more efficient checks on the origin of property.

The search for riches concentrated on weekend houses (D 26.3.69) of which there were apparently 43,000 in the whole of Yugoslavia, 72 per cent containing one to two rooms only, and 40 per cent with electricity and water supply, but 15 per cent without any amenities (Ep 10.1.72).

Partly it was true that people invested their savings in unproductive luxuries unless they were prepared to leave their money in savings accounts and be eroded. There was no possibility of investing one's savings in anything productive in Yugoslavia (cf. 92, p. 128). As late as 1976, an accountant's weekend-house was confiscated although he had earned the money with which to buy it by keeping books for about ten sports associations. The Commission for the investigation of the origin of wealth suggested confiscation and the courts confirmed it, implying that it was wrong to earn enough money to buy a second home even if one works as hard as this accountant (Ep 25.10.76).

Accusations of fraud, embezzlement, and robbery started being made in all directions. Headlines such as 'Who is stealing?' (Tanjug 25.6.72), 'Respected embezzlers' (Tanjug 21.1.72) and 'Honesty is in question' (D 4.3.72) abounded. Managers were appearing in court all over the country. 'Guilty but not according to the criminal code', reported *Dnevnik* (18.10.72) about a group of directors of the Konus industrial combine and regretted that 'unjustified riches' was not a criminal act. Simultaneously the tax administration could not cope, because some tax inspectors hardly 'knew how to hold a pencil in their hand' (Dn 26.11.72). Finally, in 1972 the communist leader Jure Bilic came forward with a plea for moderation because there was so much talk about robbery, corruption, etc. that Yugoslavia appeared to be a society of robbers (Ep 21.12.72).

Nonetheless, President Tito himself renewed the attack on criminal activity and lack of socialist morality (V 1.2.76). He said that in Yugoslavia nobody, including himself, could become rich through his salary. Many people were enriching themselves by illegal activity. The worst were 'former merchants' but many communists had learned from them and surpassed them. Quite a few did not commit illegal acts for themselves but for their enterprise. If they did that they could be certain of support from their fellow workers: these were 'group-ownership abuses' which were also the subject of a statement by the Praesidium of the CC of the YLC (JP 75, p. 177; Zupanov, V 12.11.75). On the other hand, bribes became a common feature (D 10.11.76) and the recipients were rarely prosecuted.

Backpedalling became necessary immediately after the beginning of the campaign against 'riches'. At any rate, in May 1968, communist leaders (Kraigher, S., D 7.5.68) were warning against *uravnilovka* as a return to state intervention. Somewhat later, Edvard Kardelj (K 10.1.70) suggested that a clear distinction should be made between social differences and social differentiation in the old sense. The latter was due to 'various remnants of the class society or of the etatist elements of the new society', while the former was a consequence of distribution according to labour. Social differences were rational because they gave incentives for more productive and qualified work. 'We cannot reduce high personal incomes if they originate from work, but must concentrate on the improvement of efficiency which will make it possible to raise low personal incomes', explained Kardelj. Nevertheless, some people preferred to work less, so as not to earn too much (Sefer, D 15.9.73).

Research sponsored by trade unions and conducted by Berislav Sefer showed that a redistribution of 18 per cent of the national income would make all incomes completely equal (NR 23.11.68). Kardelj claimed that by taxing away all earnings over dinars 2000 (about $ 130) a month and redistributing the proceeds everybody else would gain only dinars 18 per month (V 28.2.70). In itself, research was a great step forward because, at the start of the campaign, accusations of 'riches' were flung around without any data (Ep 28.2.72). In the end it turned out that in Slovenia the ratio between the average incomes of unqualified workers and experts was 1:2.8 and that this ratio was stable: it had increased from 1:2.76 to 1:2.81 in eight years. The span between the highest and lowest incomes in Slovenia was 1:12 and if income per member of family was taken, 1:25 (Vus 3.11.71). This ratio of 1:2.81 compared with ratios of 1:5.9 in France, 1:4.3 in Denmark, 1:3.5 in Britain, 1:2.4 in Norway and 1:1.9 in Western Germany, but caution is required regarding any international comparisons. For East European countries such data are less reliable, but it was believed that the Soviet ratio was 1:4 or even 1:6. This was the answer to 'bureaucrats' who were trying to prove that social differences had been deepened by the reform, while there were many signs that they had been reduced.

The Marxist philosopher Saksida seems to have begun research in social stratification in the mid-sixties. He came to the preliminary conclusion that in order to understand the social 'strata' it was not enough to base himself on the ownership of means of production, which was negligible in a socialist society anyway, but on the distribution of power, income, consumption and social status (96). Later others added wealth (personal consumption durables) and education (Goricar, NR 22.10.71) while intelligence and family connections should also be included. One can sympathise with those Marxists who claimed that the acceptance of this kind of strata theory is for all practical purposes anti-Marxist because it theoretically denies the existence of the working class (Goricar, NR 9.3.73). But the search for a definition of the working class at the consultation of Yugoslav sociologists bordered on the medieval disputes among the schoolmen. Nevertheless it disposed of all pretence that the abolition of the private ownership of means of production solves all but transitional and temporary problems.

The concept of 'political power' came into its own again. Where political power is absolute, political people also hold all material advantages in their hands and can 'appropriate' whatever they want (Vus 27.10.71). In Yugoslavia, power is no longer absolute, but sufficient for most of the group holding power to profit from it: two thirds of communist league members have incomes above the average. High incomes in themselves (or property for that matter) do not give much security because people are given them only on sufference from political leaders; witness the campaign for the so-called equality itself. Neither is security provided by self-management or direct democracy because it atomises the population as long as they cannot organise themselves as an opposition against the rulers (12) which, however, is a move towards representative democracy and pluralism (see p. 174).

Stane Saksida (Vus 27.10.71) came to the conclusion that social mobility in Yugoslavia was minimal. Of course, the social picture did change immediately after the war, or rather after the revolution, but the social position changed most for those who joined the communist party after the war, then for those who had been party members since before the war, less for those who participated in the liberation war without becoming communists, and hardly at all for the broad mass. On the contrary, the class of rulers rose much above the mass.

Now they are protecting their position and have erected walls around themselves. Those from the highest classes have social relations only with each other, possibly also with children of middle class parents, but never with children from the lowest class. In Slovenia, 55 per cent of the whole social structure, or 75 per cent of the population, are manual workers. Barely 40 per cent of pupils in elementary schools belong to this 'stratum', 18 per cent in secondary schools, and 16 per cent in higher schools. In the Slovene parliament, there was one single industrial worker in 1971, i.e. 0.3 per cent of the total membership, while 71.2 per cent of members belonged to the 'leading personnel'. Of course, all 'leading personnel' belong to the Marxist working class, however, as a party document said, antagonisms have arisen between various parts of the working class and the vanguard role of the League of Communists should help to overcome them.

The Slovene communist leader Vinko Hafner commented:

> Many old, but also some young, communists have grasped by now that, after so many years of work, they no longer command any support from among workers, they no longer speak the same language – or to put it more succinctly, they no longer have the same interests. (Vus 27.10.71)

13: Strikes and Unemployment

13.1 STRIKES

As originally, from an orthodox Marxist point of view, the possibility of conflicts was denied, it was claimed that any strikers would in fact be acting against themselves (see p. 55). The belief that there could not be any conflicts went so far that, for a while, no grievance procedures existed in factories (56, 8). This absence of a vent for dissatisfaction and for different interests aggravated the conflicts which inevitably occured in practice (55, pp. 185–6). Consequently, strikes or 'work stoppages' as they were called, gradually became a normal phenomenon and there were about 2000 (JP 69, p. 44) during the 1960s, which means just over 200 a year on average. After a lull, there were again 159 stoppages from 1973 till the end of 1976 in Slovenia alone (Ep 22.8.77).

The reasons for these strikes were manifold, but on the whole the conflicts were intensified by the underlying non-conflict model which confused the workers, who did not know where to direct their dissatisfaction and where to look for those responsible (who in a sense did not exist anyway) (56). The number of strikes might have been much higher and the strikes themselves much worse if there had not been, in the background, the disapproving strictures by the supreme leader maintaining that this kind of thing should not be allowed.

Semi-officially (JP 69, p. 44) strikes were said to be mainly due to unresolved problems in the distribution of income. This could take the form of one working unit resenting the treatment of another working unit. Such occurrences were particularly interesting because they led Kardelj (61) to say that it 'was illusory to believe that any system could automatically solve all problems . . . and . . . prevent all phenomena of inequality and conflict between people' (p. 63), and that 'absolute justice in distribution according to work was impossible' (p. 90). He could as well have said that no distribution according to work was possible because nobody knows how to measure work in physical terms.

Instead Kardelj said that criteria of distribution could not be made 'objective'; that there was no system which could prevent 'unsocialist relationships in practice' (p. 96). Hence conflicts and 'work stoppages', although there should not be any under 'ideal' socialist self-management (p. 90). Some groups of workers were even provoking conflicts in order to gain advantages for themselves (p. 90). And if workers were allowed 'to appropriate enterprises' revenue without limit and in a socially irresponsible way', those workers employed in 'highly accumulative' plants would be privileged and would become 'parasites living at the expense of the labour of others' (p. 93). These statements obviously meant that the possibility existed of exploitation of one worker by another even after the abolition of private ownership of means of production and the introduction of self-management. The government was trying to find a solution, but this proved very difficult (see p. 217). Another conclusion drawn was that many people 'idealised the working man and overestimated his real possibilities' (JP 69 p. 446) (see pp. 245–6).

However, it was not only the distribution of income within enterprises that caused strife, but also simply what workers considered excessively low incomes (D 15.7.71) or excessive fluctuations in monthly incomes (D 19.2.72). In many instances, workers refused to accept the results of the market. The general manager of the Ravne iron-works, which went on strike for that reason, wrote in *Delo* that the independent distribution of income within enterprises was over-idealised because some working organisations also distributed what they had gained 'by speculation or by customs duties and taxation fraud' (D 22.2.72). Nonetheless, the workers' urge to distribute in excess of enterprises' income was so strong that 'socialisation of losses or strikes' were mentioned as alternatives (Ep 22.8.77).

There were other reasons for strikes: some were directed against the leading managers who, however, refused to be made responsible for solutions which were not within their full control, or directly against local authorities and indirectly even against higher authorities. There were strikes against the decisions of the workers' councils (56). Even if the workers council represented the majority, various minorities could still feel badly treated. The homogeneity of socialist society was an 'etatist illusion' (127, p. 157). On the other hand, there were also strikes in solidarity with workers dismissed from enterprises. Workers mainly went on strike when they exhausted the regular internal procedure for changing an enterprise decision they did not like (127, p. 156). On some occasions, the reasons for strikes were quite exotic: in

Stara Pazova, a factory stopped work because of the dumping of butane bottles from Czechoslovakia (Ep 21.6.71); on another occasion a knitting factory at Lebane struck because they did not like a Belgrade television programme about their enterprise (Ep 13.11.72).

Strikes sometimes required police (militia) intervention and even became violent. In 1969, a group of about 40 workers in the open-hearth division of Jesenice iron-works locked themselves into the changing rooms to protest against a reduction in pay. The militia was called in and some of the strikers were arrested. The comment was that 'an organised society had to defend its collective interests' and that the intervention by the militia was proof that the power of the workers' council was not purely fictitious (D 19.4.69). It was also claimed that the real reason for the strike was probably not wages, but was 'of a deeper, political character' (*Glas*, Kranj, 19.7.69). Four workers — the alleged ring-leaders — were expelled from the works (D 29.4.69) and Mitja Ribicic, who had just been appointed federal premier, hailed the anti-strike actions of the Jesenice workers' council as 'an important affirmation of self-managers' and threatened everybody who tried to use 'various forms of undemocratic pressure outside the self-management system' with 'measures of revolutionary pressure' (D 28.4.69). In Jesenice (B 17.4.69) and in some other instances (B 24.8.70), the strikers were obliged to pay for the damage done to the enterprise.

The intervention of the militia was possibly more justified in the strike of 800 workers at the port of Rijeka in June 1969. There all the executives were thrown out of the Port office and beaten in the streets (*Ilustrovana Politika* 3.6.69). Similar things happened elsewhere. There were street demonstrations, physical assaults, interference with production, destruction of social property, etc. (JP 69, p. 495).

The Yugoslav communists were puzzled by the 'work stoppages', which according to doctrine should never have happened, and about which there had never been any legislation (69). However, in 1969, the need for some solution became so urgent that the Praesidium of the League of Communists had to deal with it and issued a document headed Conclusions on Conflict Situations in Working Organisations (JP 69 p. 495).

The leaders found it very difficult to explain why strikes took place under socialism. They said that there was an essential difference between Yugoslav strikers and strikers under the capitalist system. There the purpose was to change production relations, while in Yugoslavia it was not. This statement was strange as a few lines previously in the same document said that strikes could be 'anti-self-management and anti-socialist'. Kardelj (61, p. 91) added that under capitalism strikes 'were the only possible weapon in the solution of relations between workers, selling their labour power, and owners of capital as buyers of labour power'. This approach was a consequence of the Marxist misunderstanding that under capitalism there is an enormous surplus value for which workers must fight. If it is recognised that investment and taxation are necessary under any system, only what capitalists consume could be distributed among others. Workers, therefore, strike against each other because they are trying to distribute among themselves much more than there is to distribute at all. Something similar was happening Yugoslavia: the Executive Committee of the Slovene League of Communists criticised workers for believing that solutions were not dependent on their own efforts but could be found outside their workers' organisation (D 2.6.68). Fundamentally, strikes are as rational or irrational in socialism as in capitalism.

The Praesidium stated that strikes were damaging for the working class and could not be the method for resolving problems in Yugoslav society. In its view, strikes were due to bureaucratic and technocratic managerial relations, retarded socialist consciousness in workers, the inadequate material basis of self-management, the appropriation of income regardless of work results, differing business conditions, hostile elements and ideological and political remnants of the class enemy and so on. They could have simply stated that neither capitalism nor socialism can solve all human problems and that, therefore, clashes are inevitable and it would be better to bring them out into the open.

The Praesidium's solution was self-management agreements and contracts and arbitration in which trade unions should play a considerable role. Social factors outside the working organisations should be brought into the picture, but nobody should be allowed to grant anybody anything in excess of 'real possibilities'. After each strike, the responsibility for it should be apportioned, the responsible ring leaders should be punished and the working people who stopped work should be held responsible for material and social damage.

Even after this pronouncement by the Praesidium, the legal or even ideological position on strikes remained vague. For the Second Self-management Conference in 1971, a self-management code was prepared (*Sunday Times* 4.4.71) Art. 8 of which read:

> In order to restore self-management which has been weakened, in order to protect the rights and interests of the workers which have

been violated, self-managers are allowed, without suffering any consequence, to proclaim an effective stoppage of work, or to stop work.

The Code was never adopted and para. 1 of Art. 47 of the 1974 Constitution simply says:

> If a dispute arises in an organisation of associated labour between workers of different parts of the organisation, or between workers and organs of the organisation, or of the social political community, and this dispute cannot be solved in the regular way, the workers have the right and duty to express their claims through the trade-union organisation.

The Yugoslav communists kept vacillating between the propaganda value of claiming that there was freedom to strike in Yugoslavia and that there were no strikes there at all. On 4 Apr. 1971, William Shawcross wrote an article in the *Sunday Times* under the heading 'Tito gives the right to strike'; in 1974, David Lascelles reported in *The Financial Times* that workers' self-management had eliminated strikes (5.7.74). Neither report turned out to be entirely true. In 1975, it was again reported that Yugoslavs were to get the right to strike (*Observer* 6.4.75). At any rate, Yugoslav sociologists argue that the absence of labour strife does not necessarily indicate any kind of superiority—it may simply mean that all conflicts are suppressed (55, p. 199).

13.2 UNEMPLOYMENT

The elimination of overfull employment was one of the first thoughts of Yugoslav economic reformers (see pp. 14 and 41) because they were aware both of the demoralising effect of being employed without having a job to do, and of the catastrophic effect of concealed unemployment on efficiency. Chronic unemployment began in the early 1950s when those hurriedly employed in 1949 in excess of real needs were dismissed. Since then the number employed outside agriculture has risen continuously, but so has the number of unemployed, indicating that new job opportunities could not keep up with the numbers looking for employment.

In 1965 the average yearly number employed outside agriculture reached 3,662,000 persons, of which 79,000 were in the private sector

(SG 1963, p. 96). During the reform the number fell to 3,561,000 in 1967 (private sector 95,000), i.e. by 101,000 or just under 3 per cent — only to begin rising again and reaching 4,925,500 (private sector 92,000) in 1976 (SG 77, p. 114).

At the same time, the number of unemployed rose from 267,000 at the end of 1965, to 327,000 at the end of 1968, fell to 290,000 at the end of 1971 (SG 1973, p. 106) and rose to 478,000 at the end of 1974 and 665,000 at the end of 1976 (SG 77, p. 125). The figure of 750,000 unemployed was mentioned in mid-1977 (Ep 6.6.77).

Although the employment figures are yearly averages and the unemployment figures for the end of the year, the relationship between these figures may still have some significance. Unemployment as a percentage of those employed was 7 per cent in 1965, 10.6 per cent in 1974 and 13.5 per cent in 1976 (cf. Ep 23.5.77).

There is some indication that the figures for the unemployed are incomplete. Statistical tables show (e.g. SG 73, p. 106) that in the last few years more people were simply scored off the list of unemployed than found employment through employment bureaux. Apparently, many workers in search of work do not register with employment bureaux because they do not expect to get work through them (P 27.3.73). Very few of those registered were in receipt of an unemployment payment. Their number was reduced from just over 32,000 in 1967 to just over 10,000 in 1971, and this rose to 18,700 in 1976 (SG 77, p. 126). While a contribution towards the payment of unemployment benefit has to be paid by every employed person, only those whose households do not earn a certain (obviously small) amount per member receive the unemployment benefit (JP 74, p. 9). These arrangements are subject to social contracts and self-management agreements, which, as *Jugoslovenski Pregled* puts it, are the most efficient ways to overcome and resolve conflict situations when it is necessary to adjust individual wishes to objective possibilities at a certain level of social development. Hopes for the liquidation of unemployment are not high: over the last few years the average number of unfilled vacancies dropped from 83,000 in 1964 to 53,500 in 1976 (SG 77, p. 127).

To what extent concealed unemployment has fallen from its onetime level of between 15 and 20 per cent (see p. 93) is difficult to assess. Most probably Yugoslav enterprises could still produce as much as they do after dismissing between 200,000–500,000, i.e. 5 to 12 per cent. And of course some of those employed are only necessary as long as enterprises are allowed to produce for stock-piling or to erect unutilised or under-utilised plant. The number of those 'unproductively employed' is estimated at 1.5 million, i.e. about 33 per cent of the enterprise labour force (Ep 9.5.77).

13.3 WORK ABROAD

The gravity of the situation in Yugoslavia cannot be understood without taking into account the fact that from the early 1960s emigration in search of work abroad began and developed into an exodus. By 1971 there were 672,000 Yugoslavs at work abroad, of whom 71,000 were dependents, the rest active workers. This migration was shown for the first time in a table published by the SG 73, on p. 109.

Whether this figure is correct or whether it should be higher as many a Yugoslav worker abroad succeeded in evading government surveys, is difficult to say. The statistical expert Ivo Vinski (V 23.11.72) estimated that there was an under-recording of 5 per cent so that the number of workers abroad at the beginning of 1971 was about 700,000 and at the beginning of 1972 800,000. The number rose to this figure from 350,000 in 1968. Official figures indicate that, at the end of 1972, there were about one million Yugoslav workers and dependents abroad. This was about 10 per cent of the total active population (P 14.4.73) and about 20 per cent of those employed outside agriculture. For 1975, the figure was put at 1.1 million (Smole, D 21.6.75).

The official attitudes to the exodus of Yugoslav workers showed puzzlement and uncertainty. The first reaction was to prohibit such departures, but then the Praesidium of the Yugoslav trade unions expressed the opinion that it was impossible to stop the outflow of workers by administrative measures. Instead, economic conditions should be improved and wages increased (B 12.11.65). It was added that a return to 'full employment' of the kind existing before the reform would not make sense. Then 'there was little work and many skimpy wages' (B 5.12.65). Finally, a consultation organised at the Central Committee of the Yugoslav League of Communists came to the conclusion that employment abroad was an'economic necessity' (B 20.4.68).

Nevertheless, the motives of those going abroad soon began to be questioned by those left behind with a much lower living standard. An inquiry into the primary motives of emigrants (JP 71, p. 1) showed that in 38.2 per cent of cases this was to solve the accommodation problem at home; in 36.3 per cent to find employment; in 12.7 per cent to earn money for buying a small business and in 12.2 per cent to improve their skills or buy a car. A later inquiry into multiple motives (P 7.10.73) provided a different picture: 63.2 per cent were going abroad because of the low earnings in Yugoslavia and only 22.9 per cent because of unemployment. The tacit interpretation seems to have been that people went because they wanted more money (i.e. were greedy). It is true that a considerable part of those going abroad had employment before leaving, but they were replaced by others in their Yugoslav enterprise who would obviously have remained without work had their predecessors not gone.

The possibility of a 'brain drain' became a worry (D 3.5.69) and the question of how to prevent experts from leaving was raised (B 1.3.70). Most were said to be leaving because they were dissatisfied with their position in enterprises, which was also confirmed by sociologists (127, p. 74, mentions the 'mass exodus' of engineers). Vinski (V 23.11.72) showed that the percentage of qualified people was higher amongst emigrants than amongst the working population at home. In the end, the 1973 Act on Immigration provided for a migration plan to prevent the unchecked departure of experts (Sl 33/73 and Vus 20.6.73).

The large numbers of Yugoslav workers abroad were not only an ideological embarrassment for the Yugoslav communists and a drain on the Yugoslav Army, over which Tito was worried, but there was the danger that they would be politically influenced by their new surroundings (JP 73, p. 49). A supplement to Borba (30.6.70) complained that foreign police and intelligence services tolerated propagandistic, intelligence and terrorist activity by Yugoslav political exiles amongst Yugoslav workers abroad. While the third and possibly the second kinds of activity were no doubt deplorable, there was no reason why foreign authorities should try and prevent Yugoslav workers from being exposed to information not controlled by Yugoslav communists. In any case, they could not have done so even if they had wanted to, since Yugoslav workers had eyes to see and could draw their own conclusions. Tito himself pointed out in a speech (P 14.9.74) that Yugoslav workers earned far better wages abroad than at home and said that they should work as well at home as they did in Federal Germany. Then he admitted that the difference was due to the 'organisation of work'. Did he realise that, in fact, he was accusing himself? Certainly, differences in productivity between Western Europe and Yugoslavia were to a considerable degree due to historical development, but a sizeable part of the lag in catching up must be attributed to communist experiments.

Despite the much higher earnings of Yugoslav workers in Germany than at home, the Yugoslav communists were eager to accuse the host countries of 'capitalist exploitation' and push Yugoslav workers into collaboration with left-wing groups (D 17.3.73, NR 6.12.74). They should have known better than to undermine a system which helped Yugoslavia itself to overcome its difficulties. In contrast, it was in order for the Yugoslav authorities to try and obtain the best possible conditions for Yugoslav citizens abroad (B 4.8.69). The difficulty was that many Yugoslav citizens were afraid that this 'protection' would only enable the Yugoslav authorities to get hold of an unjustifiably large part of their earnings.

Discussions on how to persuade the workers abroad to come home began in the late sixties and early seventies. Some leading persons were seriously worried about the numbers leaving, but simply believed that a great economic expansion would start in the near future which would induce the workers to come back. They were not prepared to do anything more substantial than that, while many Slovene and Croat deputies were trying to obtain customs duty and other concessions for returning emigrants from the Federal Assembly which could encourage them to come back. They were also suggesting that expatriates should be lured back by better conditions for opening private businesses (D 12.3.71).

Many enterprises wanted to profit from the foreign exchange the emigrants possessed (see p. 165) which they wanted to use to buy machinery abroad. Although originally the authorities were thinking of checking on the 'origin' of foreign exchange deposited in private citizens' accounts (B 21.6.69), later the danger of frightening workers abroad off depositing their currency in Yugoslav banks led to repeated assurances that the government would not interfere with these deposits (B 26.9.71). Some enterprises wanted to introduce shares which workers abroad could buy (see p. 218), others went ahead and promised workers abroad employment if they were prepared to buy a machine for them (B 16.12.70) or to lend them foreign exchange (B 4.10.70).

In the 1970s, the remittances by workers abroad to Yugoslavia played an important role in balancing the foreign accounts (see p. 165). They amounted to over 5 per cent of the Yugoslav GSP—the peak in 1973 was 7.3 per cent—and paid for 8.6 per cent of 1975 consumption in Yugoslavia (JP 76, p. 145; JP 77, p. 325).

Eventually, the possibility of a large-scale return of workers from abroad became only too true. The depression in Western Europe deepened in 1974—to a considerable extent under the effect of agitation by left-wingers for unrealistic wages—and unemployment figures rose even in Germany. Now, the permanent discussion on how to bring the workers back was replaced by worries that they might really be sent back and by demands that Germany in particular should guarantee further employment of Yugoslav emigrant workers (D 10.1.75). By the end of 1976, about 300,000 had returned (Ep 6.12.76). The Yugoslav government tried to persuade West European governments that they should make financial contributions for the re-employment of the Yugoslav workers returning home, but so far only the Netherlands has paid 6 million guilders into a special fund (D 21.10.77).

In Yugoslav unemployment and immigration policy, the North-Western Republic of Slovenia occupies a very special position, which prompted *Ekonomska politika* to publish an article under the heading 'The tribulations of full employment' (Ep 14.4.75). The situation there displays many similarities to Switzerland. Although the figures one can find differ, according to some data there are about 80,000 Slovenes working abroad (D 5.10.74) (the population of Slovenia in 1971 was about 1,725,000) and there are as many Yugoslavs from other republics working in Slovenia (D 21.9.74). About 60 per cent of the newcomers are unskilled, but about half of them soon learn a skill. They work mainly in construction (42 per cent are employed in this branch) and in municipal services (15 per cent). They are not only prepared to accept lower jobs, they are also ready to live in makeshift accommodation, which the Slovenes refuse even if they are unemployed, in one of the still predominantly agrarian regions of Slovenia. These workers 'from other republics' are resented by Slovenes—they also have difficulty in learning Slovene—but the Slovenes are not inclined to do the work they do.

Parallel with this development, employment in Slovenia has been rising by leaps and bounds in comparison with the rest of Yugoslavia, so that according to the *Ekonomska politika* article quoted, there are two to three vacancies for one unemployed in contrast to the rest of Yugoslavia where the relationship for instance in Macedonia is 36 unemployed per unfilled vacancy. While in all the rest of Yugoslavia investment is excessively capital-intensive, the opposite is true in Slovenia because of low personal incomes, owing to the influence of equalisation tendencies (D 29.3.71). The problem could possibly be solved if the Slovenes were allowed to export their entrepreneurship to the rest of Yugoslavia, but this possibility is blocked by the system in spite of the possibility of 'cooperation' between enterprises (see p. 117).

13.4 REASONS FOR LACK OF EMPLOYMENT OPPORTUNITIES

The transition from an agricultural society to an industrial society is difficult, particularly if forced into a short period. Under any conditions, this transition inevitably leads to stresses and strains. When trying to diagnose the reasons for unemployment, *Jugoslovenski Pregled* singled out, amongst other things, the depressed situation of agriculture and the privileged position of some other branches of the economy, and the volume and direction of investment (JP 67, p. 258).

In the immediate postwar years, all sorts of pressures (including militia) (see p. 14) were used to force people off the land and to employ them indiscriminately in industrial activities and state administration. Without doubt, as an economy advances and productivity increases, the agricultural population has to be reduced, but the reduction will come by itself if productivity in agriculture in fact rises and it must come gradually. The Yugoslav communists neither saw to the improvement of agricultural productivity nor phased the transition, but wanted everything at once.

In the teeth of all economic calculation, which was disdained as a capitalist prejudice, enormous amounts were invested by concentrating on branches which needed least labour, although they were unprofitable (see p. 28). Investment was not merely too capital intensive, but often just wasted too. The 1973 conclusions of the League of Communists (JP 93, p. 49) concerning emigration did stress 'faster development of branches which require less investment per employee' as a remedy, but at this stage it is very difficult to correct the previous distortions because of the physical composition of the productive capital stock.

When 'associated labour' took over, further pressure for capital intensive investment developed, although accumulation in enterprises tended towards zero. It was in the interest of employed workers to amass capital, if obtainable, in their own enterprise if it raised their own productivity at all, rather than establish new jobs although the latter might have raised productivity by much more, but this of course would have benefited other workers. While workers will not dismiss their mates to increase their own pay (see p. 95), they are quite happy to restrict employment opportunities to achieve the same effect. Workers' management leads to greater capital intensity than appropriate and less employment (47, p. 389).

The emigration conclusions admitted that 'personal work with private means' could help in creating more employment opportunities, but in practice this private work was so hemmed in that it could hardly develop so as to help with employment. A leader in the Ljubljana *Delo* (29.3.73) said that emigrants would not be able to come home and find work as along as 'we quarrelled about dogmatic theses whether it is still socialism (for a private workshop) to employ six workers instead of five or to have a six-ton lorry instead of five-ton lorry'. The underlying ideology preferred unemployment to prosperity on the basis of private initiative.

The initial neglect of the tertiary sector could not be entirely repaired either, although the emigration conclusions called for that, but here again more scope for private initiative would have helped.

Finally, many highly qualified specialists could not find work because the posts requiring their qualifications were occupied by insufficiently qualified persons. *Jugoslovenski Pregled* (JP 67, p. 257) mentioned that, in 1967, 150,000 workers with low skills and 400,000 unskilled workers were in posts for which a higher qualification was required. Yugoslav experts employed abroad often said that they would not return home as long as Yugoslavia was dominated by (politically) 'deserving' people who no longer met the requirements of the jobs they were doing (D 29.3.71).

13.5 THE RIGHT TO WORK

All in all, in the mid-1970s, there were about 700,000 fully unemployed, 700,000 workers abroad, 500,000 in unproductive employment in manufacturing and possibly the same number in agriculture (cf. larger figures in Ep 9.5.77). This means that worthwhile work cannot be found in Yugoslavia for about a quarter of the total labour force and about one-third of the non-agricultural labour force. It is a sobering thought that the situation might have been worse had 1,700,000 people not been killed during the war according to official figures, and had not some 300–400,000 gone into political emigration immediately after the war.

Small wonder that the right to work written into all Yugoslav constitutions—e.g. Art. 36 of the 1963 Constitution, and Art. 159 of the 1974 Constitution—called forth only sarcastic remarks by young people. A student commented in 1967:

> The social ownership of means of production is then no panacea with which to cure unemployment and guarantee the right to work, the

> most fundamental of all rights. It is true, as Marx said, that unemployment is a proof that a society is incompetent but this goes not only for the incompetence of a capitalist society . . . For the time being, we are forced to send our unemployed to work in precisely those states which do not recognise the right to work . . . We are sending them into capitalist slavery! Surprisingly, we all gain from that: the worker who earns more than at home, the society because the unemployment pressure is reduced, and the State because of the improvement in the balance of payments. (46)

In 1952, President Tito said that the Soviet Union was no better than capitalist States, but he still thought that it had solved the problem of unemployment. Later on this illusion also evaporated. In 1960, Vukmanovic (121, p. 360) was telling Polish trade-unionists how Yugoslav enterprises were dismissing workers, who thus became unemployed, but added: 'Of course, the problem of unemployment develops. But it existed before too, except that it was concealed because there were many workers in enterprises who were not needed for production at all'. This evaluation also applied to Soviet enterprises.

Naturally, it was no use to keep people in employment where they were not needed, but jobs should have been generated for them. It was hardly an improvement to claim that Yugoslav unemployment was not 'the classical unemployment' (JP 67, p. 257). 'Classical' unemployment occurs when marginal enterprises are not capable of paying the existing wages; the Yugoslav unemployment developed because the communists were not capable of properly combining factors of production and generating real working places.

Yugoslav communist writers meanwhile continue to denigrate pre-war Yugoslavia because there was a (peak?) unemployment rate of 12 per cent (130,000 unemployed vs. 950,000 employed outside agriculture) (Vinski quoted in JP 74, p. 1) and because, from 1920–1935, 74,000 emigrants went abroad (119).

Part Four

More Institutional Changes (1970s)

14: Organisational Reforms

14.1 REORGANISATION OF ENTERPRISES

In March 1968, Yugoslav economists discussed two reports prepared by the Economic Institute in Zagreb (38, 39, 40) at a symposium in Opatija. The main conclusion was that the Yugoslav enterprise was over-regulated (39, p. 122 ff). Legislation still interfered with areas of the activity of working organisations that could advantageously be left to themselves. The economic system was 'slow-moving and very rigid'; the legal provisions were difficult to understand, so that they required mandatory interpretations, creating new problems; in 1965, three federal acts were published per day, not including acts at lower levels; all of which led to insecurity and uncertainty (see p. 236). The best solution would have been for the law to determine only the basic principles and a framework for the behaviour of enterprises.

The Constitutional Amendment XV, adopted in 1968 (Sl 55/68; JP 68, p.9), accepted these suggestions and provided that the members of a working organisation and its constituent parts might independently decide on which decisions they would reserve for themselves, what jurisdiction they would transfer to workers' councils and what executive, collegiate or individual managerial posts they would establish. The relative freedom of organisations led to a great diversity at the levels above the still obligatory workers' councils: some enterprises introduced administrative committees, others business committees; various consultative and auxiliary bodies such as 'collegia' of experts, commissions, committees etc. were established (JP 69, p. 427). Some of the organs were duplicated at the level of the working unit, the component part of an enterprise.

However, it soon transpired (cf. chapter 12) that under the new self-management forms also the real relationships did not correspond to self-management tenets, that the influence of leading personnel was excessive and that of workers insufficient, and that the workers were dissatisfied with their role and demanded that their self-management rights be implemented. There were clashes between parts of enterprises, domination of one part over the others, and lack of coordination (JP 70, p. 227).

To deal with these difficulties, the Federal Assembly adopted a Resolution on the Implementation of Amendment XV (JP 70, p. 233) which praised the attempt to restrict government interference and rely on the creativity of the working people, but then criticised technocratic-bureaucratic, conservative and other anti-self-management tendencies. These allegedly were causing workers to transfer decisions on important economic matters to directors and other executive organs to give members of workers' councils excessively long mandates so that participation in self-management organs was limited and to neglect the adoption of enterprise by-laws.

Then yet another Constitutional Amendment, XXI (JP 71, p. 347), was enacted by the Federal Assembly. It introduced the right to transform any part of a working organisation into a basic organisation of associated labour provided it represented an organisational whole and the results of its work could be confirmed by the market (JP 71, p. 347). These basic organisations are direct descendents of the previous 'economic units' which developed into 'working units'. One might think this was merely a change in terminology but the Federal Assembly (JP 73, p. 7) insisted that the establishment of basic organisations of associated labour and their combination into larger units was 'one of the crucial tasks' bringing about 'deep changes in the functioning of working organisations'. Everywhere action committees had to be elected to implement the constitutional amendments.

The Constitution of 1974 and the 1976 Act on Associated Labour preserved their formal independence of enterprises regarding detailed organisation, but laid down the following provisions: in the basic organisation of associated labour delegates of workers from all parts of the production process had to sit on the workers' council; in the working organisation or composite organisation of associated labour delegates of all basic organisations must represent them on the workers' council; mandates of members of workers' councils must not exceed two years and members could be re-elected only once. In contrast, the tour of duty of an individual manager or of a member of a managing body might be up to four years and they could be re-elected.

The constant flow of small and big changes in legal provisions and terminology required incessant meetings and conferences and registration of changes with courts (Ep 26.11.73). Nonetheless, reorganisations were slow to be implemented and enterprises were late in producing the set of by-laws under Amendment XV (B 12.3.71). After the promulgation of Amendment XXI, seven new acts were needed merely to adjust the previous acts on labour relations, which were now called 'mutual relations between workers'.

In spite of all this activity, at the end of 1976 there were only 419 enterprises in Slovenia consisting of basic organisations of associated labour; 2487 remained unitary (Ep 14.2.77). Moreover, investment decisions were not handed over to the basic organisations at all, but were made completely at the level of the enterprise, with funds being taken from those economic units whose retained earnings were higher than their investment needs. This was a purely book-keeping operation, since the interest charged had no significance to anyone (47, p. 377).

Many communists were worried that enterprises would 'abuse' the freedom given by Amendment XV (Ep 2.2.70) and that 'spontaneity' would become rife if the Party *de facto* gave up making decisions on matters for which ultimately it did not carry any responsibility. *Ekonomska politika* for this reason, accused the Party of behaving like a former owner who had leased his means of production out to workers (Ep 8.6.70 and 31.1.72). At the beginning of the 1970s the accusation that Party representatives were acting like 'padres' to factories was partly a joke, but in 1975 the League of Communists decided to exert its influence on enterprises by passing resolutions which would be mandatory on its members working in them (see p. 232).

In spite of constitutional guarantees for the independence of enterprises, this independence may also have been limited because self-management was given tasks with which it could not cope, as claimed by sociologists. Branko Horvat summarised the situation in mid-1973: 'Therefore all that self-management consists of is hiring and firing. I do not exaggerate if I say that self-management has been liquidated. And since it is supposed to be the driving force of our economy, it can be said that our economic power is failing' (Ep 16.7.73).

The stress on the basic organisations of associated labour was such that Art. 37 of the 1974 Constitution confirmed the workers' right to take any such fundamental unit out of an enterprise, provided this withdrawal did not harm the rest of the working organisation. It was nonetheless expected that basic organisations of associated labour would combine with other basic units 'in order to increase their revenue, improve their work and business and raise the productivity of joint social labour', as Constitutional Amendment XXII put it (JP 71, p. 350). But, as pointed out by Kardelj (61, pp. 98–9), economic incentives did not work in that direction because no proper institutional arrangements had been devised while a simple 'capital relationship' was unacceptable.

Many relationships between firms remained unsatisfactory and integration of enterprises was frequently not based on workers' interests but was due to 'informal' pressure either of political factors or of a stronger economic organisation.

According to Kardelj, this led to 'mammoth' enterprises with centralised direction, whereas a more differentiated structure would have been appropriate. Nevertheless, the faith in bigness was such that Kardelj believed that 'forced' integration, although inappropriate, did give many positive results, possibly more positive than negative. In fact, the Recommendations of the Federal Assembly on the immediate tasks with respect to the implementation of Constitutional Amendments XXI to XXIII expressly stated that the fundamental idea of the new provisions was to facilitate a faster, wider and more complete integration process in the economy (JP 73, p. 7). 'Disintegration and atomisation' were against the spirit of these Amendments.

The integration movement was given a new fillip by the 1976 Act on Associated Labour, Arts 382 to 387 of which established a framework for the so-called 'composite organisations of associated labour', based on self-management agreements. Composite organisations may be founded by organisations which are linked by the supply of inputs, or which produce similar articles, or which intend to share their revenue or have other interests in common.

During the discussion of the Act it was not clear what the aim of these provisions was (Ep 7.7.75) and fears were expressed that they would enable some enterprises to live at the expense of others (Ep 29.9.75). Then the expression 'reproduction linkage' appeared (Ep 11.8.75) and 'the association of labour and resources', meaning the circulation of capital between enterprises, became one of the main purposes quoted. Composite organisation was supposed to help 'to achieve that degree of concentration of capital which was required by the contemporary economy' (Ep 12.4.76). Funds could be transferred from one enterprise to another either against payment of interest and repayment of capital, or without either. In the latter case, the reason might be the elimination of bottlenecks or the need to safeguard supplies (Ep 23.5.77). The payments to the lending enterprise might be conditional on the successful operation of the borrowing organisation, which entails the sharing of risk and, so to speak, 'common income' (Ep 6.10.75). Such cooperation might lead to mutual influence on enterprises' business and development policy or even to mutual determination of transfer prices (Ep 12.4.76).

The cooperation of enterprises in 'reproduction units' was necessary because there was no capital market. More esoteric goals of integration which were mentioned included the need for 'the economic and moral expansion of labour' (Ep 9.4.73) or for 'concentration without alienation' (Ep 2.7.73). Sometimes 'reproduction units' were hurriedly put together under political pressure (Albreht, Ep 6.10.75), or enterprises combined without any 'special reason' to demonstrate their political diligence (Ep 8.8.77).

In this kind of integration the danger of monopoly was constantly present (Ep 12. and 26.12.77), as it was known that the possibility of pushing up prices was one of the reasons for combining (D 7.12.74). Another was to get losses covered by others (Ep 12.4.76, 8.8.77).

The 'socialisation' of losses became the more acceptable as the Act on Associated Labour stressed the social-economic content of income. Thus losses also assumed a 'social character' (Ep 15.12.77). In fact, composite organisations of labour further blurred the economic responsibility of economic units. Anybody who requested that there should be clear-cut market relations between enterprises, to show which were efficient and which not, was accused of having an 'entrepreneurial mentality' and not recognising the 'unity of the process of reproduction' (D 6.12.74, Ep 14.2.77).

14.2 AGREEMENTS AND PLANNING

Self-management agreements and social contracts were first used *ad hoc* (see p. 138) to try to restrict the distribution of income amongst workers, but were then enacted, with wider aims in mind, by Constitutional Amendment XXI, the 1974 Constitution and the Act of Associated Labour. A self-management agreement is defined as an agreement among self-management bodies, whereas a social contract is concluded between the former and political authorities.

Amendment XXI (Sl 29/71) stated that the level of personal incomes and other rights derived from work could be determined by self-management agreement, or social contract, or legal Act, in line with the general level of productivity of social labour as a whole. This limitation of free distribution of income was indubitably a reversal of the initial intentions (see p. 72). In fact, the 'White book' (26, p. 121) had claimed that social regulation of incomes would be a step backward.

Kardelj explained that it was originally hoped that distribution according to labour (61, p. 77) would be brought about by means of some system which would gradually equalise business conditions

(p. 23). The market was supposed to wither away under the influence of the 'organic development of production forces' (p. 65). These expectations had failed.

It was an illusion — Kardelj thought in 1972 — to believe that 'self-managers could solve everything by themselves' (p. 42). The struggle for 'full independence and freedom' of self-managers was waged in the name of workers' rights, while in reality it frequently served 'technocracy'. Even under self-management the absolute freedom of the worker was unreal, particularly with respect to the disposal and distribution of income (p. 60). The course of events could not be left exclusively to 'the freedom of self-managers' or 'direct action of the masses'. Such ideas had an odour of abstract liberalism (p. 38).

Distribution by the market was not distribution according to labour (p. 66) and self-management decisions by workers were 'voluntaristic', i.e. arbitrary, because they were not guided by the three components of the Yugoslav system: the market, planning and solidarity (p. 25). It was impossible to allow workers to 'appropriate' without limit out of their enterprise's income (p. 78) because this could only lead to the appearance of 'elements' of exploitation of some workers by others (p. 86). However, excessive State intervention was also 'voluntaristic' (p. 24).

An objective 'individual quantity of labour' which should presumably determine individual personal incomes did not exist in practice (p. 60). Work is not individual but social and, moreover, combined with means of production in social ownership (p. 62) so that surplus labour flowed between working organisations (p. 63). In other words, Kardelj admitted that there was no way of determining objectively the 'just' or 'correct' pay for a worker, as Marxists always claimed there was. He wrote that there was no method of establishing fully objective criteria for distribution according to labour (p. 87). Distribution according to labour was a question of social convention (pp. 61 and 87).

It was the market that befogged the social character of labour (p. 73), in particular as in Yugoslavia property was not in group ownership but in social ownership (p. 74), which apparently means that workers and the working class as a whole should have economic and political power over the entire capital stock in social ownership, which also means control over common income (p. 72). For this reason, social contracts and self-management agreements should establish criteria for the distribution of personal incomes (p. 87).

Such contracts and agreements could create a precise system within which democratic decision-making was possible (p. 56). To act as 'diligent businessman' self-managers had to be free, but they could be free only if their actions had to remain within the framework of socialist self-management and equality of working people (p. 92).

Under the influence of Kardelj's thought on the social character of labour, contracts and agreements were elevated to a general instrument of Yugoslav system which could help 'gradually to eliminate the present contradiction in Yugoslav society' (61 p. 42). They were applied to all aspects of economic and political life. Their role in integration has been mentioned already and they were also to be used for planning etc. It was hoped the rules they contained would eliminate the need for at least a substantial proportion of State legal Acts (NR 27.2.76, Ep 1.11.76).

The Yugoslav Plan for 1976–80 prescribed that relations between enterprises should depend less and less on sales and purchases but rather be regulated by agreements (Ep 5.4.76). The aim seems to be the replacement of the market by contracts, in line with Kardelj's ideas. One commentator said that in the 1970s the previous market mystique was replaced by a self-management agreement mystique (Zupanov quoted in 41, p. 332), another that the reliance on these agreements had completely abolished economic responsibility (Horvat, Ep 14.11.77).

Ekonomska politika (5.4.76) criticised this shift of emphasis, saying that the market could still contribute much more to the efficiency of the Yugoslav economy than the 'pious wishes' contained in various conclusions, regulations, contracts and agreements. According to the views of the Slovene Vice-Premier, the fulfilment of 'pious wishes' included in the social contracts would have required a GSP double the actual one as well as three times greater foreign loans than were available (Ep 21.4.75).

The normal working of the market, of course, presupposes a network of contracts — it is in reality a network of contracts, explicit or implicit. These contracts are negotiated and concluded between people having opposite interests within a legal framework which establishes the procedure and protects general interests. Yugoslavia is attempting to extend the use of contracts in two senses: (1) the contracts are to be concluded not only between people of different interests, i.e. buyers and sellers, but also between people having the same interests, e.g. between sellers on prices; (2) these one-sided contracts are elevated to general norms, with some legal provisions also to be based on contracts. This extension of the use of contracts poses problems, to say the least.

The contracts and agreements tend to narrow the jurisdiction of the individual 'associated worker' (Ep 15.11.71, 10.4.72) which would be even more restricted if the workers did not largely disregard the agreed rules, especially regarding the distribution of incomes (Ep 25.10.76, 13.6

and 10.10.77). The other danger is that the making of contracts and agreements, which is very time consuming (Ep 26.7.76), occupies managers so much that they have no time to manage production. Instead, they try to gain advantages for their enterprise by negotiating general norms which suit them (D 25.8.74).

Kardelj's doubts about the market also renewed his interest in planning, which had been overlooked because of decentralisation (61, p.22). He reaffirmed that 'society had the right to guide the market' (p. 68) and said that the 'action centralism' needed for this purpose had nothing whatever to do with previous bureaucratic centralism (p. 13). The new slogan became the unity of 'market, social planning and social solidarity of working people' (p. 25), but Kardelj hoped that 'scientific planning' would reduce the market to 'a mere technique' (p. 69).

Even before Kardelj formulated his new theories the Federal Assembly had passed a new Basic Act on Social Planning in 1970 (Sl 28/70) which had made contracts and agreements a part of the system of planning, which thus 'acquired a new quality' (JP 70, p. 33). This Act ended a long period of pragmatic adjustment of planning methods to successive reforms during which planning in fact fell into almost complete desuetude.

The new approach was taken over by the Constitution of 1974 (Arts 69 to 74) in a sufficiently vague form to prevent any harking back to the old administrative planning, while details were left to a specific Act (Kraigher, S., K 23.10.73).

The question of the meaning of what Kardelj called 'scientific planning' remains. At a symposium in Amsterdam in 1970, one Yugoslav participant said that Yugoslavia had no central planning (Samardzija in 18, p. 163) and another that the question of planning had not been solved yet: 'We cannot say which system of planning we have. The whole society is now trying to find a proper solution' (Blum in 18, p. 164).

Things had not advanced much by the time Kardelj said in 1975:

> The new system of planning can be introduced only by a plan. We must start planning so as to be able to introduce the new principles of planning . . . without waiting for the new Act on planning or even for the draft of this Act. (Ep 28.4.75)

When the 1976 Act on the Foundations of the System of Social Planning and on the Social Plan of Yugoslavia (Sl 6/76) was finally made law it did not clarify matters. It did not say what the economic methodology of planning was to be, but empowered the federal government to prescribe 'the obligatory unitary methodology' (Art. 27). What the Act did say was that in principle the plans should be worked out by 'the working class and all working people' (Art. 1) and that individual workers should take part in the formulation of the plan of their basic organisation of associated labour according to its statute (Art. 32).

The procedure of planning was to consist of self-management agreements and contracts between everybody and everybody else. They were to establish common interests and goals and regulate mutual relations, rights, obligations and responsibilities for the achievement of these common interests and goals (Art. 17). Political authorities (social-political communities) were to combine the agreements and contracts into formal plans which could also impose planning obligations on basic organisations in so far as this was consistent with the law (Art. 59), especially if the conclusion of agreements and contracts between them should be delayed (Art. 60). Sanctions could be applied against individuals who would not comply with their obligations.

After the medium-term plan for 1976–80 had been agreed by the representatives of republics and provinces in mid-1976, it was claimed that this was only the beginning and that much more work would have to be done in the form of systemic Acts, social contracts, self-management agreements, supplements and amendments (Ep 28.11.77). This was because many obscurities remained although one of the purposes of planning was to 'control the spontaneous functioning of the market and inequalities in development, in conditions of work and appropriation of income' (Art. 1). The 1976 planning Act does not seem to have improved the economic system, which was 'incomplete and inconsistent' (NR 5.12.75).

In the discussion of the Resolution on Plan Implementation in 1978, one critic said that there was no information about the planning methods used and that plans continued to be excessively ambitious (Bajt, Ep 28.11.77). Although the fundamental category of planning was to be 'income' (Art. 5) and the planning of personal incomes, i.e. an incomes policy, was provided for in Art. 6, inflationary distribution continues.

As early as 1971, *Ekonomska politika* (22.3.71) regretted that self-management agreements in combination with government controls were leading to 'an institutionalised total politicisation of the economy' so that everybody was free to take decisions without bearing the economic consequences.

14.3 CAPITAL MARKETS AND 'PAST LABOUR'

The allocation of capital remains a problem and so does the relationship between individuals and the capital of their enterprise.

The investment of capital where it contributes most to output is very difficult, not to say impossible, when all circumstances push enterprises to plough back their funds. For a while the solution was sought in a capital market, and the 1966 Federal Resolution on Economic Policy demanded that an appropriate mechanism be created (Ep 1.6.70). But it was obviously not easy to devise 'socialist' shares, although the advantages of shares for raising additional capital for enterprises were pointed out (B 3.6., 4.7.70). The sale of shares was also considered to be a way to attract back to Yugoslavia funds earned abroad by Yugoslav workers (D 14.1.71).

Eventually Kardelj came out against shareholding, arguing that private shareholding especially would mean exploitation of other people's labour (D 19.11.71). Nonetheless, he himself pursued the matter further in his booklet on the *Contradictions of Social Ownership* (61). In his view, it was compatible with socialism, indeed, it was 'a relationship most suitable for a socialist society' if one enterprise lent to another money which was then repaid with the addition of a contractually determined 'price' out of the income of the borrowing enterprise (pp. 104–6).Kardelj believed that this relationship could not turn into exploitation for two reasons: (1) because the loan would be extinguished once it had been paid off (*amortiziran*); and (2) because it did not entitle the lending collective to take part in the management of the borrowing collective (p. 95), which according to Kardelj would establish a 'capitalist property relationship'.

It is now Yugoslav practice to allow enterprises to invest in each other and even to establish some sharing in risk and management by means of self-management agreements. But this arrangement does not create an open capital market which would make it possible to obtain an overall view of how efficiently capital is used in different sectors and different enterprises.

These considerations bring us back to the question of how to establish a link between individuals and capital, so as to make them feel responsibility for its use and accumulate new capital through savings. 'Everybody's, somebody's and nobody's ownership gave Yugoslav property relations world exclusivity but also avante-garde problems' claimed a subheading in *Borba* (8.10.70). Criticising people who thus treat social capital as something separate from workers, Kardelj wrote

(61, p. 36): 'They do not understand that social property is simultaneously that kind of 'individual' property without which neither he (the worker) nor his work can be free'. These are mere words which do nothing to align workers' individual interests with their collective interests.

To counter this indeterminateness and establish a better link between items of property and individual workers, the 1971 constitutional amendments introduced Marx's term 'past labour', which in fact simply means capital; witness Kardelj's own expression 'live and past labour, viz. labour and social capital' (61, p. 94). Both the 1974 Constitution (Art. 20) and the Act on Associated Labour (Art. 126) prescribe that the worker's personal income should correspond to the contribution 'which he has made by his live and past labour to the increase in the income of his basic organisation'. Kardelj claims that past labour is not a worker's share in capital but only another measure of live labour.

It is difficult to understand what he means, and hardly surprising that 'the principle of distribution on the basis of past labour, on the basis of the size of accumulation, the administration of accumulation and management is not consistently applied in any organisation of associated labour' (Ep 18.4.77). Nobody understands what this means or, as it was put at a meeting of the CC of the Slovene LC, nobody 'understands the class and social-economic essence of past labour' (Ep 14.3.77).

What else could be expected at a time when 'associated labour' contributed to investment an amount equal to no more than depreciation even if domestic credits are included (Ep 21.4.75). According to the Praesidium of the Croat Business Chamber all new investment came from foreign sources, which is in line with the conclusions of chapter 10.

14.4 ALIENATED CAPITAL

The discussion of banks as institutions holding alienated capital first began as a dispute between republics. When the federal investment fund was turned over to the three federal specialist banks (see p. 146) whose headquarters were in Belgrade, the continued concentration of what became called the 'State' capital gave Serbia a notable preponderance in 'capital markets'. Some 30 billion dinars were involved (K 7.3.69). The Croats (V 25.11.70) were quick to point out that in 1969 Croatia produced 27.2 per cent of GSP, while its credit potential amounted to only 17.7 per cent of the total Yugoslav credit potential, whereas Serbia had

50.3 per cent of this potential compared with a contribution to GSP of 36.8 per cent.

The reply to such complaints was that it was not enough simply to decentralise banking, to move capital from the centre to the republics, but that it must be 'de-etatised', taken out of State hands at any level and returned to direct producers (K 5.11.71). Slogans such as 'a new nationalisation of banks' (NR 11.9.70) even their 'third nationalisation' (Ep 14.9.70) gained currency with the aim of returning 'alienated financial capital' to progressive producers (V 12.2.70).

The communist leader Vladimir Bakaric, a Croat, praised the great achievements of some Yugoslav banks, but then explained the Marxist viewpoint:

> However, if one considers all this realistically—these are all social resources, in fact monetary resources, which move in the sphere of surplus value. As a consequence, they (the banks) do not produce anything, they only administer surplus value. (D 19.9.70)

He said that he himself had coined the term 'nationalisation of banks' as a joke, but that he indeed advocated a closer link between banks and direct producers.

Like most things economic, banks were a subject of the constitutional amendments, as well as a reform of the Act on Banks and Credit at the beginning of 1970. The economic organisations that had invested money in a bank were given the right to 'administer' the bank and were called administrators (*upravljaci*) of the bank. They were to elect an executive committee at a general meeting of founders, where the voting was to be according to capital invested. A credit committee was to represent the bank workers.

The investment in the bank credit fund was to be permanent and would carry an entitlement to interest rates which were to be higher than the interest rates usually paid, depending on business success and in fact would be dividends. An enterprise was to be given a 'receipt' for its investment, which was to be a security that could be sold to another enterprise, but not to other banks or political authorities. The price of these receipts would be a measure of interest rates in the capital market.

On the basis of the new legal provisions, banks were to conclude 'founding agreements' as the *Ljubljanska banka*, for instance, did on 14 June 1974. The Secretary of the new bank, Joze Bencina, commented on this agreement in an interview with *Nasi Razgledi* (8.6.74): 'The bank has thus become a special organisation of associated labour instead of an alienated centre of economic power above the economy. The new bank even dispensed with the credit committee manned by specialists and transferred its functions to the executive committee so that direct producers can distribute credits via their representatives in the bank.' Bencina said: 'It is in no way essential that specialists should decide on the allocation of bank credits.' But the specialists would be consulted, of course. The interviewer insisted that this was playing with words and that credits would in reality continue to be distributed by people who did not create the resources of economic organisations; thus they would be alienated from direct producers in spite of everything. Bencina thought that ways would have to be found for the worker who created the surplus value to know exactly where his money was flowing. There would no longer be an anonymous part of the credit fund because any addition to bank resources would be immediately allocated to its 'administrators'. There would be no 'credit fund' either, it would be called 'resources for crediting' and should in fact be called 'the fund of administrators'.

In the end, the interviewer said that, in his view, these arrangements still left open many problems of 'anonymous' capital, of bank monopoly, of alienation of resources and of the efficient activity of banks.

Articles 39 and 40 of the 1974 Constitution once again contained provisions on banking which led to a series of new Acts on this subject at the end of 1976 and the beginning of 1977. Meanwhile, the Praesidium of the CC of YLC issued Conclusions on the Activity of the League of Communists and other Social and Political Factors regarding Social Relations in the Area of the Banking, Monetary and Credit Systems in accordance with the Constitution of the SFRY and the Decisions of the Tenth Congress of the YLC (JP 75, p. 283). The Conclusions demanded that workers in the organisations of associated labour should master the banking, monetary and credit systems and that the whole sphere of money should become an integral part of income relationships. The 1976–7 Acts transformed banks into 'financial associations of associated labour' (JP 77, p. 417) which were to be run by 'delegates' (see p. 234) of the basic organisations of associated labour (Ep 28.11.77).

Simultaneously, the system of central banks, which since 1972 had consisted of the National Bank, six republic national banks and two provincial national banks, was redefined. They are now managed by a Council of Governers of the National Bank of Yugoslavia under the supervision of the Federal Assembly, which also determines the system and goals of the joint monetary issue policy (JP 77, p. 417).

The monetary issue is the central problem. The Praesidium Conclusions warned that 'the monetary issue must not be turned into the issue of fictitious social capital and used to establish credit relations between the issuing institution and the users of credits'. This caution will hardly be heeded as long as one of the main preoccupations under the new monetary dispensation is 'the distribution of monetary issue' and as long as credits are being extended without the obligation of repayment (Ep 3.10.77, 2.11.76). Such attitudes are, however, entirely in line with traditional behaviour: the great debate on the 'transformation' of 'State capital' ended in a general cancelling of debts owed to banks by working organisations and social-political communities (see Sl 21/74 etc., JP 77, p. 417).

Objections to the functioning of commerce were voiced along with the objections to banks. Foreign trade and wholesale organisations especially were criticised for earning too much. The 1974 Constitution, therefore, provided, in Art. 43, that these organisations might be obliged to combine with production organisations and share their income with them (see also Arts 71 to 79 of the Act on Associated Labour). These provisions followed from the Marxist ideas on commerce (see p. 23) and artificially tried to transfer the income of trading enterprises to production enterprises instead of bringing down trading profits and costs by means of competition. *Ekonomska politika* (19.4.72) wondered whether these rules which were already contained in Constitution Amendment XXII, were not in fact directed against the market rather than just against commerce.

The endeavours to 'invent a new kind of banking', to 'rediscover what has been discovered a long time ago' (Ep 21.12.71), show that the Yugoslav communist leaders still do not comprehend what an economic system is all about. Yugoslav banks are not as rich as generally thought — only about 6 per cent of their total assets 'belong' to their founders, the rest is balanced by their liabilities, i.e. deposits of their customers (Ep 31.10.77). Of the interest charges received by *Ljubljanska banka*, for instance (NR 8.6.74), 63 per cent was paid out in interest to depositors, 13.7 per cent went on taxation and 6.9 per cent to the reserve fund, 8.7 per cent to the business fund and costs and only 7 per cent to the working collective. The interest rates they charged were lower than inflation rates so that real resources were being transferred to debtors. Nonetheless, there were demands that interest charges should be abolished so as not to burden direct producers (Ep 16.5.77). The very high gearing of Yugoslav enterprises ('borrowed' resources amount to 156 per cent of 'owned' resources (Ep 8.8.77)) and the hypertrophy of credit relations (Ep 31.10.77), are not a consequence of 'exploitation' by financial capital, but a result of the very low, not to say non-existent, accumulation of producer-managed enterprises. In 1977 enterprises borrowed more than they invested.

What can be achieved by 'nationalising' banks, by turning them over to delegates of direct producers under these circumstances? It can only make the situation worse for the 'producers' themselves. The market and financial discipline are not something that can be freely manipulated by 'wise' producers. The market reflects the wishes of these very same producers as consumers and financial discipline should force them to comply with the market, i.e. their own wishes as consumers, in their own general interest, even if it may not be in their special interest as workers in individual enterprises. The banks should place capital where it will raise output in line with demand most. The talk about 'nationalisation' of banks only means that the functioning of the system in the general interest should be flouted so that group interests would be catered for in a general scramble for credits to cover losses and bad investment. Capital placed by banks according to profitability is not 'alienated' but used in the general interest of producers who cannot see the wood of their own general interest for the trees of their special ones.

15: Constitutional Changes

15.1 NATIONALIST REVIVAL

President Tito often claimed that the communist approach had enabled the Yugoslav leadership completely to resolve the national problems of the country (D 17.10.72). For this reason, a separate Council of Nations was abolished as early as 1953 (JP 67, p. 145). In fact the virulent nationalisms in Yugoslavia had only been pushed underground and erupted as soon as the political controls were somewhat relaxed in the mid-1960s.

The communist leadership was displeased by nationalist controversies and Tito said, at the renewal of disputes, that 'Yugoslav workers did not worry about the pronunciation of words but rather about the improvement of their living standard' (B 26.3.67). The 'class aspect' of everything was the most important matter (Tito, B 29.9.70) while nationalism was 'class treason' (D 6.2.72). Tito was particularly worried by the nationalist centrifugal forces in the League of Communists itself and condemned what he called 'communist regional orientation' (B 23.9.70).

President Tito thought that all nationalist outbursts had an economic basis (B 9.11.65), but what this basis was was less clear. Nationalism created a climate in which every nation blamed all shortcomings on the others. The Croats felt exploited (34, 35 vs. Dabcevic-Kucar, B 23.6.71) and the Macedonians believed that the underdeveloped regions contributed 55 per cent to the central authorities' expenditure (Ep 11.1.71). In Slovenia, there was almost an open rebellion when a World Bank Loan for Yugoslav motorways was not used to build roads there (D 2.8.69, B 2.8.69).

The disputes continued although the transfer of financial resources through the federal budget was abolished in 1965 and a separate Fund for credits to economically underdeveloped areas was introduced (Mincev, B 17.2.65).

Regardless of transfers of resources from region to region, the distribution of GSP among republics remained almost the same with slight oscillations over the years (Ep 28.12.70, 19.7., 2.8.76, SG 77, p. 402) (see p. 36). Even though the less developed regions by now have a greater capital stock per worker in industries than the more developed ones, their productivity has remained lower and their business losses bigger than elsewhere.

After Croat students had gone on strike to demand that Croatia should be allotted more foreign exchange, Tito called a meeting of the Praesidium of the YLC in Karadjordjevo in December 1971 and dismissed the Croat Premier and the republic party secretary. Croat nationalism was driven underground again.

15.2 FEDERATION DISMANTLED

Despite its attacks on nationalism, the Yugoslav communist leadership felt the unrest amongst Yugoslav nations keenly and tried to counter it. Both the Central Committee of the Yugoslav League of Communists (JP 69, p. 5) and the Federal Assembly (JP 69, p. 149) adopted resolutions dealing with national and linguistic problems. Furthermore, the 1963 Constitution was amended several times, in April 1967 (amendments I–VI), in December 1969 (amendments VII–XIX) and in June 1971 (amendments XX–XLI) so as gradually to take account of the rising nationalist feelings.

The Amendments introduced the following main changes: the upgrading of the Council of Nations; the re-assignment of jurisdiction between federal and other authorities; the upgrading of the two autonomous units within the republic of Serbia and of the so-called nationalities, i.e. the non-Slavonic minorities; and finally, as a counterweight, the introduction of rules protecting the unity of the Yugoslav market.

Amendments I andVII–XI made the Council of Nations, consisting of 20 representatives from each republic and 10 each from the two autonomous provinces of Vojvodina and Kosovo, the main federal legislative Chamber taking part in all aspects of legislation, while the Federal Council with representation proportional to population was demoted to what was called 'the Social-Political Council', participating only in legislation concerning internal political matters.

Amendment XVI first transferred some jurisdiction from the Federation to republics, but Amendments XXX and XXXI radically changed the position by postulating that the federation would have jurisdiction only in those matters which the Constitution expressly allocated to the centre. Amendment XXXIII took the changes even further: it provided that in some instances decisions by federal bodies could be taken only if they had been previously agreed on by constituent republics and provinces. These instances included important matters such as social plans, monetary policy, foreign exchange and trade, aid to less developed regions etc. Reaching agreements amongst republics turned out to be a lengthy procedure, so that some people were afraid that its inefficiency could endanger the functioning of the institution (Ep 23.4.73). Many decisions were not taken in time, so that the government was unable to tell enterprises what kind of legal provisions and policy measures to expect (Ep 10.1.72).

The rationale behind this decentralisation was 'to strengthen real unity by avoiding centralism' (B 29.12.70). But this idea was combined with the intention to reduce State functions altogether and convert them into social functions. The secretary of the Macedonian League of Communists, Slavko Milosavlevski, proclaimed that the development of self-management would narrow down the role of constituent republics as classical State organisations (B 7.4.71).

With respect to jurisdiction in economic matters Amendment III of 1967 limited the right of the Federation to finance investment and Amendment XVI of 1968 transferred to the republics the main part of legislation on taxation. Amendments XXVIII and XXXIV of 1971 further developed this theme and provided for coordination of fiscal policy between republics and provinces, determined the source of federal finance (partly by contributions paid by republics) and regulated federal investment, in particular regarding credits for the development of underdeveloped regions. Amendment XXVII provided that the National Bank of Yugoslavia would be directed by a council of governors consisting of the Governor of the bank itself and the Governors of the national banks of all republics and provinces (see p. 221).

While in general the Amendments stressed decentralisation, Amendment XXV contained provisions for the protection of the unity of the Yugoslav market, giving enterprises and individuals equal rights for their economic activity on the whole territory of Yugoslavia. An Article on criminal offences against the unity of the Yugoslav market was included in the new Yugoslav criminal code, although there was some hesitation about how to formulate it (Ep 8., 15.1.73).

This insistence on the unity of the market was apparently a consequence of (nationalist?) attempts to make individual republics as self-sufficient as possible when decentralisation was introduced (Ep

17.6.74). But tendencies to self-sufficiency were much older than that: as early as 9 Feb. 1966, *Borba* was writing about the tendency to close territorial markets and prevent enterprises, particularly commercial ones, from establishing subsidiaries on 'foreign' territory.

However, in spite of nationalism and institutional shortcomings the integration of Yugoslav markets was considerable, as is shown in Tables 15.1 and 15.2.

Table 15.1: External flows, by republics, 1968
(percentages of GSP)

Republic	*Imports from abroad*	*Sales to other republics*	*Exports to abroad*
Bosnia and Herzegovina	7.2	34.4	6.2
Montenegro	7.1	34.3	6.2
Croatia	10.9	27.7	7.7
Macedonia	11.3	31.1	5.5
Slovenia	13.8	39.7	8.2
Serbia	8.9	24.2	6.8
Total Yugoslavia	10.2	29.4	7.1

Source: Ep 29.11.71

Table 15.2: Inter-republic flows, 1968
(Billions of dinars)

Republic	*Sales to other republics*	*Purchases from other republics*	*Balance on inter-republic trade*
Bosnia and Herzegovina	8.8	10.3	−1.5
Montenegro	1.3	2.9	−1.6
Croatia	16.4	16.8	−0.4
Macedonia	3.5	6.0	−2.5
Slovenia	14.3	9.9	+4.4
Serbia	20.6	19.0	+1.6

Source: Ep 29.11.71

The less developed regions however felt that this interpenetration of the various parts of the Yugoslav economy was working to their detriment. The president of the Central Committee of the Macedonian

League of Communists claimed that a new development fund was needed to neutralise the negative effects of the market. The fund was to be a link, not a sacrifice or aid (Cemerski, B 25.10.70). Such a Fund was included in the provisions of Amendment XXVIII where it was specified that it should be fed from obligatory loans.

15.3 'DEMOCRATIC CENTRALISM' IN THE LEAGUE OF COMMUNISTS

While the Federal State was thus being decentralised, the trend within the Yugoslav League of Communists was in the opposite direction. The Communist Party was re-named the League in 1952 at the Sixth Congress in order to underline its changed role, which was also stressed in the new Programme adopted in 1958 at the Seventh Congress. This said that 'the League of Communists was less and less a factor of power and more and more a factor for forming and developing the socialist consciousness of working people' (90, p. 226). It was suggested that the League would gradually wither away. At any rate, it did not demand for itself monopolistic rights but only wanted to struggle for the implementation of socialist principles (90, p. 227). All decisions, including those reached within the League, must be the result of 'an active socialist battle of views'. The League did not want to issue orders but to encourage citizens to be active and show initiative. Government on behalf of the people should grow into government by the people (90, p. 229).

The 1958 Programme did mention quite clearly the principle of 'democratic centralism' i.e. the rule that once a majority decision had been taken, all members of the Party had to abide by it. For anybody who remembered how it was handled during Stalin's time, this rule had sinister overtones. However, in Yugoslavia the more liberal aspects of the programme prevailed, so much so that as Tito later put it (Tito, JP 72, p. 347; Tito at X Congr., B 28.5.74) the League became a 'debating club' and 'a federalist coalition' of party factions.

In the 1960s, Tito did not seem to object to such developments, but even described them as a 'strong injection of democratism into the League of Communists and social relations' (Tito, IX Congr., B 13.3.69). At that time he also considered that 'unity of thought' as opposed to 'unity of action', in the League of Communists was no longer required (Tito, B 31.12.67). But he must have been in two minds about the state of his party as it was emerging for quite some time. His leading principle seems to be that the Communist Party must have unchallenged power, which he equates with socialism. When he saw power slipping out of the Party's hands in Hungary and Czechoslovakia, he soon reconciled himself with Soviet intervention although it could be dangerous for himself (121, p. 276; Kardelj, JP 77, p. 215). The Prague Spring must have strengthened Tito's apprehension about where the so-called 'liberalism' in Yugoslavia itself could lead.

In the summer of 1969 there was a campaign against 'pluralism' (B 4.7.69). Tito had obviously decided to begin his manoeuvres to deal with the sense of freedom that had grown in Yugoslavia over the years. He brought in as federal Prime Minister a political policeman from Slovenia, Mitja Ribicic. The new head of the central executive immediately proclaimed that the federal authorities should not be interested only in economic matters but should also be concerned with other 'spheres of our social practice', and added by way of example: 'I think that it is necessary to give more independence to the services of public and State security and to all factors responsible for legality in accordance with the Constitution and laws and fighting against anti-socialist tendencies entering the country from abroad or existing in the country' (B 1.6.69). The secret police, or security service as it was officially called, again became more prominent and was regularly praised, in particular on 13 May, Security Service day, as 'the bearer of socialisation of the defence of human rights' (Ribicic, B 13.5.73, Ep 20.5.74).

In 1971 Ribicic's tour of duty as Prime Minister came to an end and he was nominated by the Socialist Alliance as a candidate for the Slovene representation on the new Federal Praesidium. However, as Ribicic was, and is, very unpopular in Slovenia because of his participation in massacres and mass imprisonment in Slovenia in the 1940s, a group of 25 members of the Slovene parliament tried to put up another candidate, as they were entitled to by law. They were rebuked for 'undermining the authority of the League of Communists and true socialist self-management democracy' and some were expelled from the League and had to resign from the Parliament. In spite of such pressure, 33 members of the Slovene Parliament refused to vote for Ribicic (B 14.8., 10., 18.9.71, Ep 9.8.71).

A year after the dismissal of the Croat leadership, a general attack on people with independent ideas followed, under the heading of suppression of 'liberalism and technocratism' (Kardelj, B 7.4.73). After the meeting of the Executive Bureau of the Praesidium of the YCL on 18

September, President Tito issued a letter (JP 72, p. 347) which became known as 'the Letter' and was quoted for years.

It announced an ideological and political offensive by the League of Communists, which would have to be restored to an efficient organisation of revolutionary action. The Letter demanded the elimination from the ranks of the YCL of all those 'alien to the ideology and policy of the League' and the reaffirmation of democratic centralism in the relationship between the centre and the republics too. Social and State functions, in particular in the economy, education, information, administration, judiciary and security, should be reserved for 'people who would implement them in the interest of the working class and the development of self-management'. This requirement is usually referred to as the 'moral-political qualification' (*moralno-politicka podobnost*) of candidates for posts.

The axe fell almost immediately afterwards: many 'liberal' communist leaders were subjected to pressure to resign from their government and party posts, among them the most prominent three former foreign ministers, Koca Popovic, Marko Nikezic and Mirko Tepavac, and the Slovene Prime Minister Stane Kavcic (V 15.11.73). The removal of a whole generation of communist leaders was justified as being in the interest of the working class, which was also the basis for the interference of the League of Communists with everything.

The word 'class' began appearing in all sorts of contexts: the three former foreign ministers were said to have abandoned 'the class positions of our foreign policy' (Ribicic, K 22.3.73). An even more sinister use of the term occurred in a statement by the new Secretary General of the YLC, Stane Dolanc, who said: 'We must purge and reorganise the administration of justice and also education, so that they will once again have their true class character and become an instrument of the working class' (Dolanc, B 21.9.72). The press and broadcasting had a class role (B 17.5.73). The editors of many newspapers were dismissed, amongst them the editor of *Ekonomska politika*, Ljubomir Veljkovic (B 29.6.73). Only what strengthened the position of the working class could be called 'democratic' (Stambolic, V 6.5.75).

Naturally, the League of Communists equated itself with the working class. Kardelj spoke about 'the League of Communists as the organised working class' (B 19.5.73). Tito thought that 'the League of Communists must be turned into a force which will carry through what our working class demands' (B 7.5.73). He considered that the Communists should again interfere with everything (Tito B 6.4.73) and that self-management was only a specific form of the dictatorship of the proletariat (Tito B 1.12.73). (This standpoint was fully supported at the Tenth Congress of the YLC in May 1974.)

The possibility of co-existence of different ideologies was denied (B 22.3.73). Furthermore, political neutralism was declared to be equal to open resistance to the policy of the LC (B 30.5.73). A director was criticised for being interested only in the business success of his enterprise and four communists were taken to task because they voted for him to remain in his post (B 17.3.73).

Some features of the old Stalinist obscurantism cropped up again. The Slovene chief of secret police complained that foreign intelligence services were sending agents to spy on projects and test political opinion; they studied the press, even local and factory press, specialised journals and scholarly works, they organised and financed meetings of experts, inquiries, research (from demographical to speleological), 'They encouraged research, at the first glance entirely scholarly research, but frequently with a hidden other interest . . .' (D 11.5.74). Julije Drasinover, the director of the Institute for Market Research in Belgrade was sentenced to three years imprisonment for exchanging bulletins of his institute for bulletins of similar institutes in Milan and Zurich, something which had been routine under the old dispensation (B 3.10.73, NZZ 19.10.73, B 7.3.74). Professor Novica Vucic, for instance, was accused of issuing lecture notes which were 'unscientific, anti-Marxist and West-oriented' (B 29.3.73). 'Religious communities' came under fire again for their alleged political activity (Tanjug, B 8.11.74).

Against this background, the question arose of what Tito, Kardelj and their associates were going to do in the economic sphere. A reversal as in the political sphere, was widely anticipated. But they were still sufficiently horrified by the results of central planning in the 1940s to cause Tito to spend some time describing its shortcomings and inefficiency at the Ninth Congress in 1969, after having of course claimed that the administrative-centralist system was initially inevitable (Tito, JP 69, p. 103).

However, the refusal to turn back to centralist planning did not make the existing system work any better. Half 'the Letter' was devoted to economic matters: the number of enterprises working at a loss was on the increase; the findings of the Social Accountancy Service went unheeded; 'consumption mentality' was prevalent. 'The Letter' concluded by saying that the essential question was whether the working class would control the whole of social reproduction. The real problem was not working class control but that the Yugoslav communist leaders could not or would not devise a system in which sensible criteria for investment would lead to production in conformity with needs. Neither could they or would they allow people to be given incentives to perform the tasks required. To remedy this, the Praesidium of the CC of the YLC, after its meeting of 8 October 1974, resorted to political manipulation and issued Conclusions on the Implementation of Stabilisation (JP 74, p. 385) which enjoined communist organisations and individuals to take initiatives and make the Yugoslav economy function. It was admitted that 'some essential questions of the economic system and development policy were not resolved', but everybody should make an effort to find temporary solutions. The Praesidium also recognised that often mistakes were not a consequence of 'resistance to self-management', but 'of confusion, lack of experience and ignorance'. To carry out this decision the Executive Committee of the YLC began preparations for a long series of discussions with communists from various economic groupings, branches and complexes, so that clear standpoints could be elaborated and communists could engage in implementing them (Ep 10.2.75). The LC was to take direct responsibility for the solution of problems in the economy (K 28.10.74). In some instances meetings of members of the LC directly discussed what decisions to take in economic sectors (ferrous metallurgy, Ep 31.3.75) or in enterprises (Ep 29.1.77). The resolution of economic questions was said to be the main political test for communists at the time (Ep 4.8.75), which required that they should be 'one of the decisive initiators and executants of activity' (Tito, Ep 3.3.75); in short, that the LC should again become what it had once been (Ep 9.2.76).

In this spirit the CC of the YLC issued the Conclusions on the Direct Ideological-Political Tasks of the YLC in the Struggle for the Further Development of Socialist Self-Management Social-Economic Relations within Associated Labour on 17 April 1976 (JP 76, p. 165). The most important postulate included was that communists should resist any solutions ideologically alien to the LC, and any attempt to preserve old relationships under the guise of an alleged defence of self-management rights of workers if they were in fact based on techno-bureaucratic, liberalistic, group-ownership and other anti-self-management conceptions.

The final seal was put on the 'politicisation' of self-management, and the abandonment of the search for a system which would work automatically, by Kardelj on 13 June 1977. In a speech before the Praesidium of the CC of the YLC (JP 77, p. 209) he demanded that communists should resist with determination all aspects of 'the so-called spontaneity theory, that is the idea that workers–self-managers could take qualified decisions and secure their social progress merely by their own spontaneous, viz. empirical, reactions to events around themselves, without the firm support of organised forces of socialist consciousness and creativity'. The principal 'organised force of socialist consciousness' was the League of Communists. The LC did not ask for a monopoly position for itself—it always worked with the people; political monopoly existed where there were several parties but they did not work with the people. A multi-party system had been surpassed in Yugoslavia where there was to be a political system based on the 'pluralism of self-management interests'. The LC should be consistent in the struggle against real enemies of socialism and socialist self-management but flexible when it came to dealing with non-fundamental clashes of interest within self-management democracy (such as income distribution?) or when the social consciousness of the working masses lagged behind.

In other words, not only the economic but also the political system should keep the LC firmly in control, although discussions or even compromises might be allowed in less important matters. The 1974 Constitution set out to devise such a political system.

15.4 THE LONGEST CONSTITUTION IN THE WORLD

When opening the discussion on the new draft Constitution, Kardelj said: 'I would say that it is one of the longest constitutional texts in the world' (Kardelj, B 19.5.73). The final version had an introduction on Basic Principles consisting of ten sections occupying 20 pages and then 406 articles occupying 153 pages. As a rule Constitutions consist of just over 100 articles. This length was necessary, according to Kardelj (B 19.5.73) because Yugoslav practice revealed 'many deformations and negative phenomena' which were due to the spontaneity of economic life and were now to be eliminated by more adequate 'regulation and harmonisation'. Again according to Kardelj (B 22.5.73) the purpose of all this state activity was to create 'conditions for the process which Marx, Engels and Lenin called "the withering away of the State"'.

To some extent the new Constitution was simply a consolidation of the previous texts, since the numerous Amendments from 1967 till 1971 had made a patchwork of the Constitution of 1963. Nevertheless, the new Constitution meant a 'shake-up of the system' (Ep 18.12.74) and required at least thirty-three new Acts within a few months to implement the constitutional changes. This may not necessarily have implied that the enormous business of reorganising the basic organisation of associated labour would have to start all over again, but it certainly meant that everything done so far would have to be checked and rechecked. Although *Ekonomska politika* had a new loyalist management by the time it printed these reflections on 18 March 1973, irritation was ill-concealed (Ep 18.3.73). When the Amendments had been debated in 1970, the same weekly had remarked that it was 'the seventh reorganisation of the State' in 25 years (Ep 30.11.70).

But in numerous points the new Constitution went beyond mere consolidation. Following Kardelj's exposition (B 22.5.75), the main such points were: the strengthening of the subjective factors of revolution and socialism, i.e. the League of Communists, Socialist Alliance, and trade-unions; prevention of lengthy internal disputes within organisations of associated labour by enabling social organisations such as the Social Accountancy Service to intervene, along with the consolidation of internal workers' control (see p. 132); the authorities of federal organs, especially the Chamber of Republics and Provinces (see p. 225) were to issue provisional legal Acts also in these legislative areas where the consent of all republics and provinces was required (see p. 226), if they could not agree amongst themselves; the introduction of national parity in all houses of the Federal Assembly, but the abolition of such parity in the Federal executive council and Federal administration; more independence for the commune along with the prevention of its autarchic insulation.

As to wider strategy, Kardelj posited two aims for the new Constitution: one was the strengthening of the political and social-economic position of the working class; the second was to raise the working efficiency of the self-management system as such (B 19.5.73).

The method chosen to strengthen the political influence of the working class was to introduce delegates (*delegati*) instead of at least formally independent members of parliament (*poslanici*). The first move in this direction was contained in Amendment VIII of 1968, but the full introduction of the delegate system came only with the Constitution of 1974. This provided that the Federal Assembly would consist of two chambers: the federal chamber and the chamber of republics and provinces. The first consists of thirty delegates of self-management and social-political organisations in each republic and twenty each from two provinces, the second of twelve-member delegations from Assemblies of republics and eight-member delegations from Assemblies of provinces.

All delegates are subject to an imperative mandate, i.e. must vote in the Federal Assembly not according to their own view, but according to the wishes of their electors, and they can be recalled. This new arrangement was hailed to be 'perhaps one of the most important steps towards democracy in history' (Kardelj, B 1.5.72) and it was claimed that it 'opened up new horizons' (B 16.4.74). Why this change should mean much is difficult to perceive, because—as shown by the example of the 25 members of parliament in Slovenia—it can hardly be claimed that previously members of assemblies were independent. However, according to Kardelj (B 31.1.69) up till 1969 the Yugoslav parliaments had been dominated by professional politicians, while thereafter the majority of delegates and delegations would be workers (B 20.3.74).

The presumption is that 'workers' know what they want and that they all want the same, so that anybody who ventures a dissenting opinion should be recalled. However, it seems obvious that all wanting and thinking is done by individuals and that groups, let alone very large groups like 'classes' or nations, can come to a unitary view, if at all, only by means of an exchange of views and debate. Such exchanges and discussion began in Yugoslavia in the 1960s, but are now stopped. Therefore the workers are again an amorphous mass which is not allowed to formulate any views because anybody who expresses an important view different from that of the leadership is eliminated as anti-working-class. The delegational system strengthened this possibility, but did not create it. What it all amounts to is that the leadership believes that it knows what the working class wants, or at least that it knows what is in the interest of the working class since it embraces Marxism. However, there are many interpretations of Marxism, so that even if Marxism were the only answer, nobody could be sure that he was in the possession of the right interpretation. But anyway it is quite unscientific to claim that Marxism is the only or the final answer, or 'the science'. If anything, the Yugoslav experience proves that Marxism has no answer to many problems, such as economic initiative, economic responsibility and investment criteria, to name but a few. Practical solutions can, therefore, be found only in open debate, which is the scientific way, but also the political way in so far as politics wants to be rational. The delegational system has stifled the hopes for rational debate in Yugoslavia.

Kardelj said that the second strategic aim of the new Constitution was to improve the functioning of the self-management system. It will have become clear from the present study that such an improvement was overdue as some problems were not solved at all (e.g. initiative, saving) while some contradictory solutions were introduced. For instance, while the functioning of a decentralised economy necessitates incentives, in Yugoslavia income (i.e. revenue of enterprises) has become meaningless because of 'the confused circle of equalising the work of successful and unsuccessful basic organisations of associated labour bound together by self-management agreements on association' (Ep 18.4.74). Because the market was deprived of its spontaneity in this way it had to be replaced by more and more regulations and laws.

As early as 1967, *Borba* wrote approvingly about the movement of 'anti-normalism', of people who thought that in Yugoslavia everything was regulated by Acts which nevertheless contained masses of gaps and contradictions (see pp. 7 and 185). Laws only lasted from one day to the next, had no common thread, and merely reflected the passing ideas of some leading personalities. Kardelj, the main ideologist and 'legislator' defended himself by claiming that changing laws were necessary because of the rapid changes occurring in Yugoslav society (JP 71, p. 103), without, however, specifying what he thought was changing so fast, that provisions were sometimes abandoned before there was time to apply them. Further he claimed that all fears of legal regulation were unfounded (B 5.10.74).

The fiercest and best articulated attack on legal inflation in Yugoslavia came in 1972: Kosta Cavoski, in a paper published in *Gledista* (21), opened his criticism by quoting Tacitus: 'Corruptissima res publica, plurimae leges'. In his view the abundance of laws was not a consequence of the complexity of our times, but of 'spiritual sterility'. There was no legal security despite the formal granting of all sorts of freedoms and rights. They were granted with one hand and then abolished with the other by means of explanatory provisions, allegedly to implement their real content. The incessant changes in the Constitution every two years only proved that it was not patterned on any higher idea but was merely an expression of arbitrariness. Laws could become simply a weapon in the hands of 'alienated power'. Cavoski was sent to prison.

But even though Cavoski went to jail, doubts about continuous legislative changes did not die down. In 1975, the Vice-Premier of Yugoslavia, Berislav Sefer, himself (Ep 21.7.75) ventured to remark in the Federal Assembly that Yugoslavia suffered not only 'from an inflation of prices, but also from an inflation of government measures'. Enterprises were destabilised by the continuous change of legal provisions (D 5.3.69, Cemerski, B 31.5.70, Ep 4.6.76). Frequently they did not know what course to take because the rules were unclear or contradictory (Ep 13.9.71, 27.12.76). In consequence, they even more frequently simply disregarded the law (Ep 20.9.71, 27.12.76).

It was no longer entirely a joke to suggest the enactment of an 'Act on the Obligatory Implementation of Acts' (Ep 3.10.77), especially as the 1974 Constitution and the Act on Associated Labour were difficult to translate into supplementary norms and legal practice (Blazevic, D 9.6.78) as they were inspired by 'wonderful dreams' rather than by the 'awareness of reality', as Cavoski said about Yugoslav constitutional changes. What Yugoslavia needs is a simple and understandable system with more opportunity for citizens to do things independently.

16: Conclusions

16.1 QUANTITATIVE ECONOMIC CONCLUSIONS

Looking back over the 30 years of the Yugoslav economy under communist management, observers usually first mention growth rates. *The annual average rate of growth of the GSP* in the whole period was just over 6 per cent, unless the jump of 20 per cent from 1947 to 1948 is also included in the calculation, when the rate becomes 6.7 per cent. This initial jump however was possible because the economy in 1947 was still depressed following the war and was considerably below the pre-war level to which it recovered in 1948. The rate of growth per head of population was about 1 per cent lower because that was the rate of population growth over the whole period. It was about 1.3 per cent in 1948–60 and about 0.9 per cent in 1961–76. The result is respectable though not spectacular since other countries in both East and West have achieved the same. The GSP per head in 1975 was dinars 23,562, equal to $ 1385, converted at the rate $ 1 equal to dinars 17. This is 4 times more than in 1939.

The result is somewhat less impressive if the *yearly rise in personal consumption* is considered. It was explained in Part I that consumption did not reach the pre-war level until the end of the 1950s. Consequently, consumption has risen only by about 4 per cent per year if one calculates from the pre-war level. But even if this point is disregarded, consumption rose more slowly during the thirty years than total production; its rate of growth was just over 5 per cent. Even after 1960, growth of personal consumption of 6.0 per cent per year was somewhat below the GSP growth rate of 6.3 per cent.

The best time for consumption was the period between 1956 and 1965, when it was boosted by renewed utilisation of the pre-war consumer goods industry and by the commissioning of plant built in the early 1950s. For this reason it is necessary to go back to the immediate post-war period to obtain a complete picture of development. Consumption per head in 1975 was dinars 13,040, $767, which is just over twice the pre-war level.

The prime mover of the Yugoslav economy has been fixed investment, amounting to about 30 per cent of the GSP per year. As compared with the *average incremental capital–output ratio* of 7.2 in 1947–60, in 1961–75 the capital–output ratio was 5.2, but it deteriorated again from 4.8 in 1961–65 to 5.6 in 1971–75 (JP 76, p. 467). The normal capital–output ratio is about 2–3, with some countries such as the United States and Federal Germany doing much better than this.

The capital–output ratio would have more meaning if output did not also include unsaleable stocks and non-utilised capacity, both waste, probably amounting to at least 10 per cent of the GSP. A slightly better measure of capital efficiency is obtained if fixed investment is related to growth in personal consumption. The capital–personal consumption ratio for the whole period would be 6, if the entire growth of consumption is taken, and over 7, if the growth of consumption above the 1939 level is considered.

The massive investment did help to increase *gross labour productivity in industry* after the end of the 1950s. The average yearly growth of labour productivity in 1961–76 has been 4.6 per cent per year. The rate has fallen from almost 6 per cent in 1961–65 to 3.5 per cent in 1971–75. But much more serious than this decline is the complete lack of coordination of labour and capital, so that an incredibly large number of Yugoslavs has no work or cannot find work in Yugoslavia. The figure is between 15 and 25 per cent of the active population.

Therefore, the average yearly rise in personal incomes of 5 per cent after 1960, when salaries and wages attained the pre-war level, is much less significant. It is a reflection of the combination of vast amounts of capital with a limited number of workers, while some people have no opportunity to work at all. The average increase of wages and salaries over the 1939 level in 1948–76, was 2.8 per cent per year. The average personal income in 1976 was dinars 3535, equal to current $208 per month which is about 2.5 times the average pre-war income of those receiving salaries and wages.

The rate of increase in real personal incomes has fallen from 7.4 per cent in 1966–70 to 2 per cent in 1971–6, much faster than the fall in the growth of labour productivity or even personal consumption, because consumption financed by transfers from Yugoslav workers abroad has risen so much. In 1975, 8.6 per cent of expenditure on consumer goods originated from abroad.

This leads to a point which is even worse than the low efficiency of investment and the large number of unemployed; it is the fact that the Yugoslav economy is heavily dependent on support from abroad. It

Table 16.1: Yugoslav growth rates

		GSP			Personal consumption		Personal incomes: Nominal		Personal incomes: Real			Industrial labour productivity	
1947													
48		20.1											
49		8.6	6.0		6.8								
50		−10.6			−9.1	−1.1							
51		9.8			2.1								
52		−14.1			−6.9								
53	7.1	20.0	6.4		1.1	2.3	1		−3			5.4	
54		1.3			4.9		12		14	1		0	2.8
55		14.8		4.0	10.1		3		−8		4.2	3.1	
56		−6.0			1.5		10	5	2			3.0	
57		23.9			11.9		21		17			9.7	
58		1.6	8.6		4.8	7.7	5		0	7.6		0.9	5
59		17.7			9.8		17		15			5.5	
60		5.8			10.6		17		4			5.8	

61		5.7			7.3		7		0			3.9	
62		4.2			1.4		13		4			4.5	
63		12.4	7.1		9.9	7.2	18		10	6.2		10.1	6
64		11.5			11.6		25		12			7.2	
65		1.5			6.0		40		5			4.2	
66		8.5			1.7		37		12			4.7	
67		2.6			6.9		15		7			1.1	
68	6.3	4.0	6.3	6.0	3.3	5.4	9	5.0	4	7.4	4.6	6.7	5
69		10.4			7.1		15		6			7.3	
70		6.1			8.0		19		8			5.3	
71		8.8			8.3		22		5			5.5	
72		4.6			4.6		17		0			3.1	
73		5.0	6.1		2.7	5.3	16		−2	1.6		2.5	3.5
74		8.5			7.3		28		6			5.8	
75		3.6			3.4		23		−1			0.8	
76		4.0					16		4			0.8	
		ø 6.7 (1947–76)			ø 5.1 (1948–75)				ø 5.0 (1952–76)				
		ø 6.2 (1948–76)			ø 4.1 (1948–75, 1939 = 100)				ø 2.8 (1947–76, 1939 = 100)				

Sources: Column 1 and 2 – JP 57, pp. 465, 511; SG 73, p. 120, SG 77, p. 138
Column 3 – SG 73, p. 283 and SG 77, p. 310
Column 4 – SG 77, p. 87

requires free imports of between 5 and 10 per cent of the GSP (in the form of workers' remittances, or loans) to function and especially to grow at all. If it were no longer in receipt of this external subsidy, its distorted structure and general inefficiency would be shown up to the full.

To sum up, the characteristic features of Yugoslav economic development after 1945 were: a relatively high rate of growth of GSP and a lower, but still respectable rate of growth of personal consumption; both these results, however, depended on Yugoslavia's ability to finance from external sources additional absorption 5–10 per cent more than domestic production; simultaneously almost 10 per cent of Yugoslav production is waste and there is considerable unemployment.

There do not seem to be any signs that the performance of the Yugoslav economy in this respect could be improved. If anything, there are signs that in the 1970s the inconsistencies are beginning to tell and may cause more difficulties than hitherto. Yugoslav economists were unanimous that 1978 would be more problematical than 1977 and some thought that the prospects for 1979 were also worrying (EP 21.11.77).

16.2 THEORETICAL ECONOMIC CONCLUSIONS

It is not very difficult to explain the troubles of the Yugoslav economy in terms of economic theory or simple common sense.

There is no clear link between the enterprise and the workers who are expected collectively to take decisions concerning that enterprise. Workers certainly cannot participate in the initial decision to establish an enterprise and invest a certain sum of capital in it because they will only be hired and become workers at the enterprise later. Yet, the original decision is crucial and will influence the success of the enterprise for a long time.

Under capitalism, a mistake in the original investment is reflected in a fall in the value of risk capital so that anybody taking over later will start afresh because he can buy the enterprise at an adjusted price; under self-management workers take over at the book-keeping value, or at some value which has little to do with the prospect of the enterprise, but is bureaucratically determined. This saddles them with the responsibility for the original decision in which they have not participated and for which they cannot possibly be held responsible.

The same thing applies to current decisions also because workers come and go, so that the effects of decisions they have helped to take may occur when they are no longer in the enterprise and, vice versa, they may be hit by effects of decisions taken when they were not yet there. If the distribution of personal income were according to enterprises' success, the workers would feel that as far as they were concerned their incomes depended largely on luck. Therefore, they persist in the old beliefs in equal pay for equal work and disregard what enterprises can afford when they take decisions on personal incomes, the only decision they consider important.

The lack of a permanent link between the workers and the capital of an enterprise also shows in the reluctance of workers to save—to accumulate for the enterprise. Such savings are lost for them as individuals, which is the normal viewpoint for them to take. They do save out of their inflated incomes but their propensity to save what remains their own property is also too low to finance the nation's investment.

The workers do want to take decisions on personal incomes, but are not very interested in anything else. The fact is simply that nobody can take decisions on everything and do his own other job at the same time. Decision-making in each field requires much knowledge and information, which one cannot require while engaged in other work. For this reason, the real power—with the exception of wage distribution—remains in the hands of professional managers in spite of all the rights given to workers.

As for the distribution of personal incomes, the right to do this regardless of the enterprise's success, but even as long as it is within the enterprise's income, gives workers the opportunity to indulge their own sectional interests as producers at the expense of their own general interest as consumers. If the workers do not accumulate additional capital in enterprises, or do not accumulate enough new capital at all, this behaviour raises their own present consumption but does not help to raise their own and general consumption in the future.

This situation can partly be remedied by replacing the missing accumulation through monetary issue, but monetary issue is like mana from heaven so that nobody is individually interested in how it is used. Besides there are no criteria about how to invest this artificial accumulation because there are no returns on capital in enterprises and no capital markets. It is sometimes suggested that personal incomes could be restricted by taxation, but workers can resist taxation in the same way as they do financial discipline. Further, the revenue used for investment would be in government hands and there would not be any investment criteria either.

If the capital in an enterprise is owned by somebody, it is in his interest to protect it and add to it. In this way he constantly contributes to a rise in production by both saving and placing his savings where they produce most. Simultaneously his savings and management of savings continuously raised the productivity of labour so that everybody's income will grow as measured in the labour markets which will also distribute incomes and force individual enterprises to work at a given level of efficiency.

The Yugoslav — and other — communist leaders cannot and will not understand what has been said because their thinking is obscured by Marxism, a singularly confusing interpretation of economic activity. Although Marx himself clearly admits the need for capital accumulation and government revenue to finance collective consumption, he nonetheless stresses exploitation as a reality. What does exploitation mean, if the worker cannot be given the full fruit of his work under any circumstances because of the need for accumulation? That he should manage accumulation? But managing accumulation is a skilful job which implies special knowledge and information. If alienation means division of labour, even division of labour between capital management and the rest, it cannot be abolished except at the price of a drastic fall in living standards.

Somebody has to manage capital and organise production. It cannot be done collectively because collective decisions abolish responsibility and cannot be informed. In fact, our present civilisation and economic prosperity are based on individual persons acting freely within legal and moral limits, not on collectives; life had to move away from collectives to make the present prosperity possible. It is, therefore destructive to wage a class struggle against those persons most successful in managing capital and organising production, because they have contributed to the prosperity more than anybody else; they have made possible the present level of productivity, without which there is no prosperity.

Because the Yugoslav communist leaders will not accept that Marxist economics is fallacious, they cannot find any lasting solution for the failings of the Yugoslav economy. Although it is admitted that the Yugoslav economy is inefficient (cf. Sefer, Ep 23.8.76), the usual response is manipulation of words (Ep 14.2., 7.11.77) because real solutions are not acceptable to Marxists. The French socialist leader, François Mitterand, observed, during a visit to Yugoslavia, that the Yugoslav communists were word-drunk and that the term 'self-management' was used as a magic word which was believed to solve everything (NIN 11.5.77). The worst offender in this respect is Edvard Kardelj, who has no sense of reality but juggles with words to the horror of all those who have to carry out his continuous 'innovations'.

In spite of these continuous 'innovations' the system is still 'incomplete' (General Director of the Federal Institute of Social Planning, Ep 26.7.77). The system is incomplete because it is impossible to introduce collective responsibility in enterprises; without such responsibility there is no market and without a market there is no way of aligning the interests of workers as producers and as consumers. The present trend towards a convoluted form of planning by contract is an admission of the failure of the market when responsibility is collective but it will not work because it is too complicated and the Yugoslav experience shows that wholesale planning is impossible.

Nonetheless, the Yugoslav communists will insist that workers must decide on everything and that this requirement is fulfilled in their system. We have seen that it is not in fact fulfilled because Kardelj himself said that there cannot be any self-management without the guidance and even 'meddling' of the League of Communists. This in effect means that the decisions are taken by politicians and somehow imposed on the workers. Instead of the previous élite of independent businessmen, politicians etc., there is now an organised élite of party workers. The difference is that the previous élite allowed much greater freedom to everybody because the system could be relied on to work more or less automatically. Now most things—although less than under total planning—still have to be done by decree, which requires restrictions, albeit even then they are not done well.

The only respect in which workers do have a decisive word in Yugoslavia, is in the distribution of personal income without regard for the physical limits of consumption. The Yugoslav leaders would be glad if they knew how to stop this, but they have been telling workers for such a long time that they would decide on everything that they cannot be prevented from doing it now, although it is against their own wider interests. However, even the incomplete system works in such a way that workers are prevented from deciding what is physically impossible. Too much distribution automatically raises prices. Furthermore, the communist leadership is not ready to forgo accumulation and so replaces it from monetary issue which mean that decisions are again taken out of the hands of direct producers although in a roundabout way (Ep 14., 28.11.77).

There may still be the hope that, in the fullness of time, a new socialist man will be born who will not distribute excessive personal incomes. But there is no indication that human nature changes, let alone that it changes when means of production are taken into public or social ownership. Some will argue that we should wait a little longer, but how much longer? Life has to be lived now and institutions must be adapted to people as they are now. These institutions must, therefore, prevent people from overindulging, especially if, in the end, they only harm themselves.

It is sometimes claimed that whilst self-management has imperfections which the workers themselves realise, they are nonetheless in favour of self-management (cf. Kamusic in 18, p. 113), perhaps because it gives them the feeling of greater participation in power. The workers will have to realise that in self-management—and in any other system that gives them jurisdiction over capital which is not theirs—they will always pay themselves too much income and simultaneously amass capital out of inflationary issue in their enterprise because there is no mechanism and no criterion to stop them from doing this in their own sectional interest. Any such criterion would have to come from outside which then would again limit their powers and thus restrict self-management and make it meaningless. This contradiction is a consequence of the discrepancy between their sectional interest as producers and their general interest as consumers. This contradiction can be overcome only by abiding by the market and financial discipline and the rules of private ownership of capital.

For this reason, a way out of the present Yugoslav impasse may be to turn workers' management councils into workers' representative councils for the defence of producers' interests, but balanced by independent management of enterprises linked in some manner to their capital. Maybe existing enterprises should be hired out to independent managers, including foreigners if they offer better terms, while freedom to organise new enterprises is restored to individuals and groups of individuals. This would involve the abolition of the present level of five workers in private enterprises and of ten hectares for private farmers. Foreigners would have to be brought in because the performance of some of the present engineering enterprises cannot be improved without foreign expertise and foreign technology. But, above all, a simpler system with less incomprehensible rules is indicated. Whether this solution is possible as long as the country is dominated by the League of Communists, is a different matter.

16.3 POLITICAL AND MORAL CONCLUSIONS

The Yugoslav Communists have led the economy of their country into a blind alley because they 'studied exclusively pure theories of Marxism and political economy' instead of taking into account economic facts of life. Tito admitted this (K 22.6.62) and also repeatedly recognised (see p. 72, D 30.8.69) that it was easier to pull down the old system and to wage the last war then to establish a working economic system. Evidently, the former requires only fanaticism and determination, while for the latter, the understanding that is obtained from study without prejudgement is needed. Such an approach is not fostered by the prejudices of an unworldly Marxist theory.

Because of their unjustified confidence that Marxism gave them all the answers, the Yugoslav communists have done much harm to the country. They first tried the final answer of centralist planning and, when it did not work, embarked on an ever-changing experiment with self-management which is as incomplete now as it has ever been.

In order to start on this journey through a maze by trial and error, they sought absolute power and gained it by disregarding all rules of civilised behaviour and morality. When the war began, they decided to fight for power (see 32, p. 388). In Slovenia at least, they expressly prohibited anybody from fighting the enemy without accepting their command. Whoever tried to, was mercilessly 'liquidated' or driven into the hands of the enemy. They turned the war against an external foe into a civil war while, of course, denying it, as admitted by Tito himself (V 24.5.72). After the war, they killed hundreds of thousands and imprisoned hundreds of thousands more. Why was all this necessary? It was necessary so that they could apply what they wrongly thought were perfect solutions to everything.

At this juncture, there is no reason why the Yugoslav communists should hold absolute power. Their solutions have failed. Least of all is there any reason why they should try and spread their non-system to other parts of the world although some of them still think that 'it is a real prospective for mankind' (Kraigher, S., D 29.4.77). This book is an attempt to try to prevent them from disseminating confusion.

Post-Script (Beginning 1979)

By the end of 1978, the situation in Yugoslavia has not changed.

At the Eighth Congress of the Yugoslav Trade Unions in November 1978, President Tito said:

> We are confronted with the question of why almost exactly the same problems and weaknesses arise in our economy year after year (Ep 27.11.78).

His own answer was that what is laid down in the self-management agreements and contracts is never carried through; hence, the faults are not a consequence of the system, but of by-passing the system. But what if the system is being by-passed because it is unworkable?

At the end of 1978, Vladimir Bakaric described the habitual shortcomings (D 20.12.78) in a speech before the CC of YLC: the share of investment financed out of the enterprises' own resources has been reduced to 24.3 per cent in 1977 (cf. pp. 134 and 152); the relationship between owned and borrowed capital is 47.1:52.9 (cf. p. 222); therefore, a large part of what enterprises save for depreciation and accumulation is used to pay off debts—in 1976 and 1977, the debt repayment and servicing used up 63 per cent of depreciation and enterprises' accumulation (Ep 11.12.78 even mentions 77.5 per cent for 1977). It follows that the economy cannot finance its own development and is forced to incur ever larger debts both at home and abroad. According to Bakaric, decisions on 'expanded reproduction' (net investment) are to a considerable extent alienated from workers in associated labour and transferred to factors outside the economic structure. These tendencies continued in 1978.

This result is only natural (see pp. 135–6) since the workers do not save anything for their enterprises and there is no mechanism to encourage them to do so. Bakaric is not prepared to admit this, but blamed the lack of enterprises' accumulation on contributions the enterprises have to make for 'general social needs' (taxes to finance collective consumption). It is true that on average enterprises have to pay for each dinars 100 paid out in wages dinars 49.3 in contributions to education, health service, pensions etc.; dinars 11.9 in taxes; dinars 28.1 in interests, bank charges, insurance premia etc.; dinars 20.9 for their own administration; and dinars 2.4 for miscellaneous outlays, altogether dinars 112.6 (Ep 23.10.78). This amount is a heavy burden, but as Marx himself said clearly in his *Critique of the Gotha Programme*, collective needs have to be covered out of the 'newly created value' under any circumstances. Of course the expenditure on social services in Yugoslavia is lavish (see pp. 140 ff) and their efficiency low, but these excesses and inefficiency are themselves a part of the system and in all probability cannot be changed in a short time.

It therefore does not sound convincing when Bakaric says that 'workers in the organisations of associated labour defend their personal incomes, collective consumption and accumulation against the pressure from banks and the State. To achieve this, they insist on raising the prices of their products . . . .' Obviously, these price rises are immediately tapped by the State for collective consumption which is presumably what is meant by 'the pressure from the State'. They do not contribute anything to accumulation, since accumulation remains minimal. According to *Ekonomska politika* (Ep 11.12.78), the average 'reproductive capacity' (depreciation plus net savings) of Yugoslav enterprises in 1977 amounted to 7.7 per cent, and the rate of accumulation (net enterprise savings) to 3.9 per cent of the 'average utilised capital'. These two figures are so low that the gross enterprise savings cannot possibly suffice to replace the worn-out capital. All new investment finance comes from outside. What the workers are defending is their money (personal incomes) which they do so well that in 1977 the enterprises distributed 10 per cent more than their value added, thus incurring a loss of that size. The economist Ljubo Madzar put it clearly: 'The capacity for accumulation is falling because the distribution of income is not regulated. The rise of personal income has accelerated . . .' (Ep 13.11.78). Money wages rose by 19 per cent in 1977 (SG 78, p. 133) and by 17 per cent in the first nine month of 1978 (*Indeks* 12/78). Since the rise in the cost of living was 15 per cent in 1977 and 14 per cent in the first ten month of 1978, the rise in real wages amounted to 3 and 4 per cent respectively. These figures compare with the 1977 rise of labour productivity in industry of 5.8 per cent (calc. from SG 78, p. 86), but this rise may have simply been due to an improvement of the utilisation of producer good capacities because of the high growth of investment in 1977 and 1978, amounting to 31 and 39 per cent respectively in money terms.

The inflationary income distribution could perhaps somehow be lived with, but what is grave is the continuous irresponsible investment, 'mania of investment' as Bakaric called it. According to him, fixed investment in 1978 rose to 34.4 per cent of the GSP, together with investment in working capital to more than 40 per cent. Tito commented at the Eleventh Congress of the YLC (JP 78, p. 227):

> We continue to invest a lot which is good. But it is not good that there is also unprofitable investment . . .

Bakaric's somewhat convoluted judgement was:

> . . . neither the size nor the structure of investment are in line with the development plans for the income and technological interdependence of organisations of associated labour. The efficiency of investment is decreasing, which directly influences the rather slow rise in labour productivity.

What exactly this passage means is difficult to guess, but something must be very wrong with investment. Tito and Bakaric thought that the investment chaos was due to the fact that it is not workers who decide on investment. At the Eighth Congress of the Yugoslav Trade Unions, Tito said:

> Who is responsible for the excessive ambitions and for the discrepancy between desires and possibilities? Responsible are those who make decisions on investment and other matters. Despite the wide self-management and delegational basis, many decisions are in essence not taken in a self-management manner, although they formally pass through a self-management procedure.

In contrast, the Yugoslav economists participating at a discussion in Opatija (Ep 13.11.78) had little doubt that investment was haphazard because those who took decisions (whether workers or administrators) did not bear the risk and were not exposed to the sanction of the market. The cost of capital, at 11 per cent at a time when prices are rising at a rate of 15 per cent a year, does not help.

The exorbitant investment activity in 1977 and 1978 helped to raise the rates of growth to 8 per cent in 1977 (SG 78, p. 152) and 9 per cent in 1978 (NZZ 1.2.79). An economist suggested that the Yugoslavs could live better if the growth was reduced by 1 or 2 per cent (Ep 13.11.78). It is still not known what these rates mean in terms of consumption, rise in inventories and under-utilised capacities. Anyway, the growth rates could be achieved only at the expense of a payments deficit (see pp. 165–7) which rose to $1.8 billion in 1977 and $1.1 billion in 1978 (Ep 13.11.78), so that (apparently net) foreign indebtedness reached $10.8 billion in mid-1978 (Ep 23.10.78) which is equal to dinars 194.4 billion or to about 27 per cent of the estimated Yugoslav GSP in 1977 of dinars 736 billion as compared with dinars 596 billion in 1976 (SG 78, p. 153). President Tito thought that the trade deficit with Western countries—and hence the indebtedness to them—was almost unbearable and that Yugoslavia should, therefore, change its production structure and develop its own technology (JP 78, p. 228). In spite of the high investment volume, unemployment touched 760,000 in March 1978 (*Indeks*, 12/78, p. 43).

President Tito drew the conclusions at the Eleventh Congress of the YLC:

> In view of the situation, it is small wonder that our production capacities are under-utilised, that some organisations cannot sell their products, that they work at a loss, amass inventories and so forth. All this reduces the productivity of the total social labour and the possibilities of our progress.

In his speech before the Central Committee, Bakaric mentioned the 'unfavourable political atmosphere in the working class and among the working people in general' and dealt at some length with the 'work stoppages' (cf. pp. 193 ff), ascribed by him to the 'old relationships' in working organisations. According to him strikes 'are not and should not be a property of the self-management system, in which the workers decide on their own fate', but recently they have become so frequent again that the Chairman of the Yugoslav Trade Unions spoke of 'a wave of work stoppages' (B 5.11.78). Neca Jovanov, the trade-union expert on work stoppages, believes that the term 'strike' is the right word because strikes in Yugoslavia have a class character (V 2.9.78). They are due to the large discrepancy between the promises and reality, so that the workers often turn against the decisions taken by workers' councils (*Start*, Zagreb 6.9.78) and even against decisions on distribution they themselves have approved (V 2.9.78). Further, Bakaric said the following:

> Intermittent shortages of materials and products, of building and

> other materials lead to wheeling-dealing, corruption and similar things which all offer an opportunity for the actions of the extreme left etc. President Tito's remedy for all difficulties reads: Workers in basic organisations must in reality control the entire income. (JP 78, p. 228)

In opposition to this statement, Neca Jovanov considers it 'utopian' if anybody wants the workers to decide on everything. Moreover, many economists have come to the conclusion that the distribution in enterprises will have to be regulated in some way, but were clear that such regulation would be against the principles of the self-management system (Ep 13.11.78). However, even if the problem of inflationary distribution was resolved, the problems of investment criteria, rational investment and management and responsibility for the results of these activities would remain. In short there cannot be any responsible entrepreneurship in a self-management system.

Bibliography

1. Aleksic, P., *Licni rad u socijalizmu* (*Personal work in socialism*) (Belgrade, 1973).
2. Arzensek, V., 'Motivation Structure of Employees', *Teorija in praksa* (2/1971).
3. Babic, Desput, Grbic, *Sta je delegatski samoupravni sistem?—(What is the delegational selfmanagement system?)* (Zagreb, 1974).
4. Babovic, D., 'Why Do Working People Skip Meetings?' *Socijalizam* (7–8/1975).
5. Bajt, A., 'The Criterion of Profitability in our Economy', *Ekonomska revija* (3–4/1953).
6. Bajt, A., 'Short-Term and Long-Term Approaches to Investment', *Ekonomist* (2–3/1964).
7. Bajt, A., 'Uncritical Flights of Dr. Nikola Cobeljic', *Ekonomist* (1–2/1965).
8. Bajt, A., 'Income Distribution under Workers' Self-management in Yugoslavia', in Ross, A. M. (ed.), *Industrial Relations and Economic Development* (London, 1967).
9. Bajt, A., 'Inflationary Factors in the Period after the Reform', *Ekonomist* (1–2/1967).
10. Bajt, A., 'Managerial Incentives in Yugoslavia', (CESES International Seminar, Ermenonville, 1972).
11. Bakaric, V., 'Tasks of the Popular Front of Yugoslavia in connection with the Five-Year Plan and Organisational Problems', in *Drugi kongres Ljudske fronte Jugoslavije* (*Second Congress of the Popular Front of Yugoslavia*) (Ljubljana, 1947).
12. Benson, L., 'Market Socialism and Class Structure: Manual Workers and Managerial Power in the Yugoslav Enterprise', in Parkin, F. (ed.), *The Social Analysis of Class Structure* (London, 1974).
13. Bicanic, R., 'Personal Consumption in the FPRY', *Progres* (Ljubljana, 1/1957).
14. Bicanic, R., 'Economic Growth and Centralised and Decentralised Planning', in *Problems of Economic Growth* (Delhi, 1960).

15. Bicanic, R., *Economic Policy in Socialist Yugoslavia* (Cambridge, 1973).
16. Bilandzic, D., *Management of Yugoslav Economy—1945–1966* (Belgrade, 1967).
17. Bilandzic, Tankovic, *Samoupravljange 1950–1974* (*Self-management 1950–1974*) (Zagreb, 1974).
18. Broekmeyer, M. J. (ed.), *Yugoslav Workers' Self-management* (Proceedings of a symposium in Amsterdam, 7–9 January 1970) (Dordrecht, 1970).
19. Boskovic, Dasic, *Minuli rad* (*Past labour*) (Belgrade, 1973).
20. Calic, D., *Planiranje privrede FNRJ* (*Planning of the Economy of the FPRY*) (Zagreb, 1950).
21. Cavoski, K., 'The Value of Law in the Yugoslav Society', *Gledista* (5–6/1972).
22. Centro studi e Ricerche sui Problemi Economico-Sociali, *Il sistema dei prezzi nell'Est Europeo* (*The price system in Eastern Europe*) (Milan, 1967).
23. Cobeljic, N., *Politika i metodi privrednog razvoja Jugoslavije 1947–1956* (*Policy and methods of economic development of Yugoslavia 1947–1956*) (Belgrade, 1959).
24. Cobeljic, N., 'Short-Term and Long-Term Approaches to Investment', *Ekonomist* (2/1963).
25. Cobeljic, N., 'Critical Flights of Dr. Aleksander Bajt', *Ekonomist* (2–3/1964).
26. Dabcevic-Kucar, Gorupic, Lang, Mesaric, Perisin, Sirotkovic, Stipetic, 'On some Problems of the Economic System' (the so-called White book), *Ekonomski pregled* (3–5/1965).
27. Davidovic, R., 'On the Size, Structure and Distribution of the National Income', in *Ekonomska politika FNRY* (*Economic policy of the FPRY*) (Belgrade, 1957).
28. Davidovic, R., 'Distribution in the Socialist Economy—Some Principles and Methods', in Stojanovic, R. (ed.), *Yugoslav Economists and Problems of a Socialist Economy* (New York, 1964).
29. Dedijer, V., *The Battle Stalin Lost* (New York, 1964).
30. Dimitrijevic, Macesich, *Money and Finance in Contemporary Yugoslavia* (New York, 1973).
31. Djilas, M., *The Unperfect Society* (London, 1969).
32. Djilas, M., *Memoir of a Revolutionary* (New York, 1973).
33. Djodan, Dujsin (eds.), 'Reasons and Properties of Economic Development in 1961 and 1962' (the so-called Yellow book), *Ekonomski pregled* (8/1963).
34. Djodan, S., 'The Commodity-Money Model and the Regional

Development in our Conditions', *Kolo* (1968).

35. Djodan, S., 'Where Dr. Stipe Suvar Finds Nationalism and where he Does not See it', *Kolo* (1969).
36. Domar, E., 'On Collective Farms and Producer Cooperatives', *American Economic Review* (September 1966).
37. Dubravcic, D., 'Labour as Entrepreneurial Input: an Essay in the Theory of the Producer Co-operative Economy', *Economica* (August 1970).
38. Ekonomski Institut Zagreb, *Aktuelni problemi privrednih kretanja i ekonomska politika Jugoslavije* (*Topical problems of economic development and economic policy in Yugoslavia*) (Zagreb, 1968).
39. Ekonomski Institut Zagreb, *Poduzece u reformi* (*Enterprise under reform*) (Zagreb, 1968).
40. Ekonomski Institut Zagreb, *Poduzece u reformi, diskusija sa simpozija Opatija mart 1968* (*Enterprise under reform, discussion at the symposium in Opatija, March 1968*) (Zagreb, 1968).
41. Engels, F., *Herrn Eugen Duhrings Umwalzung der Wissenschaft* (*The reversal of science by Mr Eugen Duhring*) (Zurich, 1886).
42. Furubotn, Pejovich, 'Property Rights and the Behaviour of the Firm in a Socialist State: the Example of Yugoslavia', *Zeitschrift fur Nationalokonomie* (Winter 1970).
43. Furubotn, Pejovich, 'Property Rights, Economic Decentralization and the Evolution of the Yugoslav Firm 1965–1972', *The Journal of Law and Economics* (October 1973).
44. Furubotn, E. G., 'The Long-Run Analysis of Labour-Managed Firm: an Alternative Interpretation', *American Economic Review* (March 1976).
45. Galenson, Leibenstein, 'Investment Criteria, Productivity and Economic Development', *Quarterly Journal of Economics* (August 1955).
46. Gradnik, B., 'How to Materialise the Right to Work', *Tribuna*, (students' paper, 27.11.67).
47. Granick, D., *Enterprise Guidance in Eastern Europe—A Comparison of Four Socialist Countries* (Princeton, 1974).
48. Hicks, J., 'Linear Theory', in *Surveys of Economic Theory*, Vol. III (London, 1966).
49. Hoffman, Neal, *Yugoslavia and the New Communism* (New York, 1962).
50. Horvat, B., *Ekonomska teorija planske privrede* (*Economic Theory of a planned economy*) (Belgrade, 1961).
51. Horvat, B., *Ekonomska nauka i narodna privreda* (*The science of economics and the national economy*) (Zagreb, 1968).

52. Horvat, B., *Ekonomski ciklusi u Jugoslaviji* (*Economic cycles in Yugoslavia*) (Belgrade 1969).

53. Horvat, B., 'Yugoslav Economic Policy in the Post-War Period: Problems, Ideas, Institutional Development', *American Economic Review* (1971, June Supplement).

54. Jelic, B., *Planska privreda i sistem planiranja* (*A planned economy and the system of planning*) (Belgrade, 1961).

55. Jerovsek, J., *Industrijska sociologija* (Industrial sociology) (Maribor, 1972).

56. Jerovsek, J., 'Grievances Procedure in Working Organisation', *Gledista* (7–8/1972).

57. Jezernik, M., *Hierarchy of Motivation Factors in Industry* (Ljubljana, 1966).

58. *Jugoslavija 1945–1964, statisticki pregled* (*Yugoslavia 1945–1964, Statistical survey*) (Belgrade, 1965).

59. Kardelj, E., *Problemi socialisticne politike na vasi (Problems of socialist policy in the village)* (Ljubljana, 1959).

60. Kardelj, E., *Radnicka klasa, samoupravljanje i naucno-tehnicki progres (The working class, self-management and scientific-technical progress)* (Belgrade, 1969).

61. Kardelj, E., *Protislovja druzbene lastnine v sodobni socialisticni druzbi* (*Contradictions of social ownership in contemporary socialist society*) (Ljubljana, 1972).

62. Kardelj, E., *Problemi nase socialisticne graditve*, knjiga VIII (*Problems of our socialist construction*, vol. VIII) (Ljubljana, 1974).

63. 'Komunist', *Osebno delo—za ali proti (Personal work—pro's and con's)* (Celje, 1967).

64. Korac, M., 'The Basic Economic Problems of an Analysis of the Situation of Economic Groupings', *Ekonomist* (4/1964).

65. Korac, Marsenic, *Samoupravna politika dohotka u oblasti nameuske raspodele* (*Self-management incomes policy in the sphere of distribution according to purpose*) (Belgrade, 1972).

66. Kraigher, B., *O reformi* (*About the reform*) (Celje, 1967).

67. Kraigher, S., 'On Past Labour', *Socijalizam* (6/1973).

68. Krasovec, S., 'Economics and Technology', *Ekonomski zbornik* (1956).

69. Kyovski and others, *Kolektivni delovni spori na obmocju SRS 1964–1968* (*Collective labour disputes on the territory of the Socialist Republic of Slovenia 1964–1968*) (Ljubljana, 1968).

70. Lapenna, I., 'The Legal Nature of Social Ownership in Yugoslavia', *Osteuropa-Recht* (3/1962).

71. Lavric, J., 'Basic Problems of Slovene Agriculture', *Ekonomska revija* (1951).

72. Macura, M., 'Population as a Factor of Economic Development', in *Ekonomska politika FNRJ* (*Economic policy of the FPRY*) (Belgrade, 1957).

73. Marczewski, J., *Planification et croissance economique des democracies populaires (Planning and economic growth of people's democracies)* (Paris, 1956).

74. Marx, Engels, *The German Ideology* (New York, 1960).

75. Meade, J. E., 'The Theory of Labour-Managed Firms and of Profit-Sharing', *Economic Journal* (Special Issue 1972).

76. Milenkovitch, D., *Plan and Market in Yugoslav Economic Thought* (New Haven, 1971).

77. Miljanic, N., *Novac i kredit u procesu drustvene reprodukcije* (*Money and credit in the process of social reproduction*) (Zagreb, 1964).

78. Miljevic, Blagojevic, Nikolic, *Razvoj privrednog sistema FNRJ* (*Development of the economic system of the FPRY*) (Belgrade, 1956).

79. Mirkovic, M., *Uvod u ekonomiku FNRJ* (*Introduction to the economy of Yugoslavia*) (Zagreb, 1959).

80. Misic, D., 'Investment and Investment Policy in Manufacturing', in *Ekonomska politika FNRJ* (*Economic policy of the FPRY*) (Belgrade, 1957).

81. Mozina, S., 'The Interest of Selfmanagers in Decision-Making, Control, Submitting Suggestions and Obtaining Information', *Sociologija* (3/1968).

82. Nikolic, N. M., *Integracija i koordinacija u industriji—procesi samoorganizovanja industrije* (*Integration and coordination in industry—processes of self-organisation of industrial enterprises*) (Nis, 1970).

83. Pecujlic and others, *Naucno-tehnicka revolucija i samoupravljanje* (*The scientific-technical revolution and self-management*) (Belgrade, 1969).

84. Pejovich, S., 'The Firm, Monetary Policy and Property Rights in a Planned Economy', *Western Economic Journal* (September 1969).

85. Pejovich, S., 'Towards an Economic Theory of the Creation and Specification of Property Rights', *Review of Social Economy* (September 1972).

86. Peselj, B. M., 'Yugoslav Laws on Foreign Investment', *International Lawyer* (April 1968).

87. *Petletni plan za razvoj narodnega gospodarstva FLRJ 1947–1951* (*Five-year plan for the development of the national economy of FPRY 1947–1951*) (Belgrade, 1947).
88. Pilipovic, N., *Nas privredni sistem* (*Our economic system*) (Belgrade, 1965).
89. Popovic, M., *O politiki in ciljih razvoja jugoslovanskega gospodarstva 1957 do 1960 (On the policy and goals of the development of the Yugoslav economy, 1957 to 1960*) (Ljubljana, 1958).
90. *Program in statut Zveze komunistov Jugoslavije* (*Programme and statute of the League of Communists of Yugoslavia*) (Ljubljana, 1958).
91. Rakic, V., 'Distribution of the Total Revenue of Economic Organisations', in *Ekonomska politika FNRJ* (*Economic policy of the FPRY*) (Belgrade, 1958).
92. Rodic, J. L., *Problemi likvidnosti jugoslovenske privrede (Liquidity problems of the Yugoslav economy*) (Belgrade, 1972).
93. Rotar, Forstneric, *Siti in lacni Slovenci* (*Well-fed and hungry Slovenes)* (Maribor, 1969).
94. Rus, Veljko, 'Socialism and Ownership', *Perspektive* (8/1961).
95. Rus, Veljko, *Odgovornost in moc v delovnih organizacijah* (*Responsibility and power in working organisations*) (Kranj, 1972).
96. Saksida, S., 'Social stratification in Yugoslavia', *Pogledi* (10/1967).
97. Sefer, B., *Zivotni Standard u Jugoslaviji (Living standard in Yugoslavia*) (Belgrade, 1958).
98. Sefer, B., *Zivotni Standard u Jugoslaviji (Living standard in Yugoslavia*) (Zagreb, 1965).
99. Sekretariat Izvrsnega Sveta za zakonodajo in organizacijo (Secretariat for legislation and organisation of the Executive Council (of Slovenia)), *Pregled predpisov o ekonomskih instrumentih in ukrepih (A survey of provisions on economic instruments and measures*) (Ljubljana, 1956).
100. Sirc, L., *Economic Devolution in Eastern Europe* (London, 1969).
101. Sirc, L., *Outline of International Trade* (London, 1973).
102. Sirotkovic, J., 'Features of our Planning', in *Ekonomska politika FNRJ* (*Economic Policy of the FPRY*) (Belgrade, 1957).
103. Sirotkovic, Kubovic, Sefer, *Privredno planiranje u Jugoslaviji* (*Economic planning in Yugoslavia*) (Zagreb, 1959).
104. Sirotkovic, J., *Problemi privrednog planiranja u Jugoslaviji (Problems of economic planning in Yugoslavia)* (Zagreb, 1961).
105. Stojanovic, R., 'On making Investment Decisions', *Ekonomski pregled* (3–5/1965).
106. Tisma, T., *Javne finansije* (*Public finance*) (Zagreb, 1964).

107. Todorovic, D. B., 'Problems of our Balance of Payments' in *Ekonomska politika FNRJ* (*Economic policy of the FPRY*) (Belgrade, 1957).
108. Todorovic, M., *Oslobadjanje rada* (*The liberation of labour*) (Belgrade, 1965).
109. TUC General Council, *Trade Unionism in Yugoslavia* (London, 1964).
110. Turkovic, J., *Planiranje narodne privrede FNRJ* (*Planning of the national economy of the FPRY*) (Zagreb, 1950).
111. United Nations, *Economic Survey of Europe* (Geneva, 1953).
112. United Nations, *Economic Survey of Europe in 1961* (Geneva, 1962).
113. United Nations, *Economic Survey of Europe in 1962 – Economic Planning in Europe* (Geneva, 1964).
114. Vanek, J., *The General Theory of Labour-Managed Market Economies* (Ithaca, 1970).
115. Vanek, J., *The Participatory Economy* (Ithaca, 1971).
116. Vojnic, D., *Investicije i fiksni fondovi Jugoslavije* (*Investment and fixed funds in Yugoslavia*) (Zagreb, 1970).
117. Vrcelj, Dz., 'Production Capacity Utilisation in Industry', *Ekonomist* (1–2/1965).
118. Vuckovic, M., 'The Role of Credit in Our Economy', in *Ekonomska politika FNRJ* (*Economic policy of the FPRY*) (Belgrade, 1957).
119. Vuco, N., *Agrarna kriza u Jugoslaviji 1930–1934* (*The agrarian crisis in Yugoslavia 1930–1934*) (Belgrade, 1968).
120. Vujosevic, M., 'Features of the Economic System', in Markovic, Mijovic, Bulajic, *Privredni sistem i ekonomska politika Jugoslavije* (*The economic system and economic policy of Yugoslavia*) (Belgrade, 1962).
121. Vukmanovic-Tempo, S., *Revolucija koja tece* (*Continuous Revolution*, vol. II) (Belgrade, 1971).
122. Ward, B., 'The Firm in Illyria: Market Socialism', *American Economic Review* (September 1958).
123. Waterston, A., *Planning in Yugoslavia: Organisation and Implementation* (Baltimore, 1962).
124. Wiles, P., *The Political Economy of Communism* (Oxford, 1962).
125. Zarkovic, D., 'Principles of Price Policy', *Ekonomist* (3–4/1963).
126. Zellerbach Commission, *Special Report on the European Refugee*

Situation (Washington D.C., 1959).

127. Zupanov, J., *Samoupravljanje i drustvena moc* (*Self-management and social power*) (Zagreb, 1969).

128. Zupanov, J., *Samoupravno poduzece* (*Self-managed enterprise*) (Zagreb, 1971).

Index

Accumulation: not for profits, 28; in enterprises, 96; forgone, 130; insufficient, 133–7, 151; syphoned off, 137; minimum, 139; disappearing, 161, 219

Agriculture, *see* collectivisation: disorganised, 13; production cooperatives, 8, 13

Aid: foreign, 3; military, 3; conditions of, 30

Albreht, Roman, communist official, Slovene, 213

Aleksic, Predrag, professional economist, Serb, 119

Anarchy: feared, 43; because of lack of sanctions, 177; because reality ignored, 179

Antagonism, within working class, 191

Association of enterprises: prohibited then fostered, 23; encouraged, 42; cross-subsidisation, 47, 116; integration, 115–17, 211–13

Association of producers, 1, 15, 20

Atelsek, Ivan, businessman, Slovene, 186

Automatism, *see* market; economic, 2; and large systems, 42

Bajt, Aleksander, professional economist, Slovene, 9, 68, 83, 92; on cost-push, 129–30; on distribution, 136; on inflation and growth, 160; on suppressed inflation, 161

Bakaric, Vladimir, communist leader, Croat: on limitations of distribution, 72; on new nationalisation of banks, 220

Bank credit, 146–9, 150; as subsidy, 22; irresponsible demand for, 22, 150; expansion, 30, 74; under pressure, 47, 150; for investment, 88–9; to cover losses, 157–8; by party order, 159; without repayment, 222

Banks, 146–7, 151; administer funds, 28; funds handed over to, 89, 99; bad judges of investment, 89; and illiquidity, 154; alienated capital, 219–23; should be controlled by workers, 221; and consumers' interests, 223

Basic organisations of associated labour, 210–11

Bencina, Joze, bank official, Slovene, 220–1

Bester, Mara, professional economist, Slovene, 132, 133

Bicanic, Rudolf, professional economist, Croat, 2, 6, 9; on market imperfections, 23

Bigness: tendency to criticise, 27, 118–19; size of enterprises, 115

Bilandzic, Dusan, communist economist, Serb, 176

Bilic, Jure, communist leader, Croat, 189

Blazevic, Jakov, communist leader, Serb from Croatia, 237

Blum, Erik, businessman, Serb, on lack of planning, 216

Brecelj, Marjan, pre-war politician, communist official, Slovene, 22

Bureaucracy: historical necessity of, 4; interference by, 17; and investment, 29; bancocratic, 147; as trade-unionists, 180; abstract, 184

Capacities: under-utilised, 2, 4, 89, 239; change to help, 66; utilisation data, 79–82; duplication, 88, 116

Capital by Marx, 1

Capital mobility, 26–8, 130; through taxation, 96; by contract, 117; hampered by local authorities, 147; forced, 213–14; surplus labour flows, 214; and 'past labour', 218–19
Capital–output ratio, 4, 91, 239
Cavoski, Kosta, lawyer, Serb, sent to prison, 236
Cemerski, Angel, communist official, Macedonian, on regional aid, 228; on changing law, 236
Cemovic, Momcilo, communist official, Serb, 172
Child allowances, 5–6, 53–4, 143–4
Class, housing, 144; holidays, 145; relations between producers, 171; treatment of differences, 173; not believed in, 187; positions, 188; essence of 'past labour', 219; aspect most important, 224; foreign policy, 230; justice, education, press, 230
Closing of enterprises: infrequent, 47; resisted, 87; required, 95; 30 per cent, 114; and insolvency, 150; and losses, 157
Cobeljic, Nikola, communist economist, Serb, on foreign finance, 30; on investment strategy, 68
Collectivisation of agriculture, 1; revised, 14; 'cold', 64–6
Cominform, Yugoslavia: expelled from, 1; disruption by, 2, 3
Commerce: neglect of, 23; alienated capital, 222
Communes: basic units, 19; as lynchpin, 40; opposed, 41; approve wage schedules, 44; supervision by abolished, 70; extracting money, 96; discuss enterprise statutes, 105; expenditure cut, 112
Conflicts: legalisation of, 173; not possible, 193; suppressed, 197
Consciousness: of workers, 72–3; and strikes, 196; organised force of socialist, 233
Constitution: 1953, 40–1; 1963, 104–5, 233, Amendments to, 209, 210, 211, 213, 220, 225–6, 233; 1974, 210–12, 216, 219, 221, 233–7
Consumer goods: production of, 75, 84; capacity utilisation, 81
Consumption, collective, 96–7
Consumption, personal: fall in, 5; upgraded, 36; rise neglected, 48–51; and development, 54; paid from abroad, 129, 239; growth rates of, 238
Contracts and agreements: planning by, 116; control of prices by, 126; control of personal incomes, 138–40; as solution for strikes, 196; on unemployment benefits, 198; and integration, 212; and planning, 213–17; to replace legislation, 215; mystique of, 215; disregarded, 215; convoluted, 245
Corporativist (system), 138, 141; rejected, 117
Cost of living, 75, 128
Council of producers, 40–1, 105, 141–2
Criticism, dangerous, 40
Crvenkovski, Krsto, communist leader, Macedonian, on illusions, 114

Data: lack of, 7; falsified, 30; manipulated, 113
Dedijer, Vladimir, communist writer, Montenegrin, 3
Defence expenditure, 3
Democracy: to deal with problems, 174; direct atomises, 191; pluralism attacked, 229; what serves working class, 230; pluralism of self-management interests, 233
Depreciation: misused, 31; policy impedes development, 37; insufficient, 152
Development strategy: Stalinist, 7; discussed again, 67–9; Yugoslav exaggerations of, 7; key industries, 15; and investment structure, 34
Director (manager): appointment, 39, 183–4; powerful position of, 43; accepts workers' priorities, 44; dominant, 44; informal groups, 177; no formal power, 177; mani-

pulators, 177; political, 177, 183, 186; how limit power of, 180–3; improvement of quality, 183; functions of, 183; precarious social place, 184–6; few candidates for, 185–6; must not be apolitical, 186, 231; re-election of, 187; in court, 189; under 1974 Constitution, 209–10
Discipline: business, 74; payments, 152–3, 155; financial, 159, 160, 223
Discussion: encouraged, 40, 228; not allowed, 174; fear of, 175; free stopped, 235
Disinvestment, 31; should be deducted, 48
Disproportions, 2, 4, 48, 74–82, 103; and growth, 85, 89; elimination of, 105–6
Distribution: within enterprises, 18–19, 101, 140; free, 69; excessive, 71, 243, 245; limitation of, 71–2, 213; according to work, 100–1, 125, 140, 190, 193, 213–14; not correct, 136; not according to work, 138; social guidance of, 138; criteria of, 139; strikes about, 193–4
Djilas, Milovan, ex-communist leader, dissident, Montenegrin, 1, 33, 41; great error of, 188
Dolanc, Stane, communist leader, Slovene, 138, 230
Dubravcic, Dinko, professional economist, Croat, 102

Economists, dissenting suppressed, 15
Education, 145
Employment: reduction in, 4, 14; excessive under planning, 14; fear of excessive under self-management, 19; to be reduced by self-managers, 41–2; resistance to reduction in, 93; reduction in advised, 132; artificial full, 199; in Slovenia, 202
Engineering (machine-building) industry: high cost of, 4; subsidies to, 21; and foreign trade, 24, 106–7; and interest rates, 29; preferential ranking, 34; circular investment in, 35; export by, 66, 83; capacity utilisation, 79–81, 85; modernisation of, 106; and illiquidity, 154
Enterprises: economic-legal entities, 16, 92; funds of, 19; planning by, 20, 99; called economic organisations, 42–3; founding and winding up of, 46–7; more resources to, 95–6, 112; disparate results, 130; general results, 133; resources owned and borrowed, 134, 152; less taxation, 136; and losses, 159; goals and self-management, 176–8; reorganised, 209; independence in danger, 211
Entrepreneurial (management) function: avoided by workers, 44; none for investment, 88–9; not felt by workers, 158; ignored, 174–5; workers and risk, 175, 179; knowledge and information, 175, 184; mentality, 213
Equalisation of business conditions, 45, 100–1, 213–14; and strikes, 196
Executive Council, 41
Exploitation: between enterprises, 26, 117; by private artisans, 119; between groups of workers, 176, 194; continues, 187–8; of migrants, 201; and shareholding, 218; by financial capital, 223; national, 224; meaning, 244

Financial reorganisation (*sanacija*), 156–7
Fiscal policy, impossible, 87
Foreign exchange, 24, 70; convertibility, 170–2; Croat students strike about, 225
Furubotn, Eirik, US economist, 183
Future uncertainty, 92, 99

Gligorov, Kiro, communist leader, Macedonian, 97, 106, 136
Goricar, Joze, professional sociologist, Slovene, on social strata, 190
Grlickov, Aleksandar, communist leader, Macedonian, 118; defends fast growth, 92; on convertibility, 171

Growth rates: exaggerated, 31; breakneck, 33; in the first period, 48; cause distortions, 48, 89, 91; yearly figures, 75, 76, 238, 240; Horvat's defence of, 84; OECD defence of, 86; speed up history, 92; and inflation, 125, 160; breed chaos, 127; and credit expansion, 148; and structure, 160–1; due to foreign debt, 168
GSP (Gross Social Product): Marxist definition of, 31; in the first plan, 48; components of, 75

Habits, persisting, 21
Hafner, Vinko, communist official, Slovene, on chasm between communists and workers, 191–2
Holidays, 144–5; class, 145
Horvat, Branko, professional economist, Croat, 29; inventory figures, 76, 84; on monetary policy, 83–6; advocates fast growth, 84; on closing of enterprises, 87; lack of success of reform, 137; on failing self-management, 211; on agreements abolishing responsibility, 215
Housing, 51–3, 63, 144; class, 144
Human nature, 73, 245–6

Ideology: reconsidered, 2; hesitations because of, 63; progressively more progressive, 184–5; and unemployment, 204; and lending, 218
Illiquidity, 150–5; unpaid invoices, 131, 152–3, 155; due to personal incomes, 159
Illusions (and promises) 113–14; of unlimited resources, 140–1; about working man, 194; about homogeneity of working class, 194; about independent self-management, 214; about workers deciding everything, 245
Imports, 2; of consumer goods by citizens, 86; low share of consumer goods in, 170
Income of enterprises: definition of, 19, 130–1, 155; enterprises' share in, 96, 112; concept criticised, 132; contains inflation, 137; link with market not perceived, 175; meaningless, 236
Incomes of employees, 6, 51–3; of peasants, 6, 53, 65
Indebtedness: foreign, 3, 165–8; dependence on, 239–42
Inflation, 125–33; cost-push, 83, 94, 129–30; conceals losses, 93; imported, 127; and stabilisation, 160; suppressed, 161
Instruments, economic, 20
Interests of enterprises and workers, 95, 99, 131–2; no link, 73, 242; Illyrian firm, 102–3; need for alignment, 135–6; 139; no mechanism, 138; workers' in incomes, 176; and consumers, 177
Interest rate: to constrain profits, 18; as investment criterion, 28–9; as tax, 45–6, 70, 137, 149, 152; to lenders, 46; meaningless, 29, 89, 211; lower than inflation, 222
Inventories, 239; accumulating, 2, 4, 74–9, 149; import content of, 85
Investment: basic determined by plan, 20; decentralisation, 26; initial principles of, 28; lack of criteria for, 29, 88, 243; no study of, 29; waste, 33, 89; according to proper criteria, 35; amassing of under workers' councils, 69, 103, 203; predilection for, 87–92; political, 88, 169; causes losses, 92–3; guidance through taxation, 95; irrational, 99; orientation to, 113; not by basic organisations, 211
Investment finance, 30–1; sources of, 27, 134; out of working capital, 88, 90, 151–2; neglected, 88, 90; from foreign deficit, 30, 90; foreign cooperation in, 117–18
Investment funds: established, 28; in communes' hands, 41; fed from interest, 45; handed to banks, 89, 99, 148
Investment rates: unchanged, 31–3; yearly figures, 75, 76; share in GSP, 239

Investment structure, 34–6; and unemployment, 14, 203; and subsidies, 35; changed 1956, 36
Irrationality from the West, 68, 91

Jelic, B., communist economist, Croat, 23
Jerovsek, Janez, professional sociologist, Slovene: on democracy, 174; under attack, 174, 183; on control function, 179; on rule of law and responsibility, 185; on directors, 187

Kamusic, Matija, professional economist, Slovene, 176, 246
Kardelj, Edvard, communist ideologist, Slovene, died 1979, 1, 3, 7, 8, 17; on nature of prices, 22; on agriculture, 64–5; disappointed by distribution, 71; on leading social organs, 73; on distribution, 136; on EEC, 164; on foreign trade, 168; on social stratification, 173–4; on division of labour, 184; on class position, 188; on social differences, 189–90; on conflicts and justice, 193–4; on strikes, 196; on combination of enterprises, 211–12; against spontaneity, 214, 233; against shares, 218; attacks liberalism, 229; identifies party with working class, 230; on longest constitution, 233; on direct democracy, 235; on improvement of system, 235–6; and words, 245
Kavcic, Stane, liberal communist leader, Slovene, 158; dismissed, 230
Kersnic, Alojz, communist official, Slovene, 157
Kidric, Boris, communist leader, Slovene, died 1953, 1, 9, 20, 24, 26; chief planner, 3; introduces reform, 13–16; on new planning, 16–17; on control of prices, 22; on monopoly, 23
Korosic, Marijan, professional economist, Croat: on stockpiles, 81; on price control contracts, 126–7; on inflation, 126–7
Kraigher, Boris, communist leader, Slovene, died 1967: on investment control, 26, 112; economic chief 1962, 67; criticises Social Plan 1961–5, 67; against *uravnilovka* 73; on low wages, 94, 108; on taxation, 94; on instability and investment, 108; on reform and foreign exchange, 111; died in an accident, 113; last speech, 114; on interest rates, 149; on monetary policy, 149; on foreign trade, 163, 164, 168; on EEC, 164
Kraigher, Sergej, communist official, Slovene, 188, 189, 247
Krasovec, Stane, communist economist, Slovene, 8, 37
Kurtovic, Todo, communist official, Serb, 176

Labour: forced, 31; voluntary, 31
Leading social organs, *see* Party, trade unions; must help workers, 73, 214, 233
Legal provisions: flood of, 7–8, 177, sweeping abolition, 20; blamed for losses, 94; continuous change, 181, 186, 187, 210, 233–4; rule of law, 185; enterprise over-regulated, 209; changes of defended and attacked, 236–7
Losses: preservation of loss-makers, 58, 133; due to investment, 93; do not reduce pay, 93–4, 130; due to excessive wage payments, 94, 159; monopoly of, 111; definition of, 133; total of enterprises, 134, 155–60; number of enterprises, 155; cover for, 156; external financing of, 161; and foreign debt, 168; reinsurance of, 176; socialisation of, 213; of less developed bigger, 225

Madzar, Ljubo, professional economist, Croat, 84
Management board, 39; no longer mandatory, 209
Market: elements, 2; allocation little

Market (*contd.*)
influenced by, 20; more exposure to, 95; and plan, 97–100; cannot reform structure, 125; to wither away, 214; still necessary, 215
Marxism: only knowledge, 15, 247; scientific truth, 30; disturbs acceptance of market, 100; obscures relations, 180, 244; wrong definition of property, 182; division of labour, 184; three tenets of, 187; and social strata, 190–1; and distribution according to work, 214; and working class, 235; no answers, 235
Meade, James, 102
Meetings: numerous, 44, 210; talking shop, 176; resented by directors, 187
Meier, Victor, Swiss journalist, 113
Migrants, 199–202; and small enterprises, 119, 204; remittances by, 165; in Slovenia, 202; shares for, 218; dependence on, 239–42
Miljanic, Nikola, communist official, Serb from Croatia, 137
Milosavlevski, Slavko, communist official, Macedonian, on withering away of republics, 226
Mincev, Nikola, communist official, Macedonian, 146, 224
Minic, Milos, economic Minister, Serb, 67, 74; on lack of investment criteria, 88; on excessive growth, 91
Mirkovic, Mijo, professional economist, Croat, 37, 44
Misic, Dimitrije, professional economist, Serb, 36
Monetary policy, 74, 83–7, 152–3; part of planning, 98; insufficient effect of, 149; contradictory goals of, 160; goals determined by Federal Assembly, 221–2
Money supply, 30, 74, 149, 155; yearly figures, 76; replaces accumulation, 242
Monopoly, 22; and integration, 213
Moral-political qualification (obedience to Party), required for posts, 230

National income, *see* GSP; fall in, 2, 6
Nationalisation: second, 1; more late 1950s, 63; new of banks, 220
National question, 40, 104, 224–8, 234; and convertibility, 171–2; and unanimity of decisions, 172, 217, 226; and alienated capital, 219–20; and unity of Yugoslav market, 227
Nikezic, Marko, liberal communist leader, Serb, dismissed, 230
Nikolic, Milivoje, communist official, Serb, 155

Offences: cheating by enterprises, 131; economic, 189; on behalf of enterprises, 189; against unity of Yugoslav market, 226
Organisational power, 173–83, 244; not changed by words, 178; legitimisation of, 179
Ownership: public, 1; State, historical necessity, 4; social, 15, 45–6, 214; private, 92, 187; and saving, 135; changes, 152; limits power, 181–3; abuse of collective, 182; no panacea, 204–5; indeterminate hampers responsibility, 218–19

Participation: general impossible, 175; and responsibility, 179
Party (League): interference with self-management, 39–40; discusses foreign trade, 170; to lead trade unions, 180; and directors, 186–92; leading position of, 188; and workers, 191–2; guides economy, 211; and democratic centralism, 228–33; equal working class, 230; should make system function, 232
Peasants, *see* Agriculture; deprived of wheat, 13
Pejovich, Svetozar, Yugoslav economist in US, 183
Pensions, 54, 143
People's needs not profits, 97
Personal incomes, *see* Wages; not wage-earners, 44, 93, 104, 159; reduction considered unjust, 44, 158, 159; excessive, 71; explosion of,

127–36; necessary disparities in, 130; not influenced by results, 93, 130, 159; paid in advance, 131; minimum, 133; policy, 137–40; low lead to strikes, 194; yearly rise in, 239
Pilipovic, Nikola, communist journalist, Serb, 88
Planinc, Milka, communist leader, Croat, 92
Planning, centralist, 1, 247; deficiencies of, 2; little doubt on deficiencies of, 3; impossible, 3; inconsistent, 4; shortcomings of, 7–9, 231
Planning, new social, 16–7; nature of, 20; not systematic whole, 20; basic and operational, 20; criticised, 67; and market, 97–100; no methodology of, 99; by enterprises, 99; by agreement, 116, 213–17; of bank credit, 146; of foreign trade, 162; faulty, 169; methodology unknown, 216–17
Polajnar, Anton, communist official, Slovene, 156, 159
Political power: and evil, 187; and appropriation, 191; politicisation of economy, 217, 232; in Party's hand, 229; and political police, 229; and spying, 231; and war, 247
Popovic, Koca, liberal communist leader, Serb, dismissed, 230
Popovic, Milentije, communist leader, Serb, 92, 148
Pragmatism: not socialist, 63; un-Marxist, 187
Pre-war Yugoslavia: comparison with, 57; denigrated, 205
Prices: distorted by instruments, 21; disparities in, 21, 110; control of, 22, 93, 94, 107, 112, 125–6, 161; possibility of liberalisation, 23; influence of international trade on, 23, 106; industrial production, 75; re-alignment, 107–11; rising, 125–7; freezing, 1966, 126; arbitrary, 126
Private artisans, 118–21; hostile treatment of, 37
Private surgeries, 63, 143
Production cost, unknown, 44, 94, 132, 160
Productivity (efficiency): of labour, 4, 56, 127, 239; divergent by branch, 169; of capital, 4, 56–7; general, and losses 160
Professional specialists, do not want to be directors, 183; attacks on, 186; unemployed, 204
Profits, distributed by local plan, 18–19; substitute concept, 44; distribution minimal, 45; word frowned on, 132–3
Public finance, 95–7; part of planning, 98; free exchange of work, 136; in constitutional amendments, 226

Quality, deterioration of, 5; and subsidies, 21

Rates of accumulation and funds, 17–18, 28
Reform: principles 1950, 16; goals 1965, 106; will to, 113–15; could be more durable, 132; unsuccessful, 137
Regions, investment problems of, 36, 224–5
Reserve funds, 45, 47, 157
Responsibility: resented by workers, 44–5; none for investment, 88; lack of, 92, 158–9; resisted, 93–5; and right to work, 157; socialised, 159, 194, 213; no sanctions, 159, 160, 177; collective and hierarchical, 175, 244; and changing rules, 175–6; of decision-makers, 176, 242; and high incomes, 185; abolished by agreements, 215, 217; for capital, 218
Riches: Tito against, 73; attack on, 188–9
Ribicic, Mitja, communist policeman, Slovene: on protectionism, 169; on anti-strike action, 195; Prime Minister, 229; opposed by Slovenes, 229; on class foreign policy, 230

Right to work, 157, 204–5
Rodic, Jovan L., professional economist, Serb, 78
Romac, Pasko, communist official, Croat, 113
Rus, Veljko, professional sociologist, Slovene: under attack, 174, 183; on real trade unions, 179–80; on limitation of directors, 180–3; proposals by similar to contract system, 182
Rus, Vojan, professional philosopher, Slovene, 174

Safety at work, 140
Saksida, Stane, professional philosopher and sociologist, Slovene: on social strata, 190; on social mobility, 191
Samardzija, Milos, professional economist, Serb, 92, 216
Saving: private, 30, 135, 243; by enterprises, 133–5, 243; propensity to, 135, 243
Sefer, Berislav, communist official and economist, Croat, 50, 161, 190, 236
Self-management: forced on Yugoslavia, 2; burdened with previous mistakes, 41; direct by small units, 101; difficulties with, 173–8; lack of interest in, 174; lost meaning, 175; magic word, 175, 245; supposed efficiency of, 176; and enterprises' goals, 176; and consumers, 178; and control, 179; unreal, 209–10; failing, 211; must not be spontaneous, 214, 232–3; workers in favour of, 246
Sentjurc, Lidija, communist leader, Slovene, 63
Sirotkovic, Jakov, communist official and economist, Croat, 138; on clearing of debts, 154; optimist, 161
Smole, Janko, communist official, Slovene: resigns as Premier, 141; on socialisation of losses, 158; on EEC, 164; on number of migrants, 199
Social differences: stratification, 173; reasons for, 188; and social differentiation, 189–91
Social insurance, 141–3
Social justice: not for enterprises, 95; absolute impossible, 193
Sociologists: on self-management, 173–83; solutions by, 178–83
Solidarity: component of self-management, 214
Soviet model: introduction of, 1; denied, 4; not altered, 2; thoughtless reception of, 16; initially inevitable, 231
Stabilisation: expenditure within limits, 111; and responsibility, 160
Stajner, Rikard, communist official, Croat, 114
Stambolic, Petar, communist leader, Serb, 230
Stanovnik, Janez, communist official, secretary general of the UN European Economic Commission, on EEC, 164
Stojanovic, Radmila, communist economist, Serb, on investment, 67
Strikes, 55, 193–7; repressed by trade unions, 180; foreign reports on, 197
Structure of production: difficult to change, 33, 35, 113, 203; the sore point, 63; reversal 1960, 66–7; not left to markets, 125; not re-aligned, 127; and foreign trade, 164, 170
Students: demonstrations by, 188, sarcasm about right to work, 204–5
Subsidies, 21–2; cross-subsidisation, 45, 47, 116, 158, 212; for exports, 169
Supek, Rudi, new left sociologist, Croat, on workers' interest in incomes, 176
System: search for, 15; shortcomings of, 160, 231; formal and reality, 174–5, 176; equilibrium of, 175; technical and social, 175; 'romantic' facade of, 178; incomplete and inconsistent, 217, 245; to fulfil needs, 232; needs improvement, 235

Taxation: progressive of wages, 18, 19, 243; to steer economy, 20; in-

direct, 21, 30; called 'contribution', 70; shifts to personal incomes, 96; reform 1965, 111–12; paid in advance, 151
Technocracy, 174; and strikes, 196; criticised, 210; for independent self-management, 214, 232; and liberalism attacked, 229
Technology: most advanced, 37–8; and association, 115, 116; busy with, 186
Tepavac, Mirko, liberal communist official, Serb, 230
Terminology: new words for old concepts, 132; changes in, 210; 'past labour', 219; manipulation of, 244
Tito, Josip Broz-, Marshal and President, Croat, 1, 2, 7; on consumption, 5; rejects scarcity prices, 8; introduces reform, 15; on excessive stress on market, 20; cuts investment, 35; on reconstruction of old plants, 37; encourages dismissals, 42; on abolition of 'wages', 44; on pensioners, 54; on criminals, 55, 189; on strikes, 55; on women, 63; on peasants' mistrust, 65; criticises planning, 67; supports wider jurisdiction for workers' councils, 70; on capacity utilisation, 89; on low standard, 94; talks to artisans, 119; exonerates workers, 138, 160; on limited resources, 141; on foreign trade, 162–3; on tourism, 165; perturbed by distribution, 71–2; against riches and *uravnilovka*, 73; on inventories, 74; on sterile investment, 89; on foreign debt, 165; on better wages abroad, 200; on Soviet employment, 205; on national question, 224; on the Party, 228–9; 'the Letter' by, 230; on self-management as dictatorship of proletariat, 230–1; on shortcomings of centralist planning. 231; on communists as initiators, 232; on limited knowledge, 247
Todorovic, Mijalko, communist leader, Serb, 33, 35, 74; on equalisation of business conditions, 101; on failures, 115
Trade: international, 22–5, 162–4; and reform 1965, 106, 111; protectionism, 169; export of naked labour, 169; self-managed, 172
Tripalo, Mika, liberal communist leader, Croat, 95
Turnover of workers, 55, 73, 93, 131, 133
Trade unions: supervision by abolished, 70; approve wage schedules, 44; against cost-push theory, 138; real as bargaining partners, 179–80; on migrants, 199

Unemployment, 2, 197–9; concealed, 14, 93, 198–9; rising, 42; reasons for, 203; and Soviet Union, 205
Uravnilovka, criticised, 73, 137, 189

Vanek, Jaroslav, US economist, 102; on accumulation, 136
Veljkovic, Ljubomir, editor *Ekonomska politika*, Serb, dismissed, 230
Veselinov, Jovan, communist leader, Serb, 13, 40
Vinski, Ivo, professional statistician, Croat, 199, 200, 205
Vlahovic, Veljko, communist leader, Serb, 185
Vojnic, Dragomir, professional economist, Croat, 91
Vrcelj, Dz., professional statistician, Croat, 79
Vucic, Novica, professional economist, Serb, 231
Vuckovic, M., professional economist, Serb, 29, 146
Vukmanovic-Tempo, Svetozar, 9, 15, 21, 28, 29, 33, 37; economic Minister, 3; on ficticious data, 30; on forced labour, 31; on profitable investment, 35; to Nasser on investment, 68; leader of trade unions, 69; on measurement of labour, 101; on unemployment, 205
Vukovic, Dusan, communist official, Montenegrin, 108, 114

Wages, *see* Personal incomes; low, 5, 51–4; consequence of, 54–5; trauma of, 174; accounting, 18; determined by by-laws, 19; minimum, 20; fear of excessive payment of, 43, 96; parity of, 94, 130, 179, 343
Workers' council 39, 209; jurisdiction extended, 69; not much influence, 175; composition of, 210
Workers' self-management, *see* Self-management; Act on, 1; organisation of, 39–41; cannot use jurisdiction, 175
Working organisations: outside economy, 43; self-management contradiction, 175

Zupanov, Josip, professional sociologist, Croat: on directors, 183; on criminality, 189; on mystique of contracts, 215